노래로 배우는 한국어 1

English(영어)
translation(번역판)

• 노래 (noun) : song; music; singing
A composition created by setting rhythmical lyrics to music; or the act of singing such a piece of music.

• 로 : no equivalent expression
A postpositional particle that indicates a method or way to do something.

• 배우다 (verb) : learn
To obtain new knowledge.

• -는 : no equivalent expression
An ending of a word that makes the preceding statement function as an adnominal phrase and implies that an event or action is happening in the present.

• 한국어 (noun) : Korean; Korean language
The language used by the Korean people.

※ 이 책의 폰트는 '함초롬 바탕체'를 사용하였습니다.

< 저자(author) >

㈜한글2119연구소

• 연구개발전담부서

• ISO 9001 : 품질경영시스템 인증

• ISO 14001 : 환경경영시스템 인증

• 이메일(e-mail) : gjh0675@naver.com

< 동영상(video) 자료(material) >

HANPUK_english(translation)
https://www.youtube.com/@HANPUK_English

HANPUK

제 2024153361 호

연구개발전담부서 인정서

1. 전담부서명: 연구개발전담부서

[소속기업명: (주)한글2119연구소]

2. 소　재　지: 인천광역시 부평구 마장로264번길 33
상가동 제지하층 제2호 (산곡동, 뉴서울아파트)

3. 신고 연월일: 2024년 05월 02일

과학기술정보통신부

「기초연구진흥 및 기술개발지원에 관한 법률」 제14조의 2제1항 및 같은 법 시행령 제27조제1항에 따라 위와 같이 기업의 연구개발전담부서로 인정합니다.

2024년 5월 13일

한국산업기술진흥협회장

G-CERTI *Certificate*

hereby certifies that

Hangul 2119 Research Institute Co., Ltd.

Rm. 2, Lower level, Sangga-dong, 33, Majang-ro 264beon-gil, Bupyeong-gu, Incheon, Korea

meets the Standard Requirements & Scope as following

ISO 9001:2015
Quality Management Systems

Creation of Media Content, Publication of Korean Paper and Electronic Textbooks, Production and Release of Albums for Korean Language Education

Certificate No: GIS-6934-QC
Initial Date : 2024-05-21
Expiry Date : 2027-05-20

Code : 08, 39
Issue Date : 2024-05-21
Valid Period : 2024-05-21 ~ 2027-05-20

Signed for and on behalf of GCERTI
President I.K.Cho

Certificate of Registration Certificate of Registration

G-CERTI *certificate*

hereby certifies that

Hangul 2119 Research Institute Co., Ltd.

Rm. 2, Lower level, Sangga-dong, 33, Majang-ro 264beon-gil, Bupyeong-gu, Incheon, Korea

meets the Standard Requirements & Scope as following

ISO 14001:2015
Environmental Management Systems

Creation of Media Content, Publication of Korean Paper and Electronic Textbooks, Production and Release of Albums for Korean Language Education

Certificate No	: GIS-6934-EC	Code	: 08, 39
Initial Date	: 2024-05-21	Issue Date	: 2024-05-21
Expiry Date	: 2027-05-20	Valid Period	: 2024-05-21 ~ 2027-05-20

Signed for and on behalf of GCERTI
President I.K.Cho

< 목차(table of contents) >

< 1 >

한글송

한글(Hangul) 송(song)

[발음(pronunciation)]

< 전주(introductory instrumental accompaniment) >

바 빠 파 다 따 타 가 까 카 자 짜 차 사 싸 하 마 나 아 라
바 빠 파 다 따 타 가 까 카 자 짜 차 사 싸 하 마 나 아 라
ba ppa pa da tta ta ga kka ka ja jja cha sa ssa ha ma na a ra

자음 열아홉 개 소리
자음 여라홉 개 소리
jaeum yeorahop gae sori

아 어 오 우 으 이 애 에 외 위 야 여 요 유 얘 예 와 워 왜 웨 의
아 어 오 우 으 이 애 에 외 위 야 여 요 유 얘 예 와 워 왜 웨 의
a eo o u eu i ae e oe wi ya yeo yo yu yae ye wa wo wae we ui

모음 스물한 개 소리
모음 스물한 개 소리
moeum seumulhan gae sori

< 1 절(verse) >

다 같이 말해 봐
다 가치 말해 봐
da gachi malhae bwa

아설순치후
아설순치후
aseolsunchihu

다 함께 불러 봐
다 함께 불러 봐
da hamkke bulleo bwa

아설순치후
아설순치후
aseolsunchihu

우리 모두 느껴 봐
우리 모두 느껴 봐
uri modu neukkyeo bwa

발음 기관을 본뜬
바름 기과늘 본뜬
bareum gigwaneul bontteun

기역, 니은, 미음, 시옷, 이응
기역, 니은, 미음, 시옫, 이응
giyeok, nieun, mieum, siot, ieung

다섯 글자
다섣 글짜
daseot geulja

세상의 모든 소리를 들어 봐
세상에 모든 소리를 드러 봐
sesange modeun sorireul deureo bwa

또 하고 싶은 말을 다 외쳐 봐
또 하고 시픈 마를 다 외처 봐
tto hago sipeun mareul da oecheo bwa

신비로운 사연
신비로운 사연
sinbiroun sayeon

감추었던 비밀
감추얻떤 비밀
gamchueotdeon bimil

진실을 전해 줘
진시를 전해 줘
jinsireul jeonhae jwo

< 후렴(refrain) >

아 야 어 여 오 요 우 유 으 이
아 야 어 여 오 요 우 유 으 이
a ya eo yeo o yo u yu eu i

가 나 다 라 마 바 사 아 자 차 카 타 파 하
가 나 다 라 마 바 사 아 자 차 카 타 파 하
ga na da ra ma ba sa a ja cha ka ta pa ha

이제부터 들려 줘 너의 마음을
이제부터 들려 줘 너에 마으믈
ijebuteo deullyeo jwo neoe maeumeul

지금부터 전해 줘 너의 사랑을
지금부터 전해 줘 너에 사랑을
jigeumbuteo jeonhae jwo neoe sarangeul

아 야 어 여 오 요 우 유 으 이
아 야 어 여 오 요 우 유 으 이
a ya eo yeo o yo u yu eu i

가 나 다 라 마 바 사 아 자 차 카 타 파 하
가 나 다 라 마 바 사 아 자 차 카 타 파 하
ga na da ra ma ba sa a ja cha ka ta pa ha

모음 스물하나에 자음 열아홉을 더해
모음 스물하나에 자음 여라호블 더해
moeum seumulhanae jaeum yeorahobeul deohae

마흔 가지 소리로 세상을 느껴 봐
마흔 가지 소리로 세상을 느껴 봐
maheun gaji soriro sesangeul neukkyeo bwa

< 2 절(verse) >

하늘과 땅이 만나 ㅗ, ㅜ
하늘과 땅이 만나 ㅗ, ㅜ
haneulgwa ttangi manna o, u

사람과 만난다면 ㅏ, ㅓ
사람과 만난다면 ㅏ, ㅓ
saramgwa mannandamyeon a, eo

하루면은 충분해
하루며는 충분해
harumyeoneun chungbunhae

하늘, 땅, 사람을 본뜬
하늘, 땅, 사라믈 본뜬
haneul, ttang, sarameul bontteun

아 어 오 우 야 여 요 유 으 이
아 어 오 우 야 여 요 유 으 이
a eo o u ya yeo yo yu eu i

열 글자
열 글짜
yeol geulja

세상의 모든 소리를 들어 봐
세상에 모든 소리를 드러 봐
sesange modeun sorireul deureo bwa

또 하고 싶은 말을 다 외쳐 봐
또 하고 시픈 마를 다 외처 봐
tto hago sipeun mareul da oecheo bwa

신비로운 사연
신비로운 사연
sinbiroun sayeon

감추었던 비밀
감추얻떤 비밀
gamchueotdeon bimil

진실을 전해 줘
진시를 전해 줘
jinsireul jeonhae jwo

< 후렴(refrain) >

아 어 오 우 야 여 요 유 으 이
아 어 오 우 야 여 요 유 으 이
a eo o u ya yeo yo yu eu i

가 나 다 라 마 바 사 아 자 차 카 타 파 하
가 나 다 라 마 바 사 아 자 차 카 타 파 하
ga na da ra ma ba sa a ja cha ka ta pa ha

이제부터 들려 줘 너의 마음을
이제부터 들려 줘 너에 마으믈
ijebuteo deullyeo jwo neoe maeumeul

지금부터 전해 줘 너의 사랑을
지금부터 전해 줘 너에 사랑을
jigeumbuteo jeonhae jwo neoe sarangeul

아 어 오 우 야 여 요 유 으 이
아 어 오 우 야 여 요 유 으 이
a eo o u ya yeo yo yu eu i

가 나 다 라 마 바 사 아 자 차 카 타 파 하
가 나 다 라 마 바 사 아 자 차 카 타 파 하
ga na da ra ma ba sa a ja cha ka ta pa ha

모음 스물하나에 자음 열아홉을 더해
모음 스물하나에 자음 여라호블 더해
moeum seumulhanae jaeum yeorahobeul deohae

마흔 가지 소리로 세상을 느껴 봐
마흔 가지 소리로 세상을 느껴 봐
maheun gaji soriro sesangeul neukkyeo bwa

들려 줘요
들려 줘요
deullyeo jwoyo

이 소리 들리나요.
이 소리 들리나요.
i sori deullinayo.

달콤하게, 부드럽게 우리 모두 말해 봐요.
달콤하게, 부드럽께 우리 모두 말해 봐요.
dalkomhage, budeureopge uri modu malhae bwayo.

< 전주(introductory instrumental accompaniment) >

바 빠 파 다 따 타 가 까 카 자 짜 차 사 싸 하 마 나 아 라

ㅂ : 한글 자모의 여섯째 글자. 이름은 '비읍'으로, 소리를 낼 때의 입술 모양은 'ㅁ'과 같지만 더 세게 발음되므로 'ㅁ'에 획을 더해서 만든 글자이다.

b; p

The sixth consonant of the Korean alphabet pronounced bieup, which is made by adding strokes to 'ㅁ', as the lips look the same as those of 'ㅁ' but 'ㅂ' is pronounced more strongly.

ㅃ : 한글 자모 'ㅂ'을 겹쳐 쓴 글자. 이름은 쌍비읍으로, 'ㅂ'의 된소리이다.

pp

The consonant of the Korean alphabet consisting of two 'ㅂ' which creates a stronger sound than a single 'ㅂ'.

ㅍ : 한글 자모의 열셋째 글자. 이름은 '피읖'으로, 'ㅁ, ㅂ'보다 소리가 거세게 나므로 'ㅁ'에 획을 더하여 만든 글자이다.

p

The 13th consonant of the Korean alphabet pronounced pieup, which is made by adding a stroke to 'ㅁ', as it is pronounced more strongly than 'ㅁ' and 'ㅂ.'

ㄷ : 한글 자모의 셋째 글자. 이름은 '디귿'으로, 소리를 낼 때 혀의 모습은 'ㄴ'과 같지만 더 세게 발음되므로 한 획을 더해 만든 글자이다.

d

The third consonant of the Korean alphabet pronounced digeut, which is made by adding a stroke to 'ㄴ', as the tongue looks the same as that of 'ㄴ' but 'ㄷ' is pronounced more strongly.

ㄸ : 한글 자모 'ㄷ'을 겹쳐 쓴 글자. 이름은 쌍디귿으로, 'ㄷ'의 된소리이다.

tt

The consonant in the Korean alphabet consisting of two 'ㄷ' which creates a stronger sound than a single'ㄷ'.

ㅌ : 한글 자모의 열두째 글자. 이름은 '티읕'으로, 'ㄷ'보다 소리가 거세게 나므로 'ㄷ'에 한 획을 더하여 만든 글자이다.

t

The 12th consonant of the Korean alphabet pronounced tieut, which is made by adding a stroke to 'ㄷ', as it is pronounced more strongly than 'ㄷ.'

ㄱ : 한글 자모의 첫째 글자. 이름은 기역으로 소리를 낼 때 혀뿌리가 목구멍을 막는 모양을 본떠 만든 글자이다.

g

The first consonant of the Korean alphabet pronounced giyeok, the sound of which is created by imitating the root of one's tongue blocking one's throat.

ㄲ : 한글 자모 'ㄱ'을 겹쳐 쓴 글자. 이름은 쌍기역으로, 'ㄱ'의 된소리이다.

kk

The consonant in the Korean alphabet consisting of two 'ㄱ' which creates a stronger sound than a single 'ㄱ'.

ㅋ : 한글 자모의 열한째 글자. 이름은 '키읔'으로 'ㄱ'보다 소리가 거세게 나므로 'ㄱ'에 한 획을 더하여 만든 글자이다.

k

The 11th consonant of the Korean alphabet pronounced kieuk, which is made by adding a stroke to 'ㄱ', as it is pronounced more strongly than 'ㄱ.'

ㅈ : 한글 자모의 아홉째 글자. 이름은 '지읒'으로, 'ㅅ'보다 소리가 더 세게 나므로 'ㅅ'에 한 획을 더해 만든 글자이다.

j

The ninth consonant of the Korean alphabet pronounced jieut, which is made by adding a stroke to 'ㅅ', as the tongue is shaped the same as that of 'ㅅ' but 'ㅈ' is pronounced more strongly.

ㅉ : 한글 자모 'ㅈ'을 겹쳐 쓴 글자. 이름은 쌍지읒으로, 'ㅈ'의 된소리이다.

jj

The consonant in the Korean alphabet consisting of two 'ㅈ' which creates a stronger sound than a single 'ㅈ'.

ㅊ : 한글 자모의 열째 글자. 이름은 '치읓'으로 '지읒'보다 소리가 거세게 나므로 '지읒'에 한 획을 더해서 만든 글자이다.

ch

The 10th consonant of the Korean alphabet pronounced chieut, which is made by adding a stroke to 'ㅈ', as it is pronounced more strongly than 'ㅈ.'

ㅅ : 한글 자모의 일곱째 글자. 이름은 '시옷'으로 이의 모양을 본떠서 만든 글자이다.

s

The seventh consonant of the Korean alphabet pronounced siot, the sound of which is created by imitating the shape of teeth.

ㅆ : 한글 자모 'ㅅ'을 겹쳐 쓴 글자. 이름은 쌍시옷으로, 'ㅅ'의 된소리이다.

ss

The consonant in the Korean alphabet consisting of two 'ㅅ', which is called double siot and which creates a stronger sound than a single 'ㅅ'.

ㅎ : 한글 자모의 열넷째 글자. 이름은 '히읗'으로, 이 글자의 소리는 목청에서 나므로 목구멍을 본떠 만든 'ㅇ'의 경우와 같지만 'ㅇ'보다 더 세게 나므로 'ㅇ'에 획을 더하여 만든 글자이다.

h

The 14th consonant of the Korean alphabet pronounced hieut, which is made by adding a stroke to 'ㅇ', as its sound comes from one's vocal cords like 'ㅇ,' which is created by imitating the shape of a throat, but pronounced more strongly than 'ㅇ.'

ㅁ : 한글 자모의 다섯째 글자. 이름은 '미음'으로, 소리를 낼 때 다물어지는 두 입술 모양을 본떠서 만든 글자이다.

m

The fifth consonant of the Korean alphabet pronounced mieum, the sound of which is created by imitating the closed shape of the lips.

ㄴ : 한글 자모의 둘째 글자. 이름은 '니은'으로 소리를 낼 때 혀끝이 윗잇몸에 붙는 모양을 본떠 만든 글자이다.

n

The second consonant of the Korean alphabet pronounced nieun, the sound of which is created by imitating the tip of the tongue reaching the upper gum.

ㅇ : 한글 자모의 여덟째 글자. 이름은 '이응'으로 목구멍의 모양을 본떠서 만든 글자이다. 초성으로 쓰일 때 소리가 없다.

ng

The eighth consonant of the Korean alphabet pronounced ieung or not pronounced at all when used as the first consonant letter, the sound of which is created by imitating the shape of a throat.

ㄹ : 한글 자모의 넷째 글자. 이름은 '리을'로 혀끝을 윗잇몸에 가볍게 대었다가 떼면서 내는 소리를 나타낸다.

r; l

The fourth consonant in the Korean alphabet pronounced rieul, the sound of which is created by lightly touching the tip of the tongue to the upper gum and then lowering it.

자음 열아홉 개 소리

자음 (noun) : 목, 입, 혀 등의 발음 기관에 의해 장애를 받으며 나는 소리.

consonant

A sound in which the air is partially or completely blocked by the movement of the throat, mouth, tongue, etc.

열아홉 : 19

개 (noun) : 낱으로 떨어진 물건을 세는 단위.
gae (no equivalent expression)
A bound noun that serves as a unit for counting the number of objects that are available as a single piece.

소리 (noun) : 물체가 진동하여 생긴 음파가 귀에 들리는 것.
sound; noise
Sound wave heard by the ear that is created when an object vibrates.

아 어 오 우 으 이 애 에 외 위 야 여 요 유 얘 예 와 워 왜 웨 의

ㅏ : 한글 자모의 열다섯째 글자. 이름은 '아'이고 중성으로 쓴다.
a
The first vowel of the Korean alphabet pronounced 'a' and used as a medial.

ㅓ : 한글 자모의 열일곱째 글자. 이름은 '어'이고 중성으로 쓴다.
eo
The third vowel of the Korean alphabet pronounced 'eo' and used as a middle vowel letter.

ㅗ : 한글 자모의 열아홉째 글자. 이름은 '오'이고 중성으로 쓴다.
o
The fifth vowel of the Korean alphabet pronounced 'o' and used as a middle vowel letter.

ㅜ : 한글 자모의 스물한째 글자. 이름은 '우'이고 중성으로 쓴다.
u
The seventh vowel of the Korean alphabet pronounced 'u' and used as a middle vowel letter.

ㅡ : 한글 자모의 스물셋째 글자. 이름은 '으'이고 중성으로 쓴다.
eu
The ninth vowel of the Korean alphabet pronounced 'eu' and used as a middle vowel letter.

ㅣ : 한글 자모의 스물넷째 글자. 이름은 '이'이고 중성으로 쓴다.
i
The 10th vowel of the Korean alphabet pronounced 'i' and used as a middle vowel letter.

ㅐ : 한글 자모 'ㅏ'와 'ㅣ'를 모아 쓴 글자. 이름은 '애'이고 중성으로 쓴다.
ae
The compound vowel of the Korean alphabet pronounced 'ae', which is made by adding 'ㅣ' to 'ㅏ' and used as a medial.

ㅔ : 한글 자모 'ㅓ'와 'ㅣ'를 모아 쓴 글자. 이름은 '에'이고 중성으로 쓴다.
e
The compound vowel of the Korean alphabet pronounced 'e', which is made by adding 'ㅣ' to 'ㅓ' and used as a middle vowel letter.

ㅚ : 한글 자모 'ㅗ'와 'ㅣ'를 모아 쓴 글자. 이름은 '외'이고 중성으로 쓴다.
oe
The compound vowel of the Korean alphabet pronounced 'oe', which is made by adding 'ㅣ' to 'ㅗ' and used as a middle vowel letter.

ㅟ : 한글 자모 'ㅜ'와 'ㅣ'를 모아 쓴 글자. 이름은 '위'이고 중성으로 쓴다.
wi
The compound vowel of the Korean alphabet pronounced 'wi', which is made by adding 'ㅣ' to 'ㅜ' and used as a middle vowel letter.

ㅑ : 한글 자모의 열여섯째 글자. 이름은 '야'이고 중성으로 쓴다.
ya
The second vowel of the Korean alphabet pronounced 'ya' and used as a medial.

ㅕ : 한글 자모의 열여덟째 글자. 이름은 '여'이고 중성으로 쓴다.
yeo
The fourth vowel of the Korean alphabet pronounced 'yeo' and used as a middle vowel letter.

ㅛ : 한글 자모의 스무째 글자. 이름은 '요'이고 중성으로 쓴다.
yo
The sixth vowel of the Korean alphabet pronounced 'yo' and used as a middle vowel letter.

ㅠ : 한글 자모의 스물두째 글자. 이름은 '유'이고 중성으로 쓴다.
yu
The eighth vowel of the Korean alphabet pronounced 'yu' and used as a middle vowel letter.

ㅒ : 한글 자모 'ㅑ'와 'ㅣ'를 모아 쓴 글자. 이름은 '얘'이고 중성으로 쓴다.
yae
The compound vowel of the Korean alphabet pronounced 'yae', which is made by adding 'ㅣ' to 'ㅑ' and used as a middle vowel letter.

ㅖ : 한글 자모 'ㅕ'와 'ㅣ'를 모아 쓴 글자. 이름은 '예'이고 중성으로 쓴다.
ye
The compound vowel of the Korean alphabet pronounced 'ye', which is made by adding 'ㅣ' to 'ㅕ' and used as a middle vowel letter.

ㅘ : 한글 자모 'ㅗ'와 'ㅏ'를 모아 쓴 글자. 이름은 '와'이고 중성으로 쓴다.
wa
The compound vowel of the Korean alphabet pronounced 'wa', which is made by adding 'ㅐ' to 'ㅗ' and used as a middle vowel letter.

ㅝ : 한글 자모 'ㅜ'와 'ㅓ'를 모아 쓴 글자. 이름은 '워'이고 중성으로 쓴다.
wo
The compound vowel of the Korean alphabet pronounced 'wo', which is made by adding 'ㅓ' to 'ㅜ' and used as a middle vowel letter.

ㅙ : 한글 자모 'ㅗ'와 'ㅐ'를 모아 쓴 글자. 이름은 '왜'이고 중성으로 쓴다.
wae
The compound vowel of the Korean alphabet pronounced 'wae', which is made by adding 'ㅐ' to 'ㅗ' and used as a middle vowel letter.

ㅞ : 한글 자모 'ㅜ'와 'ㅔ'를 모아 쓴 글자. 이름은 '웨'이고 중성으로 쓴다.
we
The compound vowel of the Korean alphabet pronounced 'we', which is made by adding 'ㅔ' to 'ㅜ' and used as a middle vowel letter.

ㅢ : 한글 자모 'ㅡ'와 'ㅣ'를 모아 쓴 글자. 이름은 '의'이고 중성으로 쓴다.
ui
The compound vowel of the Korean alphabet pronounced 'ui', which is made by adding 'ㅣ' to 'ㅡ' and used as a middle vowel letter.

모음 스물한 개 소리

모음 (noun) : 사람이 목청을 울려 내는 소리로, 공기의 흐름이 방해를 받지 않고 나는 소리.
vowel
A sound made by vibrating one's vocal cords without obstructing the flow of air.

스물한 : 21

개 (noun) : 낱으로 떨어진 물건을 세는 단위.
gae (no equivalent expression)
A bound noun that serves as a unit for counting the number of objects that are available as a single piece.

소리 (noun) : 물체가 진동하여 생긴 음파가 귀에 들리는 것.
sound; noise
Sound wave heard by the ear that is created when an object vibrates.

< 1 절(verse) >

다 같이 말하+[여 보]+아.
말해 봐

다 (adverb) : 남거나 빠진 것이 없이 모두.
all; everything
With nothing left over or missing.

같이 (adverb) : 둘 이상이 함께.
together
With each other.

말하다 (verb) : 어떤 사실이나 자신의 생각 또는 느낌을 말로 나타내다.
say; tell; speak; talk
To verbally present a fact or one's thoughts or feelings.

-여 보다 : 앞의 말이 나타내는 행동을 시험 삼아 함을 나타내는 표현.
-yeo boda (no equivalent expression)
An expression used to indicate that one does the act mentioned in the preceding statement, as a test.

-아 : (두루낮춤으로) 어떤 사실을 서술하거나 물음, 명령, 권유를 나타내는 종결 어미.
-a (no equivalent expression)
(informal addressee-lowering) A sentence-final ending used to describe a certain fact, ask a question, **give an order**, or advise.

아설순치후

아 → 어금니 (noun) : 송곳니의 안쪽에 있는 크고 가운데가 오목한 이.
molar
A big tooth with a depressed center that is located behind the cuspid.

설 → 혀 (noun) : 사람이나 동물의 입 안 아래쪽에 있는 길고 붉은 살덩어리.
tongue
The long, red piece of flesh that is in the lower interior part of a human or animal mouth.

순 → 입술 (noun) : 사람의 입 주위를 둘러싸고 있는 붉고 부드러운 살.
lips
The red and soft flesh that surrounds the opening of the mouth.

치 → 이 (noun) : 사람이나 동물의 입 안에 있으며 무엇을 물거나 음식물을 씹는 일을 하는 기관.
tooth
A part in the human or animal mouth that is used to bite something or chew food.

후 → 목구멍 (noun) : 목 안쪽에서 몸속으로 나 있는 깊숙한 구멍.
throat
A deep opening inside the neck that leads to other inside parts of the body.

다 함께 부르(불ㄹ)+[어 보]+아.
불러 봐

다 (adverb) : 남거나 빠진 것이 없이 모두.
all; everything
With nothing left over or missing.

함께 (adverb) : 여럿이서 한꺼번에 같이.
together; along with
In the state of several people being all together.

부르다 (verb) : 곡조에 따라 노래하다.
sing
To sing to a tune.

-어 보다 : 앞의 말이 나타내는 행동을 시험 삼아 함을 나타내는 표현.
-eo boda (no equivalent expression)
An expression used to indicate that one does the act mentioned in the preceding statement, as a test.

-아 : (두루낮춤으로) 어떤 사실을 서술하거나 물음, 명령, 권유를 나타내는 종결 어미.
-a (no equivalent expression)
(informal addressee-lowering) A sentence-final ending used to describe a certain fact, ask a question, **give an order**, or advise.

아설순치후

아 → 어금니 (noun) : 송곳니의 안쪽에 있는 크고 가운데가 오목한 이.
molar
A big tooth with a depressed center that is located behind the cuspid.

설 → 혀 (noun) : 사람이나 동물의 입 안 아래쪽에 있는 길고 붉은 살덩어리.
tongue
The long, red piece of flesh that is in the lower interior part of a human or animal mouth.

순 → 입술 (noun) : 사람의 입 주위를 둘러싸고 있는 붉고 부드러운 살.
lips
The red and soft flesh that surrounds the opening of the mouth.

치 → 이 (noun) : 사람이나 동물의 입 안에 있으며 무엇을 물거나 음식물을 씹는 일을 하는 기관.
tooth
A part in the human or animal mouth that is used to bite something or chew food.

후 → 목구멍 (noun) : 목 안쪽에서 몸속으로 나 있는 깊숙한 구멍.
throat
A deep opening inside the neck that leads to other inside parts of the body.

우리 모두 느끼+[어 보]+아.
느껴 봐

우리 (pronoun) : 말하는 사람이 자기와 듣는 사람 또는 이를 포함한 여러 사람들을 가리키는 말.
we
A pronoun used when the speaker refers to himself/herself and the listener or listeners, or a group of people including the speaker and listener or listeners.

모두 (adverb) : 빠짐없이 다.
all of
Everyone or everything without exception.

느끼다 (verb) : 특정한 대상이나 상황을 어떻다고 생각하거나 인식하다.
think
To think about or perceive a certain subject or situation in a certain way.

-어 보다 : 앞의 말이 나타내는 행동을 시험 삼아 함을 나타내는 표현.
-eo boda (no equivalent expression)
An expression used to indicate that one does the act mentioned in the preceding statement, as a test.

-아 : (두루낮춤으로) 어떤 사실을 서술하거나 물음, 명령, 권유를 나타내는 종결 어미.
-a (no equivalent expression)
(informal addressee-lowering) A sentence-final ending used to describe a certain fact, ask a question, **give an order**, or advise.

발음 기관+을 본뜨+ㄴ 기역, 니은, 미음, 시옷, 이응
본뜬

발음 기관 (noun) : 말소리를 내는 데 쓰는 신체의 각 부분.
pronunciation organ
Each bodily organ which is used to speak or make a sound.

을 : 동작이 직접적으로 영향을 미치는 대상을 나타내는 조사.
eul (no equivalent expression)
A postpositional particle used to indicate the subject that an action has a direct influence on.

본뜨다 (verb) : 이미 있는 것을 그대로 따라서 만들다.
imitate; copy
To duplicate something by copying exactly an existing object.

-ㄴ : 앞의 말이 관형어의 기능을 하게 만들고 사건이나 동작이 완료되어 그 상태가 유지되고 있음을 나타내는 어미.
-n (no equivalent expression)
An ending of a word that makes the preceding statement function as an adnominal phrase and indicates that an event or action has been completed and its state continues.

기역 (noun) : 한글 자모 'ㄱ'의 이름.
giyeok
The name of the consonant 'ㄱ' in the Korean alphabet.

니은 (noun) : 한글 자모 'ㄴ'의 이름.
nieun
The name of the consonant 'ㄴ' in the Korean alphabet.

미음 (noun) : 한글 자모 'ㅁ'의 이름.
mieum
The name of the consonant 'ㅁ' in the Korean alphabet.

시옷 (noun) : 한글 자모 'ㅅ'의 이름.
siot
The name of the consonant 'ㅅ' in the Korean alphabet.

이응 (noun) : 한글 자모 'ㅇ'의 이름.
ieung
The name of the consonant 'ㅇ' in the Korean alphabet.

다섯 글자

다섯 (determiner) : 넷에 하나를 더한 수의.
five
Of the number that is the sum of four and one.

글자 (noun) : 말을 적는 기호.
letter; character
A sign used to write down a spoken word.

세상+의 모든 소리+를 듣(들)+[어 보]+아.
들어 봐

세상 (noun) : 지구 위 전체.
world
The entire space on earth.

의 : 앞의 말이 뒤의 말에 대하여 소유, 소속, 소재, 관계, 기원, 주체의 관계를 가짐을 나타내는 조사.
ui (no equivalent expression)
A postpositional particle used to indicate that the referent of the following word is owned by, belongs to, is related to, originates from, or is the object of what the preceding word indicates.

모든 (determiner) : 빠지거나 남는 것 없이 전부인.
every
All without exception or without anything or anyone left.

소리 (noun) : 물체가 진동하여 생긴 음파가 귀에 들리는 것.
sound; noise
Sound wave heard by the ear that is created when an object vibrates.

를 : 동작이 직접적으로 영향을 미치는 대상을 나타내는 조사.
reul (no equivalent expression)
A postpositional particle used to indicate the subject that an act has a direct influence on.

듣다 (verb) : 귀로 소리를 알아차리다.
hear
To sense a sound with ears.

-어 보다 : 앞의 말이 나타내는 행동을 시험 삼아 함을 나타내는 표현.
-eo boda (no equivalent expression)
An expression used to indicate that one does the act mentioned in the preceding statement, as a test.

-아 : (두루낮춤으로) 어떤 사실을 서술하거나 물음, 명령, 권유를 나타내는 종결 어미.
-a (no equivalent expression)
(informal addressee-lowering) A sentence-final ending used to describe a certain fact, ask a question, **give an order**, or advise.

또 하+[고 싶]+은 말+을 다 외치+[어 보]+아.
외쳐 봐

또 (adverb) : 그 밖에 더.
moreover; besides
In addition to that.

하다 (verb) : 어떤 행동이나 동작, 활동 등을 행하다.
do; perform
To perform a certain move, action, activity, etc.

-고 싶다 : 앞의 말이 나타내는 행동을 하기를 원함을 나타내는 표현.
-go sipda (no equivalent expression)
An expression used to state that the speaker wants to do the act mentioned in the preceding statement.

-은 : 앞의 말이 관형어의 기능을 하게 만들고 현재의 상태를 나타내는 어미.
-eun (no equivalent expression)
An ending of a word that makes the preceding word function as an adnominal phrase and refers to the present state.

말 (noun) : 생각이나 느낌을 표현하고 전달하는 사람의 소리.
speech; words
Human voice through which thoughts or feelings are expressed and conveyed.

을 : 동작이 직접적으로 영향을 미치는 대상을 나타내는 조사.
eul (no equivalent expression)
A postpositional particle used to indicate the subject that an action has a direct influence on.

다 (adverb) : 남거나 빠진 것이 없이 모두.
all; everything
With nothing left over or missing.

외치다 (verb) : 큰 소리를 지르다.
cry out; shout
To yell in a loud voice.

-어 보다 : 앞의 말이 나타내는 행동을 시험 삼아 함을 나타내는 표현.
-eo boda (no equivalent expression)
An expression used to indicate that one does the act mentioned in the preceding statement, as a test.

-아 : (두루낮춤으로) 어떤 사실을 서술하거나 물음, 명령, 권유를 나타내는 종결 어미.
-a (no equivalent expression)
(informal addressee-lowering) A sentence-final ending used to describe a certain fact, ask a question, **give an order**, or advise.

신비롭(신비로우)+ㄴ 사연, 감추+었던 비밀
신비로운

신비롭다 (adjective) : 보통의 생각으로는 이해할 수 없을 정도로 놀랍고 신기한 느낌이 있다.
mysterious
Surprising and amazing to the extent that one cannot understand with one's common sense.

-ㄴ : 앞의 말이 관형어의 기능을 하게 만들고 현재의 상태를 나타내는 어미.
-n (no equivalent expression)
An ending of a word that makes the preceding statement function as an adnominal phrase and refers to the present state.

사연 (noun) : 일어난 일의 앞뒤 사정과 까닭.
story; circumstances
The situation and cause of an event or action.

감추다 (verb) : 어떤 사실이나 감정을 남이 모르도록 알리지 않고 비밀로 하다.
hide; conceal
To keep a certain fact or emotion secret from someone.

-었던 : 과거의 사건이나 상태를 다시 떠올리거나 그 사건이나 상태가 완료되지 않고 중단되었다는 의미를 나타내는 표현.
-eotdeon (no equivalent expression)
An expression used to recall a past incident or state, and indicate that the incident or state is suspended, not completed.

비밀 (noun) : 숨기고 있어 남이 모르는 일.
secret; covertness
A hidden thing unknown to others.

진실+을 전하+[여 주]+어.
전해 줘

진실 (noun) : 순수하고 거짓이 없는 마음.
truth; sincerity
A pure and sincere feeling.

을 : 동작이 직접적으로 영향을 미치는 대상을 나타내는 조사.
eul (no equivalent expression)
A postpositional particle used to indicate the subject that an action has a direct influence on.

전하다 (verb) : 어떤 소식, 생각 등을 상대에게 알리다.
deliver; pass on; tell
To convey some news, thought, etc., to another.

-여 주다 : 남을 위해 앞의 말이 나타내는 행동을 함을 나타내는 표현.
-yeo juda (no equivalent expression)
An expression used to indicate that one does the act mentioned in the preceding statement for someone.

-어 : (두루낮춤으로) 어떤 사실을 서술하거나 물음, 명령, 권유를 나타내는 종결 어미.
-eo (no equivalent expression)
(informal addressee-lowering) A sentence-final ending used to describe a certain fact, ask a question, **give an order**, or advise.

< 후렴(refrain) >

아 야 어 여 오 요 우 유 으 이

가 나 다 라 마 바 사 아 자 차 카 타 파 하

이제+부터 들리+[어 주]+어 너+의 마음+을.
들려 줘

이제 (noun) : 말하고 있는 바로 이때.
now
This moment being spoken of.

부터 : 어떤 일의 시작이나 처음을 나타내는 조사.
buteo (no equivalent expression)
A postpositional particle that indicates the start or beginning of something.

들리다 (verb) : 듣게 하다.
tell something; have something heard
To have someone listen to something.

-어 주다 : 남을 위해 앞의 말이 나타내는 행동을 함을 나타내는 표현.
-eo juda (no equivalent expression)
An expression used to indicate that one does the act mentioned in the preceding statement for someone.

-어 : (두루낮춤으로) 어떤 사실을 서술하거나 물음, 명령, 권유를 나타내는 종결 어미.
-eo (no equivalent expression)
(informal addressee-lowering) A sentence-final ending used to describe a certain fact, ask a question, give an order, or advise.

너 (pronoun) : 듣는 사람이 친구나 아랫사람일 때, 그 사람을 가리키는 말.
no equivalent expression
A pronoun used to indicate the listener when he/she is the same age or younger.

의 : 앞의 말이 뒤의 말에 대하여 소유, 소속, 소재, 관계, 기원, 주체의 관계를 가짐을 나타내는 조사.
ui (no equivalent expression)
A postpositional particle used to indicate that the referent of the following word is owned by, belongs to, is related to, originates from, or is the object of what the preceding word indicates.

마음 (noun) : 기분이나 느낌.
mood; feeling
A mood or feeling.

을 : 동작이 직접적으로 영향을 미치는 대상을 나타내는 조사.
eul (no equivalent expression)
A postpositional particle used to indicate the subject that an action has a direct influence on.

지금+부터 전하+[여 주]+어 너+의 사랑+을.
전해 줘

지금 (noun) : 말을 하고 있는 바로 이때.
now
The present moment as one speaks.

부터 : 어떤 일의 시작이나 처음을 나타내는 조사.
buteo (no equivalent expression)
A postpositional particle that indicates the start or beginning of something.

전하다 (verb) : 어떤 소식, 생각 등을 상대에게 알리다.
deliver; pass on; tell
To convey some news, thought, etc., to another.

-여 주다 : 남을 위해 앞의 말이 나타내는 행동을 함을 나타내는 표현.
-yeo juda (no equivalent expression)
An expression used to indicate that one does the act mentioned in the preceding statement for someone.

-어 : (두루낮춤으로) 어떤 사실을 서술하거나 물음, 명령, 권유를 나타내는 종결 어미.
-eo (no equivalent expression)
(informal addressee-lowering) A sentence-final ending used to describe a certain fact, ask a question, **give an order**, or advise.

너 (pronoun) : 듣는 사람이 친구나 아랫사람일 때, 그 사람을 가리키는 말.
no equivalent expression
A pronoun used to indicate the listener when he/she is the same age or younger.

의 : 앞의 말이 뒤의 말에 대하여 소유, 소속, 소재, 관계, 기원, 주체의 관계를 가짐을 나타내는 조사.
ui (no equivalent expression)
A postpositional particle used to indicate that the referent of the following word is owned by, belongs to, is related to, originates from, or is the object of what the preceding word indicates.

사랑 (noun) : 아끼고 소중히 여겨 정성을 다해 위하는 마음.
love
The attitude of sincerely caring about someone out of affection.

을 : 동작이 직접적으로 영향을 미치는 대상을 나타내는 조사.
eul (no equivalent expression)
A postpositional particle used to indicate the subject that an action has a direct influence on.

아 야 어 여 오 요 우 유 으 이

가 나 다 라 마 바 사 아 자 차 카 타 파 하

모음 스물하나+에 자음 열아홉+을 더하+여
더해

모음 (noun) : 사람이 목청을 울려 내는 소리로, 공기의 흐름이 방해를 받지 않고 나는 소리.
vowel
A sound made by vibrating one's vocal cords without obstructing the flow of air.

스물하나 : 21

에 : 앞말에 무엇이 더해짐을 나타내는 조사.
to
A postpositional particle to indicate that something is added to the preceding statement.

자음 (noun) : 목, 입, 혀 등의 발음 기관에 의해 장애를 받으며 나는 소리.
consonant
A sound in which the air is partially or completely blocked by the movement of the throat, mouth, tongue, etc.

열아홉 : 19

을 : 동작 대상의 수량이나 동작의 순서를 나타내는 조사.
eul (no equivalent expression)
A postpositional particle referring to the amount of a subject or the steps of an action.

더하다 (verb) : 보태어 늘리거나 많게 하다.
add; increase
To add or increase.

-여 : 앞의 말이 뒤의 말보다 먼저 일어났거나 뒤의 말에 대한 방법이나 수단이 됨을 나타내는 연결 어미.
-yeo (no equivalent expression)
A connective ending used when the preceding statement happened before the following statement, or was the ways or means to the following statement.

마흔 가지 소리+로 세상+을 느끼+[어 보]+아.
느껴 봐

마흔 (determiner) : 열의 네 배가 되는 수의.
forty
Being a number equaling ten times four.

가지 (noun) : 사물의 종류를 헤아리는 말.
kind; sort
A bound noun used to indicate the type of a thing.

소리 (noun) : 물체가 진동하여 생긴 음파가 귀에 들리는 것.
sound; noise
Sound wave heard by the ear that is created when an object vibrates.

로 : 어떤 일의 수단이나 도구를 나타내는 조사.
ro (no equivalent expression)
A postpositional particle that indicates a tool or means for something.

세상 (noun) : 지구 위 전체.
world
The entire space on earth.

을 : 동작이 직접적으로 영향을 미치는 대상을 나타내는 조사.
eul (no equivalent expression)
A postpositional particle used to indicate the subject that an action has a direct influence on.

느끼다 (verb) : 특정한 대상이나 상황을 어떻다고 생각하거나 인식하다.
think
To think about or perceive a certain subject or situation in a certain way.

-어 보다 : 앞의 말이 나타내는 행동을 시험 삼아 함을 나타내는 표현.
-eo boda (no equivalent expression)
An expression used to indicate that one does the act mentioned in the preceding statement, as a test.

-아 : (두루낮춤으로) 어떤 사실을 서술하거나 물음, 명령, 권유를 나타내는 종결 어미.
-a (no equivalent expression)
(informal addressee-lowering) A sentence-final ending used to describe a certain fact, ask a question, **give an order**, or advise.

< 2 절(verse) >

하늘+과 땅+이 만나+(아) ㅗ, ㅜ
만나

하늘 (noun) : 땅 위로 펼쳐진 무한히 넓은 공간.
sky
The vast, limitless space that unfolds above the ground.

과 : 앞과 뒤의 명사를 같은 자격으로 이어 줄 때 쓰는 조사.
gwa (no equivalent expression)
A postpositional particle used to list the preceding and following nouns.

땅 (noun) : 지구에서 물로 된 부분이 아닌 흙이나 돌로 된 부분.
ground; land
The part of the earth that consists of soil or stones instead of water.

이 : 어떤 상태나 상황의 대상이나 동작의 주체를 나타내는 조사.
i (no equivalent expression)
A postpositional particle referring to a subject under a certain state or situation, or the agent of an action.

만나다 (verb) : 선이나 길, 강 등이 서로 마주 닿거나 연결되다.
meet; join
For a line, road, river, etc. to adjoin or be connected with each other.

-아 : 앞의 말이 뒤의 말보다 먼저 일어났거나 뒤의 말에 대한 방법이나 수단이 됨을 나타내는 연결 어미.
-a (no equivalent expression)
A connective ending used when the preceding statement happened before the following statement or was the ways or means to the following statement.

ㅗ (noun) : 한글 자모의 열아홉째 글자. 이름은 '오'이고 중성으로 쓴다.
o
The fifth vowel of the Korean alphabet pronounced 'o' and used as a middle vowel letter.

ㅜ (noun) : 한글 자모의 스물한째 글자. 이름은 '우'이고 중성으로 쓴다.
u
The seventh vowel of the Korean alphabet pronounced 'u' and used as a middle vowel letter.

사람+과 만나+ㄴ다면 ㅏ, ㅓ

만난다면

사람 (noun) : 생각할 수 있으며 언어와 도구를 만들어 사용하고 사회를 이루어 사는 존재.
human; man
A being that is capable of thinking, makes and uses languages and tools and lives by forming a society with others.

과 : 누군가를 상대로 하여 어떤 일을 할 때 그 상대임을 나타내는 조사.
gwa (no equivalent expression)
A postpositional word referring to the person when doing something with him/her.

만나다 (verb) : 선이나 길, 강 등이 서로 마주 닿거나 연결되다.
meet; join
For a line, road, river, etc. to adjoin or be connected with each other.

-ㄴ다면 : 어떠한 사실이나 상황을 가정하는 뜻을 나타내는 연결 어미.
-ndamyeon (no equivalent expression)
A connective ending used when assuming a certain fact or situation.

ㅏ (noun) : 한글 자모의 열다섯째 글자. 이름은 '아'이고 중성으로 쓴다.
a
The first vowel of the Korean alphabet pronounced 'a' and used as a medial.

ㅓ (noun) : 한글 자모의 열일곱째 글자. 이름은 '어'이고 중성으로 쓴다.
eo
The third vowel of the Korean alphabet pronounced 'eo' and used as a middle vowel letter.

하루+(이)+면+은 충분하+여.
하루면은 충분해

하루 (noun) : 밤 열두 시부터 다음 날 밤 열두 시까지의 스물네 시간.
day
The 24 hours from midnight to the following midnight.

이다 : 주어가 지시하는 대상의 속성이나 부류를 지정하는 뜻을 나타내는 서술격 조사.
ida (no equivalent expression)
A predicate particle indicating the meaning of the attribute or category of the thing that the subject of the sentence refers to.

-면 : 뒤에 오는 말에 대한 근거나 조건이 됨을 나타내는 연결 어미.
-myeon (no equivalent expression)
A connective ending used when the preceding statement becomes the reason or condition of the following statement.

은 : 강조의 뜻을 나타내는 조사.
eun (no equivalent expression)
A postpositional particle used to indicate an emphasis.

충분하다 (adjective) : 모자라지 않고 넉넉하다.
sufficient; enough
Being ample, without shortage.

-여 : (두루낮춤으로) 어떤 사실을 서술하거나 물음, 명령, 권유를 나타내는 종결 어미.
-yeo (no equivalent expression)
(informal addressee-lowering) A sentence-final ending used to **describe** a certain fact, ask a question, give an order, or advise.

하늘, 땅, 사람+을 본뜨+ㄴ 아 어 오 우 야 여 요 유 으 이
본뜬

하늘 (noun) : 땅 위로 펼쳐진 무한히 넓은 공간.
sky
The vast, limitless space that unfolds above the ground.

땅 (noun) : 지구에서 물로 된 부분이 아닌 흙이나 돌로 된 부분.
ground; land
The part of the earth that consists of soil or stones instead of water.

사람 (noun) : 생각할 수 있으며 언어와 도구를 만들어 사용하고 사회를 이루어 사는 존재.
human; man
A being that is capable of thinking, makes and uses languages and tools and lives by forming a society with others.

을 : 동작이 직접적으로 영향을 미치는 대상을 나타내는 조사.
eul (no equivalent expression)
A postpositional particle used to indicate the subject that an action has a direct influence on.

본뜨다 (verb) : 이미 있는 것을 그대로 따라서 만들다.
imitate; copy
To duplicate something by copying exactly an existing object.

-ㄴ : 앞의 말이 관형어의 기능을 하게 만들고 사건이나 동작이 완료되어 그 상태가 유지되고 있음을 나타내는 어미.
-n (no equivalent expression)
An ending of a word that makes the preceding statement function as an adnominal phrase and indicates that an event or action has been completed and its state continues.

아 (noun) : 한글 자모의 열다섯째 글자. 이름은 '아'이고 중성으로 쓴다.
a
The first vowel of the Korean alphabet pronounced 'a' and used as a medial.

어 (noun) : 한글 자모의 열일곱째 글자. 이름은 '어'이고 중성으로 쓴다.
eo
The third vowel of the Korean alphabet pronounced 'eo' and used as a middle vowel letter.

오 (noun) : 한글 자모의 열아홉째 글자. 이름은 '오'이고 중성으로 쓴다.
o
The fifth vowel of the Korean alphabet pronounced 'o' and used as a middle vowel letter.

우 (noun) : 한글 자모의 스물한째 글자. 이름은 '우'이고 중성으로 쓴다.
u
The seventh vowel of the Korean alphabet pronounced 'u' and used as a middle vowel letter.

야 (noun) : 한글 자모의 열여섯째 글자. 이름은 '야'이고 중성으로 쓴다.
ya
The second vowel of the Korean alphabet pronounced 'ya' and used as a medial.

여 (noun) : 한글 자모의 열여덟째 글자. 이름은 '여'이고 중성으로 쓴다.
yeo
The fourth vowel of the Korean alphabet pronounced 'yeo' and used as a middle vowel letter.

요 (noun) : 한글 자모의 스무째 글자. 이름은 '요'이고 중성으로 쓴다.
yo
The sixth vowel of the Korean alphabet pronounced 'yo' and used as a middle vowel letter.

유 (noun) : 한글 자모의 스물두째 글자. 이름은 '유'이고 중성으로 쓴다.
yu
The eighth vowel of the Korean alphabet pronounced 'yu' and used as a middle vowel letter.

으 (noun) : 한글 자모의 스물셋째 글자. 이름은 '으'이고 중성으로 쓴다.
eu
The ninth vowel of the Korean alphabet pronounced 'eu' and used as a middle vowel letter.

이 (noun) : 한글 자모의 스물넷째 글자. 이름은 '이'이고 중성으로 쓴다.
i
The 10th vowel of the Korean alphabet pronounced 'i' and used as a middle vowel letter.

열 글자

열 (determiner) : 아홉에 하나를 더한 수의.
ten
Equal to 9 + 1.

글자 (noun) : 말을 적는 기호.
letter; character
A sign used to write down a spoken word.

세상+의 모든 소리+를 듣(들)+[어 보]+아.
들어 봐

세상 (noun) : 지구 위 전체.
world
The entire space on earth.

의 : 앞의 말이 뒤의 말에 대하여 소유, 소속, 소재, 관계, 기원, 주체의 관계를 가짐을 나타내는 조사.
ui (no equivalent expression)
A postpositional particle used to indicate that the referent of the following word is owned by, belongs to, is related to, originates from, or is the object of what the preceding word indicates.

모든 (determiner) : 빠지거나 남는 것 없이 전부인.
every
All without exception or without anything or anyone left.

소리 (noun) : 물체가 진동하여 생긴 음파가 귀에 들리는 것.
sound; noise
Sound wave heard by the ear that is created when an object vibrates.

를 : 동작이 직접적으로 영향을 미치는 대상을 나타내는 조사.
reul (no equivalent expression)
A postpositional particle used to indicate the subject that an act has a direct influence on.

듣다 (verb) : 귀로 소리를 알아차리다.
hear
To sense a sound with ears.

-어 보다 : 앞의 말이 나타내는 행동을 시험 삼아 함을 나타내는 표현.
-eo boda (no equivalent expression)
An expression used to indicate that one does the act mentioned in the preceding statement, as a test.

-아 : (두루낮춤으로) 어떤 사실을 서술하거나 물음, 명령, 권유를 나타내는 종결 어미.
-a (no equivalent expression)
(informal addressee-lowering) A sentence-final ending used to describe a certain fact, ask a question, **give an order**, or advise.

또 하+[고 싶]+은 말+을 다 외치+[어 보]+아.
외쳐 봐

또 (adverb) : 그 밖에 더.
moreover; besides
In addition to that.

하다 (verb) : 어떤 행동이나 동작, 활동 등을 행하다.
do; perform
To perform a certain move, action, activity, etc.

-고 싶다 : 앞의 말이 나타내는 행동을 하기를 원함을 나타내는 표현.
-go sipda (no equivalent expression)
An expression used to state that the speaker wants to do the act mentioned in the preceding statement.

-은 : 앞의 말이 관형어의 기능을 하게 만들고 현재의 상태를 나타내는 어미.
-eun (no equivalent expression)
An ending of a word that makes the preceding word function as an adnominal phrase and refers to the present state.

말 (noun) : 생각이나 느낌을 표현하고 전달하는 사람의 소리.
speech; words
Human voice through which thoughts or feelings are expressed and conveyed.

을 : 동작이 직접적으로 영향을 미치는 대상을 나타내는 조사.
eul (no equivalent expression)
A postpositional particle used to indicate the subject that an action has a direct influence on.

다 (adverb) : 남거나 빠진 것이 없이 모두.
all; everything
With nothing left over or missing.

외치다 (verb) : 큰 소리를 지르다.
cry out; shout
To yell in a loud voice.

-어 보다 : 앞의 말이 나타내는 행동을 시험 삼아 함을 나타내는 표현.
-eo boda (no equivalent expression)
An expression used to indicate that one does the act mentioned in the preceding statement, as a test.

-아 : (두루낮춤으로) 어떤 사실을 서술하거나 물음, 명령, 권유를 나타내는 종결 어미.
-a (no equivalent expression)
(informal addressee-lowering) A sentence-final ending used to describe a certain fact, ask a question, **give an order**, or advise.

신비롭(신비로우)+ㄴ 사연, 감추+었던 비밀
신비로운

신비롭다 (adjective) : 보통의 생각으로는 이해할 수 없을 정도로 놀랍고 신기한 느낌이 있다.
mysterious
Surprising and amazing to the extent that one cannot understand with one's common sense.

-ㄴ : 앞의 말이 관형어의 기능을 하게 만들고 현재의 상태를 나타내는 어미.
-n (no equivalent expression)
An ending of a word that makes the preceding statement function as an adnominal phrase and refers to the present state.

사연 (noun) : 일어난 일의 앞뒤 사정과 까닭.
story; circumstances
The situation and cause of an event or action.

감추다 (verb) : 어떤 사실이나 감정을 남이 모르도록 알리지 않고 비밀로 하다.
hide; conceal
To keep a certain fact or emotion secret from someone.

-었던 : 과거의 사건이나 상태를 다시 떠올리거나 그 사건이나 상태가 완료되지 않고 중단되었다는 의미를 나타내는 표현.
-eotdeon (no equivalent expression)
An expression used to recall a past incident or state, and indicate that the incident or state is suspended, not completed.

비밀 (noun) : 숨기고 있어 남이 모르는 일.
secret; covertness
A hidden thing unknown to others.

진실+을 전하+[여 주]+어.
전해 줘

진실 (noun) : 순수하고 거짓이 없는 마음.
truth; sincerity
A pure and sincere feeling.

을 : 동작이 직접적으로 영향을 미치는 대상을 나타내는 조사.
eul (no equivalent expression)
A postpositional particle used to indicate the subject that an action has a direct influence on.

전하다 (verb) : 어떤 소식, 생각 등을 상대에게 알리다.
deliver; pass on; tell
To convey some news, thought, etc., to another.

-여 주다 : 남을 위해 앞의 말이 나타내는 행동을 함을 나타내는 표현.
-yeo juda (no equivalent expression)
An expression used to indicate that one does the act mentioned in the preceding statement for someone.

-어 : (두루낮춤으로) 어떤 사실을 서술하거나 물음, 명령, 권유를 나타내는 종결 어미.
-eo (no equivalent expression)
(informal addressee-lowering) A sentence-final ending used to describe a certain fact, ask a question, **give an order**, or advise.

< 후렴(refrain) >

아 야 어 여 오 요 우 유 으 이

가 나 다 라 마 바 사 아 자 차 카 타 파 하

이제+부터 들리+[어 주]+어 너+의 마음+을.
들려 줘

이제 (noun) : 말하고 있는 바로 이때.
now
This moment being spoken of.

부터 : 어떤 일의 시작이나 처음을 나타내는 조사.
buteo (no equivalent expression)
A postpositional particle that indicates the start or beginning of something.

들리다 (verb) : 듣게 하다.
tell something; have something heard
To have someone listen to something.

-어 주다 : 남을 위해 앞의 말이 나타내는 행동을 함을 나타내는 표현.
-eo juda (no equivalent expression)
An expression used to indicate that one does the act mentioned in the preceding statement for someone.

-어 : (두루낮춤으로) 어떤 사실을 서술하거나 물음, 명령, 권유를 나타내는 종결 어미.
-eo (no equivalent expression)
(informal addressee-lowering) A sentence-final ending used to describe a certain fact, ask a question, give an order, or advise.

너 (pronoun) : 듣는 사람이 친구나 아랫사람일 때, 그 사람을 가리키는 말.
no equivalent expression
A pronoun used to indicate the listener when he/she is the same age or younger.

의 : 앞의 말이 뒤의 말에 대하여 소유, 소속, 소재, 관계, 기원, 주체의 관계를 가짐을 나타내는 조사.
ui (no equivalent expression)
A postpositional particle used to indicate that the referent of the following word is owned by, belongs to, is related to, originates from, or is the object of what the preceding word indicates.

마음 (noun) : 기분이나 느낌.
mood; feeling
A mood or feeling.

을 : 동작이 직접적으로 영향을 미치는 대상을 나타내는 조사.
eul (no equivalent expression)
A postpositional particle used to indicate the subject that an action has a direct influence on.

지금+부터 전하+[여 주]+어 너+의 사랑+을.
전해 줘

지금 (noun) : 말을 하고 있는 바로 이때.
now
The present moment as one speaks.

부터 : 어떤 일의 시작이나 처음을 나타내는 조사.
buteo (no equivalent expression)
A postpositional particle that indicates the start or beginning of something.

전하다 (verb) : 어떤 소식, 생각 등을 상대에게 알리다.
deliver; pass on; tell
To convey some news, thought, etc., to another.

-여 주다 : 남을 위해 앞의 말이 나타내는 행동을 함을 나타내는 표현.
-yeo juda (no equivalent expression)
An expression used to indicate that one does the act mentioned in the preceding statement for someone.

-어 : (두루낮춤으로) 어떤 사실을 서술하거나 물음, 명령, 권유를 나타내는 종결 어미.
-eo (no equivalent expression)
(informal addressee-lowering) A sentence-final ending used to describe a certain fact, ask a question, **give an order**, or advise.

너 (pronoun) : 듣는 사람이 친구나 아랫사람일 때, 그 사람을 가리키는 말.
no equivalent expression
A pronoun used to indicate the listener when he/she is the same age or younger.

의 : 앞의 말이 뒤의 말에 대하여 소유, 소속, 소재, 관계, 기원, 주체의 관계를 가짐을 나타내는 조사.
ui (no equivalent expression)
A postpositional particle used to indicate that the referent of the following word is owned by, belongs to, is related to, originates from, or is the object of what the preceding word indicates.

사랑 (noun) : 아끼고 소중히 여겨 정성을 다해 위하는 마음.
love
The attitude of sincerely caring about someone out of affection.

을 : 동작이 직접적으로 영향을 미치는 대상을 나타내는 조사.
eul (no equivalent expression)
A postpositional particle used to indicate the subject that an action has a direct influence on.

아 야 어 여 오 요 우 유 으 이

가 나 다 라 마 바 사 아 자 차 카 타 파 하

모음 스물하나+에 자음 열아홉+을 더하+여

더해

모음 (noun) : 사람이 목청을 울려 내는 소리로, 공기의 흐름이 방해를 받지 않고 나는 소리.
vowel
A sound made by vibrating one's vocal cords without obstructing the flow of air.

스물하나 : 21

에 : 앞말에 무엇이 더해짐을 나타내는 조사.
to
A postpositional particle to indicate that something is added to the preceding statement.

자음 (noun) : 목, 입, 혀 등의 발음 기관에 의해 장애를 받으며 나는 소리.
consonant
A sound in which the air is partially or completely blocked by the movement of the throat, mouth, tongue, etc.

열아홉 : 19

을 : 동작 대상의 수량이나 동작의 순서를 나타내는 조사.
eul (no equivalent expression)
A postpositional particle referring to the amount of a subject or the steps of an action.

더하다 (verb) : 보태어 늘리거나 많게 하다.
add; increase
To add or increase.

-여 : 앞의 말이 뒤의 말보다 먼저 일어났거나 뒤의 말에 대한 방법이나 수단이 됨을 나타내는 연결 어미.
-yeo (no equivalent expression)
A connective ending used when the preceding statement happened before the following statement, or was the ways or means to the following statement.

마흔 가지 소리+로 세상+을 느끼+[어 보]+아.
느껴 봐

마흔 (determiner) : 열의 네 배가 되는 수의.
forty
Being a number equaling ten times four.

가지 (noun) : 사물의 종류를 헤아리는 말.
kind; sort
A bound noun used to indicate the type of a thing.

소리 (noun) : 물체가 진동하여 생긴 음파가 귀에 들리는 것.
sound; noise
Sound wave heard by the ear that is created when an object vibrates.

로 : 어떤 일의 수단이나 도구를 나타내는 조사.
ro (no equivalent expression)
A postpositional particle that indicates a tool or means for something.

세상 (noun) : 지구 위 전체.
world
The entire space on earth.

을 : 동작이 직접적으로 영향을 미치는 대상을 나타내는 조사.
eul (no equivalent expression)
A postpositional particle used to indicate the subject that an action has a direct influence on.

느끼다 (verb) : 특정한 대상이나 상황을 어떻다고 생각하거나 인식하다.
think
To think about or perceive a certain subject or situation in a certain way.

-어 보다 : 앞의 말이 나타내는 행동을 시험 삼아 함을 나타내는 표현.
-eo boda (no equivalent expression)
An expression used to indicate that one does the act mentioned in the preceding statement, as a test.

-아 : (두루낮춤으로) 어떤 사실을 서술하거나 물음, 명령, 권유를 나타내는 종결 어미.
-a (no equivalent expression)
(informal addressee-lowering) A sentence-final ending used to describe a certain fact, ask a question, **give an order**, or advise.

< 후렴(refrain) >

들리+[어 주]+어요.
들려 줘요

들리다 (verb) : 듣게 하다.
tell something; have something heard
To have someone listen to something.

-어 주다 : 남을 위해 앞의 말이 나타내는 행동을 함을 나타내는 표현.
-eo juda (no equivalent expression)
An expression used to indicate that one does the act mentioned in the preceding statement for someone.

-어요 : (두루높임으로) 어떤 사실을 서술하거나 질문, 명령, 권유함을 나타내는 종결 어미.
-eoyo (no equivalent expression)
(informal addressee-raising) A sentence-final ending used to describe a certain fact, ask a question, **give an order**, or advise.

이 소리 들리+나요?

이 (determiner) : 말하는 사람에게 가까이 있거나 말하는 사람이 생각하고 있는 대상을 가리키는 말.
this
A pronoun used to indicate something near the speaker or what the speaker is thinking.

소리 (noun) : 물체가 진동하여 생긴 음파가 귀에 들리는 것.
sound; noise
Sound wave heard by the ear that is created when an object vibrates.

들리다 (verb) : 소리가 귀를 통해 알아차려지다.
be heard; be audible
For a sound to be heard and recognized through one's ears.

-나요 : (두루높임으로) 앞의 내용에 대해 상대방에게 물어볼 때 쓰는 표현.
-nayo (no equivalent expression)
(informal addressee-raising) An expression used to ask the listener about the preceding content.

달콤하+게, 부드럽+게 우리 모두 말하+[여 보]+아요.
말해 봐요

달콤하다 (adjective) : 느낌이 좋고 기분이 좋다.
pleasant feeling
Pleasant sensation; good feeling

-게 : 앞의 말이 뒤에서 가리키는 일의 목적이나 결과, 방식, 정도 등이 됨을 나타내는 연결 어미.
-ge (no equivalent expression)
A connective ending used when the preceding statement is the purpose, result, **method**, amount, etc., of something mentioned in the following statement.

부드럽다 (adjective) : 성격이나 마음씨, 태도 등이 다정하고 따뜻하다.
soft; gentle
One's personality, heart, attitude, etc., being kind and warm.

-게 : 앞의 말이 뒤에서 가리키는 일의 목적이나 결과, 방식, 정도 등이 됨을 나타내는 연결 어미.
-ge (no equivalent expression)
A connective ending used when the preceding statement is the purpose, result, **method**, amount, etc., of something mentioned in the following statement.

우리 (pronoun) : 말하는 사람이 자기와 듣는 사람 또는 이를 포함한 여러 사람들을 가리키는 말.
we
A pronoun used when the speaker refers to himself/herself and the listener or listeners, or a group of people including the speaker and listener or listeners.

모두 (adverb) : 빠짐없이 다.
all of
Everyone or everything without exception.

말하다 (verb) : 어떤 사실이나 자신의 생각 또는 느낌을 말로 나타내다.
say; tell; speak; talk
To verbally present a fact or one's thoughts or feelings.

-여 보다 : 앞의 말이 나타내는 행동을 시험 삼아 함을 나타내는 표현.
-yeo boda (no equivalent expression)
An expression used to indicate that one does the act mentioned in the preceding statement, as a test.

-아요 : (두루높임으로) 어떤 사실을 서술하거나 질문, 명령, 권유함을 나타내는 종결 어미.
-ayo (no equivalent expression)
(informal addressee-raising) A sentence-final ending used to describe a certain fact, ask a question, **give an order**, or advise.

아 야 어 여 오 요 우 유 으 이

가 나 다 라 마 바 사 아 자 차 카 타 파 하

이제+부터 들리+[어 주]+어 너+의 마음+을.
들려 줘

이제 (noun) : 말하고 있는 바로 이때.
now
This moment being spoken of.

부터 : 어떤 일의 시작이나 처음을 나타내는 조사.
buteo (no equivalent expression)
A postpositional particle that indicates the start or beginning of something.

들리다 (verb) : 듣게 하다.
tell something; have something heard
To have someone listen to something.

-어 주다 : 남을 위해 앞의 말이 나타내는 행동을 함을 나타내는 표현.
-eo juda (no equivalent expression)
An expression used to indicate that one does the act mentioned in the preceding statement for someone.

-어 : (두루낮춤으로) 어떤 사실을 서술하거나 물음, 명령, 권유를 나타내는 종결 어미.
-eo (no equivalent expression)
(informal addressee-lowering) A sentence-final ending used to describe a certain fact, ask a question, give an order, or advise.

너 (pronoun) : 듣는 사람이 친구나 아랫사람일 때, 그 사람을 가리키는 말.
no equivalent expression
A pronoun used to indicate the listener when he/she is the same age or younger.

의 : 앞의 말이 뒤의 말에 대하여 소유, 소속, 소재, 관계, 기원, 주체의 관계를 가짐을 나타내는 조사.
ui (no equivalent expression)
A postpositional particle used to indicate that the referent of the following word is owned by, belongs to, is related to, originates from, or is the object of what the preceding word indicates.

마음 (noun) : 기분이나 느낌.
mood; feeling
A mood or feeling.

을 : 동작이 직접적으로 영향을 미치는 대상을 나타내는 조사.
eul (no equivalent expression)
A postpositional particle used to indicate the subject that an action has a direct influence on.

지금+부터 전하+[여 주]+어 너+의 사랑+을.

전해 줘

지금 (noun) : 말을 하고 있는 바로 이때.
now
The present moment as one speaks.

부터 : 어떤 일의 시작이나 처음을 나타내는 조사.
buteo (no equivalent expression)
A postpositional particle that indicates the start or beginning of something.

전하다 (verb) : 어떤 소식, 생각 등을 상대에게 알리다.
deliver; pass on; tell
To convey some news, thought, etc., to another.

-여 주다 : 남을 위해 앞의 말이 나타내는 행동을 함을 나타내는 표현.
-yeo juda (no equivalent expression)
An expression used to indicate that one does the act mentioned in the preceding statement for someone.

-어 : (두루낮춤으로) 어떤 사실을 서술하거나 물음, 명령, 권유를 나타내는 종결 어미.
-eo (no equivalent expression)
(informal addressee-lowering) A sentence-final ending used to describe a certain fact, ask a question, **give an order**, or advise.

너 (pronoun) : 듣는 사람이 친구나 아랫사람일 때, 그 사람을 가리키는 말.
no equivalent expression
A pronoun used to indicate the listener when he/she is the same age or younger.

의 : 앞의 말이 뒤의 말에 대하여 소유, 소속, 소재, 관계, 기원, 주체의 관계를 가짐을 나타내는 조사.
ui (no equivalent expression)
A postpositional particle used to indicate that the referent of the following word is owned by, belongs to, is related to, originates from, or is the object of what the preceding word indicates.

사랑 (noun) : 아끼고 소중히 여겨 정성을 다해 위하는 마음.
love
The attitude of sincerely caring about someone out of affection.

을 : 동작이 직접적으로 영향을 미치는 대상을 나타내는 조사.
eul (no equivalent expression)
A postpositional particle used to indicate the subject that an action has a direct influence on.

아 야 어 여 오 요 우 유 으 이

가 나 다 라 마 바 사 아 자 차 카 타 파 하

모음 스물하나+에 자음 열아홉+을 더하+여
더해

모음 (noun) : 사람이 목청을 울려 내는 소리로, 공기의 흐름이 방해를 받지 않고 나는 소리.
vowel
A sound made by vibrating one's vocal cords without obstructing the flow of air.

스물하나 : 21

에 : 앞말에 무엇이 더해짐을 나타내는 조사.
to
A postpositional particle to indicate that something is added to the preceding statement.

자음 (noun) : 목, 입, 혀 등의 발음 기관에 의해 장애를 받으며 나는 소리.
consonant
A sound in which the air is partially or completely blocked by the movement of the throat, mouth, tongue, etc.

열아홉 : 19

을 : 동작 대상의 수량이나 동작의 순서를 나타내는 조사.
eul (no equivalent expression)
A postpositional particle referring to the amount of a subject or the steps of an action.

더하다 (verb) : 보태어 늘리거나 많게 하다.
add; increase
To add or increase.

-여 : 앞의 말이 뒤의 말보다 먼저 일어났거나 뒤의 말에 대한 방법이나 수단이 됨을 나타내는 연결 어미.
-yeo (no equivalent expression)
A connective ending used when the preceding statement happened before the following statement, or was the ways or means to the following statement.

마흔 가지 소리+로 세상+을 느끼+[어 보]+아.
느껴 봐

마흔 (determiner) : 열의 네 배가 되는 수의.
forty
Being a number equaling ten times four.

가지 (noun) : 사물의 종류를 헤아리는 말.
kind; sort
A bound noun used to indicate the type of a thing.

소리 (noun) : 물체가 진동하여 생긴 음파가 귀에 들리는 것.
sound; noise
Sound wave heard by the ear that is created when an object vibrates.

로 : 어떤 일의 수단이나 도구를 나타내는 조사.
ro (no equivalent expression)
A postpositional particle that indicates a tool or means for something.

세상 (noun) : 지구 위 전체.
world
The entire space on earth.

을 : 동작이 직접적으로 영향을 미치는 대상을 나타내는 조사.
eul (no equivalent expression)
A postpositional particle used to indicate the subject that an action has a direct influence on.

느끼다 (verb) : 특정한 대상이나 상황을 어떻다고 생각하거나 인식하다.
think
To think about or perceive a certain subject or situation in a certain way.

-어 보다 : 앞의 말이 나타내는 행동을 시험 삼아 함을 나타내는 표현.
-eo boda (no equivalent expression)
An expression used to indicate that one does the act mentioned in the preceding statement, as a test.

-아 : (두루낮춤으로) 어떤 사실을 서술하거나 물음, 명령, 권유를 나타내는 종결 어미.
-a (no equivalent expression)
(informal addressee-lowering) A sentence-final ending used to describe a certain fact, ask a question, **give an order**, or advise.

< 2 >

과일송

과일(fruit) 송(song)

[발음(pronunciation)]

< 1 절(verse) >

맛있는 과일 과일 과일
마신는 과일 과일 과일
masinneun gwail gwail gwail

아삭아삭 과일 과일
아삭아삭 과일 과일
asagasak gwail gwail

먹고 싶어 과일 과일
먹꼬 시퍼 과일 과일
meokgo sipeo gwail gwail

빨간색 딸기 사과 앵두
빨간색 딸기 사과 앵두
ppalgansaek ttalgi sagwa aengdu

노란색 참외 레몬 망고
노란색 참외 레몬 망고
noransaek chamoe remon manggo

초록색 수박 매실 멜론
초록쌕 수박 매실 멜론
choroksaek subak maesil mellon

보라색 포도 자두 오디
보라색 포도 자두 오디
borasaek podo jadu odi

맛이 어때요?
마시 어때요?
masi eottaeyo?

달아요 달아요 달아요
다라요 다라요 다라요
darayo darayo darayo

맛이 어때요?
마시 어때요?
masi eottaeyo?

달콤해 달콤해 달콤해
달콤해 달콤해 달콤해
dalkomhae dalkomhae dalkomhae

어때요? 어때요?
어때요? 어때요?
eottaeyo? eottaeyo?

달아요 셔요 달콤해 새콤해
다라요 셔요 달콤해 새콤해
darayo syeoyo dalkomhae saekomhae

< 2 절(verse) >

맛있는 과일 과일 과일
마신는 과일 과일 과일
masinneun gwail gwail gwail

아삭아삭 과일 과일
아삭아삭 과일 과일
asagasak gwail gwail

먹고 싶어 과일 과일
먹꼬 시퍼 과일 과일
meokgo sipeo gwail gwail

빨간색 딸기 사과 앵두
빨간색 딸기 사과 앵두
ppalgansaek ttalgi sagwa aengdu

노란색 참외 레몬 망고
노란색 참외 레몬 망고
noransaek chamoe remon manggo

초록색 수박 매실 멜론
초록쌕 수박 매실 멜론
choroksaek subak maesil mellon

보라색 포도 자두 오디
보라색 포도 자두 오디
borasaek podo jadu odi

맛이 어때요?
마시 어때요?
masi eottaeyo?

셔요 셔요 셔요
셔요 셔요 셔요
syeoyo syeoyo syeoyo

맛이 어때요?
마시 어때요?
masi eottaeyo?

새콤해 새콤해 새콤해
새콤해 새콤해 새콤해
saekomhae saekomhae saekomhae

어때요? 어때요?
어때요? 어때요?
eottaeyo? eottaeyo?

달아요 셔요 달콤해 새콤해
다라요 셔요 달콤해 새콤해
darayo syeoyo dalkomhae saekomhae

맛있는 과일 과일 과일
마신는 과일 과일 과일
masinneun gwail gwail gwail

아삭아삭 과일 과일
아삭아삭 과일 과일
asagasak gwail gwail

먹고 싶어 과일 과일
먹꼬 시퍼 과일 과일
meokgo sipeo gwail gwail

맛있는 과일 과일 과일
마신는 과일 과일 과일
masinneun gwail gwail gwail

아삭아삭 과일 과일
아삭아삭 과일 과일
asagasak gwail gwail

먹고 싶어 과일 과일
먹꼬 시퍼 과일 과일
meokgo sipeo gwail gwail

먹고 싶어 과일 과일
먹꼬 시퍼 과일 과일
meokgo sipeo gwail gwail

< 1 절(verse) >

맛있+는 과일 과일 과일.

맛있다 (adjective) : 맛이 좋다.
tasty; delicious
Tasting good.

-는 : 앞의 말이 관형어의 기능을 하게 만들고 사건이나 동작이 현재 일어남을 나타내는 어미.
-neun (no equivalent expression)
An ending of a word that makes the preceding statement function as an adnominal phrase and implies that an event or action is happening in the present.

과일 (noun) : 사과, 배, 포도, 밤 등과 같이 나뭇가지나 줄기에 열리는 먹을 수 있는 열매.
fruit
Edible fruit that grows on the stem or branch of a tree, such as apples, pears, grapes, chestnuts, etc.

아삭아삭 과일 과일.

아삭아삭 (adverb) : 연하고 싱싱한 과일이나 채소를 베어 물 때 나는 소리.
crunch
A word imitating the sound made when taking a bite out of a fresh fruit or vegetable.

과일 (noun) : 사과, 배, 포도, 밤 등과 같이 나뭇가지나 줄기에 열리는 먹을 수 있는 열매.
fruit
Edible fruit that grows on the stem or branch of a tree, such as apples, pears, grapes, chestnuts, etc.

먹+[고 싶]+어, 과일 과일.

먹다 (verb) : 음식 등을 입을 통하여 배 속에 들여보내다.
eat; have; consume; take
To put food into one's mouth and take it in one's stomach.

-고 싶다 : 앞의 말이 나타내는 행동을 하기를 원함을 나타내는 표현.
-go sipda (no equivalent expression)
An expression used to state that the speaker wants to do the act mentioned in the preceding statement.

-어 : (두루낮춤으로) 어떤 사실을 서술하거나 물음, 명령, 권유를 나타내는 종결 어미.
-eo (no equivalent expression)
(informal addressee-lowering) A sentence-final ending used to **describe a certain fact**, ask a question, give an order, or advise.

과일 (noun) : 사과, 배, 포도, 밤 등과 같이 나뭇가지나 줄기에 열리는 먹을 수 있는 열매.
fruit
Edible fruit that grows on the stem or branch of a tree, such as apples, pears, grapes, chestnuts, etc.

빨간색 딸기 사과 앵두.

빨간색 (noun) : 흐르는 피나 잘 익은 사과, 고추처럼 붉은 색.
red color
A red color like that of blood, or a ripe apple or red pepper.

딸기 (noun) : 줄기가 땅 위로 뻗으며, 겉에 씨가 박혀 있는 빨간 열매가 열리는 여러해살이풀. 또는 그 열매.
strawberry
A perennial plant that stretches its stems on the ground and bears a red fruit with seeds stuck on the outside, or the fruit.

사과 (noun) : 모양이 둥글고 붉으며 새콤하고 단맛이 나는 과일.
apple
A round-shaped sweet and sour fruit with red skin.

앵두 (noun) : 모양이 작고 둥글며 달콤하면서 신맛을 지닌 붉은색 과일.
cherry
A sweet and sour, red fruit that is small and round in shape.

노란색 참외 레몬 망고.

노란색 (noun) : 병아리나 바나나와 같은 색.
yellow
The color of a chick or banana.

참외 (noun) : 색이 노랗고 단맛이 나며 주로 여름에 먹는 열매.
oriental melon
A yellow, sweet fruit that is usually eaten in the summer.

레몬 (noun) : 신맛이 강하고 새콤한 향기가 나는 타원형의 노란색 열매.
lemon
A yellow, oval fruit that tastes and smells very sour.

망고 (noun) : 타원형에 과육이 노랗고 부드러우며 단맛이 나는 열대 과일.
mango
An oval tropical sweet fruit, of which the pulp is yellow and soft.

초록색 수박 매실 멜론.

초록색 (noun) : 파랑과 노랑의 중간인, 짙은 풀과 같은 색.
green
The color of dark grass, between blue and yellow.

수박 (noun) : 둥글고 크며 초록 빛깔에 검푸른 줄무늬가 있으며 속이 붉고 수분이 많은 과일.
watermelon
A big, green, round fruit with blackish blue stripes on it which contains red, watery flesh.

매실 (noun) : 달고 신맛이 나며 술이나 음료 등을 만들어 먹는 초록색의 둥근 열매.
plum
A green round fruit that tastes sweet and sour, and that is made into an alcoholic drink or beverage.

멜론 (noun) : 동그랗고 보통 녹색이며 겉에 그물 모양의 무늬가 있는, 향기가 좋고 단맛이 나는 과일.
melon
A fragrant, sweet fruit that is round, usually green, and has a net-like pattern on the outside.

보라색 포도 자두 오디.

보라색 (noun) : 파랑과 빨강을 섞은 색.
violet; purple
A mixed color of red and blue.

포도 (noun) : 달면서도 약간 신맛이 나는 작은 열매가 뭉쳐서 송이를 이루는 보라색 과일.
grape
Purple, small fruits forming a bundle, tasting sweet and a little sour.

자두 (noun) : 살구보다 조금 크고 새콤하고 달콤한 맛이 나는 붉은색 과일.
plum; prune
A red fruit, a little bigger than an apricot, which tastes sour and sweet.

오디 (noun) : 뽕나무의 열매.
mulberry
The fruit of a mulberry tree.

맛+이 어떻+어요?
어때요

맛 (noun) : 음식 등을 혀에 댈 때 느껴지는 감각.
taste
A sensation that is felt when touching one's tongue to food, etc.

이 : 어떤 상태나 상황의 대상이나 동작의 주체를 나타내는 조사.
i (no equivalent expression)
A postpositional particle referring to a subject under a certain state or situation, or the agent of an action.

어떻다 (adjective) : 생각, 느낌, 상태, 형편 등이 어찌 되어 있다.
such
Being such in one's thoughts, feelings, state, situation, etc.

-어요 : (두루높임으로) 어떤 사실을 서술하거나 질문, 명령, 권유함을 나타내는 종결 어미.
-eoyo (no equivalent expression)
(informal addressee-raising) A sentence-final ending used to describe a certain fact, **ask a question**, give an order, or advise.

달+아요. 달+아요. 달+아요.

달다 (adjective) : 꿀이나 설탕의 맛과 같다.
sweet
Tasting like honey or sugar.

-아요 : (두루높임으로) 어떤 사실을 서술하거나 질문, 명령, 권유함을 나타내는 종결 어미.
-ayo (no equivalent expression)
(informal addressee-raising) A sentence-final ending used to **describe a certain fact**, ask a question, give an order, or advise.

맛+이 어떻+어요?
어때요

맛 (noun) : 음식 등을 혀에 댈 때 느껴지는 감각.
taste
A sensation that is felt when touching one's tongue to food, etc.

이 : 어떤 상태나 상황의 대상이나 동작의 주체를 나타내는 조사.
i (no equivalent expression)
A postpositional particle referring to a subject under a certain state or situation, or the agent of an action.

어떻다 (adjective) : 생각, 느낌, 상태, 형편 등이 어찌 되어 있다.
such
Being such in one's thoughts, feelings, state, situation, etc.

-어요 : (두루높임으로) 어떤 사실을 서술하거나 질문, 명령, 권유함을 나타내는 종결 어미.
-eoyo (no equivalent expression)
(informal addressee-raising) A sentence-final ending used to describe a certain fact, **ask a question**, give an order, or advise.

달콤하+여. 달콤하+여. 달콤하+여.
달콤해 달콤해 달콤해

달콤하다 (adjective) : 맛이나 냄새가 기분 좋게 달다.
sweet; luscious
Tasting or smelling sweet.

-여 : (두루낮춤으로) 어떤 사실을 서술하거나 물음, 명령, 권유를 나타내는 종결 어미.
-yeo (no equivalent expression)
(informal addressee-lowering) A sentence-final ending used to **describe a certain fact**, ask a question, give an order, or advise.

어떻+어요? 어떻+어요?
어때요 어때요

어떻다 (adjective) : 생각, 느낌, 상태, 형편 등이 어찌 되어 있다.
such
Being such in one's thoughts, feelings, state, situation, etc.

-어요 : (두루높임으로) 어떤 사실을 서술하거나 질문, 명령, 권유함을 나타내는 종결 어미.
-eoyo (no equivalent expression)
(informal addressee-raising) A sentence-final ending used to describe a certain fact, **ask a question**, give an order, or advise.

달+아요. 시+어요. 달콤하+여. 새콤하+여.
셔요 달콤해 새콤해

달다 (adjective) : 꿀이나 설탕의 맛과 같다.
sweet
Tasting like honey or sugar.

-아요 : (두루높임으로) 어떤 사실을 서술하거나 질문, 명령, 권유함을 나타내는 종결 어미.
-ayo (no equivalent expression)
(informal addressee-raising) A sentence-final ending used to **describe a certain fact**, ask a question, give an order, or advise.

시다 (adjective) : 맛이 식초와 같다.
sour
Tasting vinegary.

-어요 : (두루높임으로) 어떤 사실을 서술하거나 질문, 명령, 권유함을 나타내는 종결 어미.
-eoyo (no equivalent expression)
(informal addressee-raising) A sentence-final ending used to **describe a certain fact**, ask a question, give an order, or advise.

달콤하다 (adjective) : 맛이나 냄새가 기분 좋게 달다.
sweet; luscious
Tasting or smelling sweet.

-여 : (두루낮춤으로) 어떤 사실을 서술하거나 물음, 명령, 권유를 나타내는 종결 어미.
-yeo (no equivalent expression)
(informal addressee-lowering) A sentence-final ending used to **describe a certain fact**, ask a question, give an order, or advise.

새콤하다 (adjective) : 맛이 조금 시면서 상큼하다.
sour; tangy
A flavor being a little sour and fresh.

-여 : (두루낮춤으로) 어떤 사실을 서술하거나 물음, 명령, 권유를 나타내는 종결 어미.
-yeo (no equivalent expression)
(informal addressee-lowering) A sentence-final ending used to **describe a certain fact**, ask a question, give an order, or advise.

< 2 절(verse) >

맛있+는 과일 과일 과일.

맛있다 (adjective) : 맛이 좋다.
tasty; delicious
Tasting good.

-는 : 앞의 말이 관형어의 기능을 하게 만들고 사건이나 동작이 현재 일어남을 나타내는 어미.
-neun (no equivalent expression)
An ending of a word that makes the preceding statement function as an adnominal phrase and implies that an event or action is happening in the present.

과일 (noun) : 사과, 배, 포도, 밤 등과 같이 나뭇가지나 줄기에 열리는 먹을 수 있는 열매.
fruit
Edible fruit that grows on the stem or branch of a tree, such as apples, pears, grapes, chestnuts, etc.

아삭아삭 과일 과일.

아삭아삭 (adverb) : 연하고 싱싱한 과일이나 채소를 베어 물 때 나는 소리.
crunch
A word imitating the sound made when taking a bite out of a fresh fruit or vegetable.

과일 (noun) : 사과, 배, 포도, 밤 등과 같이 나뭇가지나 줄기에 열리는 먹을 수 있는 열매.
fruit
Edible fruit that grows on the stem or branch of a tree, such as apples, pears, grapes, chestnuts, etc.

먹+[고 싶]+어, 과일 과일.

먹다 (verb) : 음식 등을 입을 통하여 배 속에 들여보내다.
eat; have; consume; take
To put food into one's mouth and take it in one's stomach.

-고 싶다 : 앞의 말이 나타내는 행동을 하기를 원함을 나타내는 표현.
-go sipda (no equivalent expression)
An expression used to state that the speaker wants to do the act mentioned in the preceding statement.

-어 : (두루낮춤으로) 어떤 사실을 서술하거나 물음, 명령, 권유를 나타내는 종결 어미.
-eo (no equivalent expression)
(informal addressee-lowering) A sentence-final ending used to **describe a certain fact**, ask a question, give an order, or advise.

과일 (noun) : 사과, 배, 포도, 밤 등과 같이 나뭇가지나 줄기에 열리는 먹을 수 있는 열매.
fruit
Edible fruit that grows on the stem or branch of a tree, such as apples, pears, grapes, chestnuts, etc.

빨간색 딸기 사과 앵두.

빨간색 (noun) : 흐르는 피나 잘 익은 사과, 고추처럼 붉은 색.
red color
A red color like that of blood, or a ripe apple or red pepper.

딸기 (noun) : 줄기가 땅 위로 뻗으며, 겉에 씨가 박혀 있는 빨간 열매가 열리는 여러해살이풀. 또는 그 열매.
strawberry
A perennial plant that stretches its stems on the ground and bears a red fruit with seeds stuck on the outside, or the fruit.

사과 (noun) : 모양이 둥글고 붉으며 새콤하고 단맛이 나는 과일.
apple
A round-shaped sweet and sour fruit with red skin.

앵두 (noun) : 모양이 작고 둥글며 달콤하면서 신맛을 지닌 붉은색 과일.
cherry
A sweet and sour, red fruit that is small and round in shape.

노란색 참외 레몬 망고.

노란색 (noun) : 병아리나 바나나와 같은 색.
yellow
The color of a chick or banana.

참외 (noun) : 색이 노랗고 단맛이 나며 주로 여름에 먹는 열매.
oriental melon
A yellow, sweet fruit that is usually eaten in the summer.

레몬 (noun) : 신맛이 강하고 새콤한 향기가 나는 타원형의 노란색 열매.
lemon
A yellow, oval fruit that tastes and smells very sour.

망고 (noun) : 타원형에 과육이 노랗고 부드러우며 단맛이 나는 열대 과일.
mango
An oval tropical sweet fruit, of which the pulp is yellow and soft.

초록색 수박 매실 멜론.

초록색 (noun) : 파랑과 노랑의 중간인, 짙은 풀과 같은 색.
green
The color of dark grass, between blue and yellow.

수박 (noun) : 둥글고 크며 초록 빛깔에 검푸른 줄무늬가 있으며 속이 붉고 수분이 많은 과일.
watermelon
A big, green, round fruit with blackish blue stripes on it which contains red, watery flesh.

매실 (noun) : 달고 신맛이 나며 술이나 음료 등을 만들어 먹는 초록색의 둥근 열매.
plum
A green round fruit that tastes sweet and sour, and that is made into an alcoholic drink or beverage.

멜론 (noun) : 동그랗고 보통 녹색이며 겉에 그물 모양의 무늬가 있는, 향기가 좋고 단맛이 나는 과일.
melon
A fragrant, sweet fruit that is round, usually green, and has a net-like pattern on the outside.

보라색 포도 자두 오디.

보라색 (noun) : 파랑과 빨강을 섞은 색.
violet; purple
A mixed color of red and blue.

포도 (noun) : 달면서도 약간 신맛이 나는 작은 열매가 뭉쳐서 송이를 이루는 보라색 과일.
grape
Purple, small fruits forming a bundle, tasting sweet and a little sour.

자두 (noun) : 살구보다 조금 크고 새콤하고 달콤한 맛이 나는 붉은색 과일.
plum; prune
A red fruit, a little bigger than an apricot, which tastes sour and sweet.

오디 (noun) : 뽕나무의 열매.
mulberry
The fruit of a mulberry tree.

맛+이 어떻+어요?
어때요

맛 (noun) : 음식 등을 혀에 댈 때 느껴지는 감각.
taste
A sensation that is felt when touching one's tongue to food, etc.

이 : 어떤 상태나 상황의 대상이나 동작의 주체를 나타내는 조사.
i (no equivalent expression)
A postpositional particle referring to a subject under a certain state or situation, or the agent of an action.

어떻다 (adjective) : 생각, 느낌, 상태, 형편 등이 어찌 되어 있다.
such
Being such in one's thoughts, feelings, state, situation, etc.

-어요 : (두루높임으로) 어떤 사실을 서술하거나 질문, 명령, 권유함을 나타내는 종결 어미.
-eoyo (no equivalent expression)
(informal addressee-raising) A sentence-final ending used to describe a certain fact, **ask a question**, give an order, or advise.

시+어요. 시+어요. 시+어요.
셔요 셔요 셔요

시다 (adjective) : 맛이 식초와 같다.
sour
Tasting vinegary.

-어요 : (두루높임으로) 어떤 사실을 서술하거나 질문, 명령, 권유함을 나타내는 종결 어미.
-eoyo (no equivalent expression)
(informal addressee-raising) A sentence-final ending used to **describe a certain fact**, ask a question, give an order, or advise.

맛+이 어떻+어요?
어때요

맛 (noun) : 음식 등을 혀에 댈 때 느껴지는 감각.
taste
A sensation that is felt when touching one's tongue to food, etc.

이 : 어떤 상태나 상황의 대상이나 동작의 주체를 나타내는 조사.
i (no equivalent expression)
A postpositional particle referring to a subject under a certain state or situation, or the agent of an action.

어떻다 (adjective) : 생각, 느낌, 상태, 형편 등이 어찌 되어 있다.
such
Being such in one's thoughts, feelings, state, situation, etc.

-어요 : (두루높임으로) 어떤 사실을 서술하거나 질문, 명령, 권유함을 나타내는 종결 어미.
-eoyo (no equivalent expression)
(informal addressee-raising) A sentence-final ending used to describe a certain fact, **ask a question**, give an order, or advise.

새콤하+여. 새콤하+여. 새콤하+여.
새콤해 새콤해 새콤해

새콤하다 (adjective) : 맛이 조금 시면서 상큼하다.
sour; tangy
A flavor being a little sour and fresh.

-여 : (두루낮춤으로) 어떤 사실을 서술하거나 물음, 명령, 권유를 나타내는 종결 어미.
-yeo (no equivalent expression)
(informal addressee-lowering) A sentence-final ending used to **describe a certain fact**, ask a question, give an order, or advise.

어떻+어요? 어떻+어요?
어때요 어때요

어떻다 (adjective) : 생각, 느낌, 상태, 형편 등이 어찌 되어 있다.
such
Being such in one's thoughts, feelings, state, situation, etc.

-어요 : (두루높임으로) 어떤 사실을 서술하거나 질문, 명령, 권유함을 나타내는 종결 어미.
-eoyo (no equivalent expression)
(informal addressee-raising) A sentence-final ending used to describe a certain fact, **ask a question**, give an order, or advise.

달+아요. 시+어요. 달콤하+여. 새콤하+여.
셔요 달콤해 새콤해

달다 (adjective) : 꿀이나 설탕의 맛과 같다.
sweet
Tasting like honey or sugar.

-아요 : (두루높임으로) 어떤 사실을 서술하거나 질문, 명령, 권유함을 나타내는 종결 어미.
-ayo (no equivalent expression)
(informal addressee-raising) A sentence-final ending used to **describe a certain fact**, ask a question, give an order, or advise.

시다 (adjective) : 맛이 식초와 같다.
sour
Tasting vinegary.

-어요 : (두루높임으로) 어떤 사실을 서술하거나 질문, 명령, 권유함을 나타내는 종결 어미.
-eoyo (no equivalent expression)
(informal addressee-raising) A sentence-final ending used to **describe a certain fact**, ask a question, give an order, or advise.

달콤하다 (adjective) : 맛이나 냄새가 기분 좋게 달다.
sweet; luscious
Tasting or smelling sweet.

-여 : (두루낮춤으로) 어떤 사실을 서술하거나 물음, 명령, 권유를 나타내는 종결 어미.
-yeo (no equivalent expression)
(informal addressee-lowering) A sentence-final ending used to **describe a certain fact**, ask a question, give an order, or advise.

새콤하다 (adjective) : 맛이 조금 시면서 상큼하다.
sour; tangy
A flavor being a little sour and fresh.

-여 : (두루낮춤으로) 어떤 사실을 서술하거나 물음, 명령, 권유를 나타내는 종결 어미.
-yeo (no equivalent expression)
(informal addressee-lowering) A sentence-final ending used to **describe a certain fact**, ask a question, give an order, or advise.

맛있+는 과일 과일 과일.

맛있다 (adjective) : 맛이 좋다.
tasty; delicious
Tasting good.

-는 : 앞의 말이 관형어의 기능을 하게 만들고 사건이나 동작이 현재 일어남을 나타내는 어미.
-neun (no equivalent expression)
An ending of a word that makes the preceding statement function as an adnominal phrase and implies that an event or action is happening in the present.

과일 (noun) : 사과, 배, 포도, 밤 등과 같이 나뭇가지나 줄기에 열리는 먹을 수 있는 열매.
fruit
Edible fruit that grows on the stem or branch of a tree, such as apples, pears, grapes, chestnuts, etc.

아삭아삭 과일 과일.

아삭아삭 (adverb) : 연하고 싱싱한 과일이나 채소를 베어 물 때 나는 소리.
crunch
A word imitating the sound made when taking a bite out of a fresh fruit or vegetable.

과일 (noun) : 사과, 배, 포도, 밤 등과 같이 나뭇가지나 줄기에 열리는 먹을 수 있는 열매.
fruit
Edible fruit that grows on the stem or branch of a tree, such as apples, pears, grapes, chestnuts, etc.

먹+[고 싶]+어, 과일 과일.

먹다 (verb) : 음식 등을 입을 통하여 배 속에 들여보내다.
eat; have; consume; take
To put food into one's mouth and take it in one's stomach.

-고 싶다 : 앞의 말이 나타내는 행동을 하기를 원함을 나타내는 표현.
-go sipda (no equivalent expression)
An expression used to state that the speaker wants to do the act mentioned in the preceding statement.

-어 : (두루낮춤으로) 어떤 사실을 서술하거나 물음, 명령, 권유를 나타내는 종결 어미.
-eo (no equivalent expression)
(informal addressee-lowering) A sentence-final ending used to **describe a certain fact**, ask a question, give an order, or advise.

과일 (noun) : 사과, 배, 포도, 밤 등과 같이 나뭇가지나 줄기에 열리는 먹을 수 있는 열매.
fruit
Edible fruit that grows on the stem or branch of a tree, such as apples, pears, grapes, chestnuts, etc.

맛있+는 과일 과일 과일.

맛있다 (adjective) : 맛이 좋다.
tasty; delicious
Tasting good.

-는 : 앞의 말이 관형어의 기능을 하게 만들고 사건이나 동작이 현재 일어남을 나타내는 어미.
-neun (no equivalent expression)
An ending of a word that makes the preceding statement function as an adnominal phrase and implies that an event or action is happening in the present.

과일 (noun) : 사과, 배, 포도, 밤 등과 같이 나뭇가지나 줄기에 열리는 먹을 수 있는 열매.
fruit
Edible fruit that grows on the stem or branch of a tree, such as apples, pears, grapes, chestnuts, etc.

아삭아삭 과일 과일.

아삭아삭 (adverb) : 연하고 싱싱한 과일이나 채소를 베어 물 때 나는 소리.
crunch
A word imitating the sound made when taking a bite out of a fresh fruit or vegetable.

과일 (noun) : 사과, 배, 포도, 밤 등과 같이 나뭇가지나 줄기에 열리는 먹을 수 있는 열매.
fruit
Edible fruit that grows on the stem or branch of a tree, such as apples, pears, grapes, chestnuts, etc.

먹+[고 싶]+어, 과일 과일.

먹다 (verb) : 음식 등을 입을 통하여 배 속에 들여보내다.
eat; have; consume; take
To put food into one's mouth and take it in one's stomach.

-고 싶다 : 앞의 말이 나타내는 행동을 하기를 원함을 나타내는 표현.
-go sipda (no equivalent expression)
An expression used to state that the speaker wants to do the act mentioned in the preceding statement.

-어 : (두루낮춤으로) 어떤 사실을 서술하거나 물음, 명령, 권유를 나타내는 종결 어미.
-eo (no equivalent expression)
(informal addressee-lowering) A sentence-final ending used to **describe a certain fact**, ask a question, give an order, or advise.

과일 (noun) : 사과, 배, 포도, 밤 등과 같이 나뭇가지나 줄기에 열리는 먹을 수 있는 열매.
fruit
Edible fruit that grows on the stem or branch of a tree, such as apples, pears, grapes, chestnuts, etc.

먹+[고 싶]+어, 과일 과일.

먹다 (verb) : 음식 등을 입을 통하여 배 속에 들여보내다.
eat; have; consume; take
To put food into one's mouth and take it in one's stomach.

-고 싶다 : 앞의 말이 나타내는 행동을 하기를 원함을 나타내는 표현.
-go sipda (no equivalent expression)
An expression used to state that the speaker wants to do the act mentioned in the preceding statement.

-어 : (두루낮춤으로) 어떤 사실을 서술하거나 물음, 명령, 권유를 나타내는 종결 어미.
-eo (no equivalent expression)
(informal addressee-lowering) A sentence-final ending used to **describe a certain fact**, ask a question, give an order, or advise.

과일 (noun) : 사과, 배, 포도, 밤 등과 같이 나뭇가지나 줄기에 열리는 먹을 수 있는 열매.

fruit

Edible fruit that grows on the stem or branch of a tree, such as apples, pears, grapes, chestnuts, etc.

< 3 >

신체송

신체(body) 송(song)

[발음(pronunciation)]

< 1 절(verse) >

머리, 어깨, 무릎, 발, 무릎, 발, 머리, 어깨, 무릎, 발, 무릎, 발
머리, 어깨, 무릅, 발, 무릅, 발, 머리, 어깨, 무릅, 발, 무릅, 발
meori, eokkae, mureup, bal, mureup, bal, meori, eokkae, mureup, bal, mureup, bal

머리, 어깨, 무릎, 발, 머리, 어깨, 무릎, 발
머리, 어깨, 무릅, 발, 머리, 어깨, 무릅, 발
meori, eokkae, mureup, bal, meori, eokkae, mureup, bal

머리, 어깨, 무릎, 발, 머리, 어깨, 무릎, 발
머리, 어깨, 무릅, 발, 머리, 어깨, 무릅, 발
meori, eokkae, mureup, bal, meori, eokkae, mureup, bal

머리, 머리, 머리카락
머리, 머리, 머리카락
meori, meori, meorikarak

얼굴, 얼굴, 얼굴, 이마
얼굴, 얼굴, 얼굴, 이마
eolgul, eolgul, eolgul, ima

눈, 코, 입, 귀, 눈, 코, 입, 귀
눈, 코, 입, 귀, 눈, 코, 입, 귀
nun, ko, ip, gwi, nun, ko, ip, gwi

머리, 머리, 머리카락
머리, 머리, 머리카락
meori, meori, meorikarak

얼굴, 얼굴, 얼굴, 이마
얼굴, 얼굴, 얼굴, 이마
eolgul, eolgul, eolgul, ima

눈, 코, 입, 귀, 눈, 코, 입, 귀
눈, 코, 입, 귀, 눈, 코, 입, 귀
nun, ko, ip, gwi, nun, ko, ip, gwi

신나게 흔들어요
신나게 흔드러요
sinnage heundeureoyo

다 함께 춤을 춰요
다 함께 추믈 춰요
da hamkke chumeul chwoyo

즐겁게 흔들어요
즐겁께 흔드러요
jeulgeopge heundeureoyo

우리 모두 춤을 춰요
우리 모두 추믈 춰요
uri modu chumeul chwoyo

< 2 절(verse) >

머리, 어깨, 무릎, 발, 무릎, 발, 머리, 어깨, 무릎, 발, 무릎, 발
머리, 어깨, 무릅, 발, 무릅, 발, 머리, 어깨, 무릅, 발, 무릅, 발
meori, eokkae, mureup, bal, mureup, bal, meori, eokkae, mureup, bal, mureup, bal

머리, 어깨, 무릎, 발, 머리, 어깨, 무릎, 발
머리, 어깨, 무릅, 발, 머리, 어깨, 무릅, 발
meori, eokkae, mureup, bal, meori, eokkae, mureup, bal

팔, 팔, 팔, 손
팔, 팔, 팔, 손
pal, pal, pal, son

다리, 다리, 다리, 발
다리, 다리, 다리, 발
dari, dari, dari, bal

가슴, 허리, 엉덩이, 가슴, 허리, 엉덩이
가슴, 허리, 엉덩이, 가슴, 허리, 엉덩이
gaseum, heori, eongdeongi, gaseum, heori, eongdeongi

팔, 팔, 팔, 손
팔, 팔, 팔, 손
pal, pal, pal, son

다리, 다리, 다리, 발
다리, 다리, 다리, 발
dari, dari, dari, bal

가슴, 허리, 엉덩이, 가슴, 허리, 엉덩이
가슴, 허리, 엉덩이, 가슴, 허리, 엉덩이
gaseum, heori, eongdeongi, gaseum, heori, eongdeongi

신나게 흔들어요
신나게 흔드러요
sinnage heundeureoyo

다 함께 춤을 춰요
다 함께 추믈 춰요
da hamkke chumeul chwoyo

즐겁게 흔들어요
즐겁께 흔드러요
jeulgeopge heundeureoyo

우리 모두 춤을 춰요
우리 모두 추믈 춰요
uri modu chumeul chwoyo

< 3 절(verse) >

머리, 어깨, 무릎, 발, 무릎, 발, 머리, 어깨, 무릎, 발, 무릎, 발
머리, 어깨, 무릅, 발, 무릅, 발, 머리, 어깨, 무릅, 발, 무릅, 발
meori, eokkae, mureup, bal, mureup, bal, meori, eokkae, mureup, bal, mureup, bal

머리, 어깨, 무릎, 발, 머리, 어깨, 무릎, 발
머리, 어깨, 무릅, 발, 머리, 어깨, 무릅, 발
meori, eokkae, mureup, bal, meori, eokkae, mureup, bal

< 1 절(verse) >

머리, 어깨, 무릎, 발, 무릎, 발, 머리, 어깨, 무릎, 발, 무릎, 발

머리 (noun) : 사람이나 동물의 몸에서 얼굴과 머리털이 있는 부분을 모두 포함한 목 위의 부분.
head
A part of the human or animal body above the neck that includes the face and hair.

어깨 (noun) : 목의 아래 끝에서 팔의 위 끝에 이르는 몸의 부분.
shoulder
The body part between the lower end of the neck and the upper end of the arm.

무릎 (noun) : 허벅지와 종아리 사이에 앞쪽으로 둥글게 튀어나온 부분.
knee
The round, protruded part between the thigh and the calf.

발 (noun) : 사람이나 동물의 다리 맨 끝부분.
foot
The bottom most part of a human's or animal's leg.

머리, 어깨, 무릎, 발, 머리, 어깨, 무릎, 발

머리 (noun) : 사람이나 동물의 몸에서 얼굴과 머리털이 있는 부분을 모두 포함한 목 위의 부분.
head
A part of the human or animal body above the neck that includes the face and hair.

어깨 (noun) : 목의 아래 끝에서 팔의 위 끝에 이르는 몸의 부분.
shoulder
The body part between the lower end of the neck and the upper end of the arm.

무릎 (noun) : 허벅지와 종아리 사이에 앞쪽으로 둥글게 튀어나온 부분.
knee
The round, protruded part between the thigh and the calf.

발 (noun) : 사람이나 동물의 다리 맨 끝부분.
foot
The bottom most part of a human's or animal's leg.

머리, 어깨, 무릎, 발, 머리, 어깨, 무릎, 발

머리 (noun) : 사람이나 동물의 몸에서 얼굴과 머리털이 있는 부분을 모두 포함한 목 위의 부분.
head
A part of the human or animal body above the neck that includes the face and hair.

어깨 (noun) : 목의 아래 끝에서 팔의 위 끝에 이르는 몸의 부분.
shoulder
The body part between the lower end of the neck and the upper end of the arm.

무릎 (noun) : 허벅지와 종아리 사이에 앞쪽으로 둥글게 튀어나온 부분.
knee
The round, protruded part between the thigh and the calf.

발 (noun) : 사람이나 동물의 다리 맨 끝부분.
foot
The bottom most part of a human's or animal's leg.

머리, 머리, 머리카락

머리 (noun) : 사람이나 동물의 몸에서 얼굴과 머리털이 있는 부분을 모두 포함한 목 위의 부분.
head
A part of the human or animal body above the neck that includes the face and hair.

머리카락 (noun) : 머리털 하나하나.
hair
Each and every hair.

얼굴, 얼굴, 얼굴, 이마

얼굴 (noun) : 눈, 코, 입이 있는 머리의 앞쪽 부분.
face
The front part of the head that has the eyes, nose and mouth.

이마 (noun) : 얼굴의 눈썹 위부터 머리카락이 난 아래까지의 부분.
forehead
The part of the face from the hairline to the eyebrows.

눈, 코, 입, 귀, 눈, 코, 입, 귀

눈 (noun) : 사람이나 동물의 얼굴에 있으며 빛의 자극을 받아 물체를 볼 수 있는 감각 기관.
eye
The sensory organ on the face of a person or animal that can see an object when stimulated by the light.

코 (noun) : 숨을 쉬고 냄새를 맡는 몸의 한 부분.
nose
The body part that is used for breathing and smelling.

입 (noun) : 음식을 먹고 소리를 내는 기관으로 입술에서 목구멍까지의 부분.
mouth
A bodily organ extending from the lips to the throat that one uses to eat and make sounds.

귀 (noun) : 사람이나 동물의 머리 양옆에 있어 소리를 듣는 몸의 한 부분.
ear
The part of a human or animal's body that hears sounds, located on both sides of the head.

머리, 머리, 머리카락

머리 (noun) : 사람이나 동물의 몸에서 얼굴과 머리털이 있는 부분을 모두 포함한 목 위의 부분.
head
A part of the human or animal body above the neck that includes the face and hair.

머리카락 (noun) : 머리털 하나하나.
hair
Each and every hair.

얼굴, 얼굴, 얼굴, 이마

얼굴 (noun) : 눈, 코, 입이 있는 머리의 앞쪽 부분.
face
The front part of the head that has the eyes, nose and mouth.

이마 (noun) : 얼굴의 눈썹 위부터 머리카락이 난 아래까지의 부분.
forehead
The part of the face from the hairline to the eyebrows.

눈, 코, 입, 귀, 눈, 코, 입, 귀

눈 (noun) : 사람이나 동물의 얼굴에 있으며 빛의 자극을 받아 물체를 볼 수 있는 감각 기관.
eye
The sensory organ on the face of a person or animal that can see an object when stimulated by the light.

코 (noun) : 숨을 쉬고 냄새를 맡는 몸의 한 부분.
nose
The body part that is used for breathing and smelling.

입 (noun) : 음식을 먹고 소리를 내는 기관으로 입술에서 목구멍까지의 부분.
mouth
A bodily organ extending from the lips to the throat that one uses to eat and make sounds.

귀 (noun) : 사람이나 동물의 머리 양옆에 있어 소리를 듣는 몸의 한 부분.
ear
The part of a human or animal's body that hears sounds, located on both sides of the head.

신나+게 흔들+어요.

신나다 (verb) : 흥이 나고 기분이 아주 좋아지다.
become happy; become delighted; become elated
To get excited and come to feel very good.

-게 : 앞의 말이 뒤에서 가리키는 일의 목적이나 결과, 방식, 정도 등이 됨을 나타내는 연결 어미.
-ge (no equivalent expression)
A connective ending used when the preceding statement is the purpose, result, method, amount, etc., of something mentioned in the following statement. **<method>**

흔들다 (verb) : 무엇을 좌우, 앞뒤로 자꾸 움직이게 하다.
wave; sway; flap; wag; shake
To make something move from side to side and back and forth, repeatedly.

-어요 : (두루높임으로) 어떤 사실을 서술하거나 질문, 명령, 권유함을 나타내는 종결 어미.
-eoyo (no equivalent expression)
(informal addressee-raising) A sentence-final ending used to describe a certain fact, ask a question, give an order, or advise. **<give an order>**

다 함께 춤+을 추+어요.
춰요

다 (adverb) : 남거나 빠진 것이 없이 모두.
all; everything
With nothing left over or missing.

함께 (adverb) : 여럿이서 한꺼번에 같이.
together; along with
In the state of several people being all together.

춤 (noun) : 음악이나 규칙적인 박자에 맞춰 몸을 움직이는 것.
dance
An act of moving one's body to music or a regular beat.

을 : 서술어의 명사형 목적어임을 나타내는 조사.
no equivalent expression
A postpositional particle that indicates the noun object of the predicate.

추다 (verb) : 춤 동작을 하다.
dance
To perform the movements of a dance.

-어요 : (두루높임으로) 어떤 사실을 서술하거나 질문, 명령, 권유함을 나타내는 종결 어미.
-eoyo (no equivalent expression)
(informal addressee-raising) A sentence-final ending used to describe a certain fact, ask a question, give an order, or advise. **<give an order>**

즐겁+게 흔들+어요.

즐겁다 (adjective) : 마음에 들어 흐뭇하고 기쁘다.
joyful; pleasant
Pleased and satisfied with something.

-게 : 앞의 말이 뒤에서 가리키는 일의 목적이나 결과, 방식, 정도 등이 됨을 나타내는 연결 어미.
-ge (no equivalent expression)
A connective ending used when the preceding statement is the purpose, result, method, amount, etc., of something mentioned in the following statement. **<method>**

흔들다 (verb) : 무엇을 좌우, 앞뒤로 자꾸 움직이게 하다.
wave; sway; flap; wag; shake
To make something move from side to side and back and forth, repeatedly.

-어요 : (두루높임으로) 어떤 사실을 서술하거나 질문, 명령, 권유함을 나타내는 종결 어미.
-eoyo (no equivalent expression)
(informal addressee-raising) A sentence-final ending used to describe a certain fact, ask a question, give an order, or advise. **<give an order>**

우리 모두 춤+을 추+어요.

춰요

우리 (pronoun) : 말하는 사람이 자기와 듣는 사람 또는 이를 포함한 여러 사람들을 가리키는 말.
we
A pronoun used when the speaker refers to himself/herself and the listener or listeners, or a group of people including the speaker and listener or listeners.

모두 (adverb) : 빠짐없이 다.
all of
Everyone or everything without exception.

춤 (noun) : 음악이나 규칙적인 박자에 맞춰 몸을 움직이는 것.
dance
An act of moving one's body to music or a regular beat.

을 : 서술어의 명사형 목적어임을 나타내는 조사.
no equivalent expression
A postpositional particle that indicates the noun object of the predicate.

추다 (verb) : 춤 동작을 하다.
dance
To perform the movements of a dance.

-어요 : (두루높임으로) 어떤 사실을 서술하거나 질문, 명령, 권유함을 나타내는 종결 어미.
-eoyo (no equivalent expression)
(informal addressee-raising) A sentence-final ending used to describe a certain fact, ask a question, give an order, or advise. **<give an order>**

< 2 절(verse) >

머리, 어깨, 무릎, 발, 무릎, 발, 머리, 어깨, 무릎, 발, 무릎, 발

머리 (noun) : 사람이나 동물의 몸에서 얼굴과 머리털이 있는 부분을 모두 포함한 목 위의 부분.
head
A part of the human or animal body above the neck that includes the face and hair.

어깨 (noun) : 목의 아래 끝에서 팔의 위 끝에 이르는 몸의 부분.
shoulder
The body part between the lower end of the neck and the upper end of the arm.

무릎 (noun) : 허벅지와 종아리 사이에 앞쪽으로 둥글게 튀어나온 부분.
knee
The round, protruded part between the thigh and the calf.

발 (noun) : 사람이나 동물의 다리 맨 끝부분.
foot
The bottom most part of a human's or animal's leg.

머리, 어깨, 무릎, 발, 머리, 어깨, 무릎, 발

머리 (noun) : 사람이나 동물의 몸에서 얼굴과 머리털이 있는 부분을 모두 포함한 목 위의 부분.
head
A part of the human or animal body above the neck that includes the face and hair.

어깨 (noun) : 목의 아래 끝에서 팔의 위 끝에 이르는 몸의 부분.
shoulder
The body part between the lower end of the neck and the upper end of the arm.

무릎 (noun) : 허벅지와 종아리 사이에 앞쪽으로 둥글게 튀어나온 부분.
knee
The round, protruded part between the thigh and the calf.

발 (noun) : 사람이나 동물의 다리 맨 끝부분.
foot
The bottom most part of a human's or animal's leg.

머리, 어깨, 무릎, 발, 머리, 어깨, 무릎, 발

머리 (noun) : 사람이나 동물의 몸에서 얼굴과 머리털이 있는 부분을 모두 포함한 목 위의 부분.
head
A part of the human or animal body above the neck that includes the face and hair.

어깨 (noun) : 목의 아래 끝에서 팔의 위 끝에 이르는 몸의 부분.
shoulder
The body part between the lower end of the neck and the upper end of the arm.

무릎 (noun) : 허벅지와 종아리 사이에 앞쪽으로 둥글게 튀어나온 부분.
knee
The round, protruded part between the thigh and the calf.

발 (noun) : 사람이나 동물의 다리 맨 끝부분.
foot
The bottom most part of a human's or animal's leg.

팔, 팔, 팔, 손

팔 (noun) : 어깨에서 손목까지의 신체 부위.
arm
The body part from the shoulder to the wrist.

손 (noun) : 팔목 끝에 있으며 무엇을 만지거나 잡을 때 쓰는 몸의 부분.
hand
A body part connected at the end of the wrist that is used to touch or grab something.

다리, 다리, 다리, 발

다리 (noun) : 사람이나 동물의 몸통 아래에 붙어, 서고 걷고 뛰는 일을 하는 신체 부위.
leg
A body part attached to the bottom of the torso of a person or animal that is used to walk or run.

발 (noun) : 사람이나 동물의 다리 맨 끝부분.
foot
The bottom most part of a human's or animal's leg.

가슴, 허리, 엉덩이, 가슴, 허리, 엉덩이

가슴 (noun) : 인간이나 동물의 목과 배 사이에 있는 몸의 앞 부분.
chest
The front part of a human or animal's body, between the neck and the abdomen.

허리 (noun) : 사람이나 동물의 신체에서 갈비뼈 아래에서 엉덩이뼈까지의 부분.
waist
The part between the ribs and hip bones in the human or animal body.

엉덩이 (noun) : 허리와 허벅지 사이의 부분으로 앉았을 때 바닥에 닿는, 살이 많은 부위.
butt; buttocks
The fleshy part between the waist and thigh that touches the floor when one is sitting.

팔, 팔, 팔, 손

팔 (noun) : 어깨에서 손목까지의 신체 부위.
arm
The body part from the shoulder to the wrist.

손 (noun) : 팔목 끝에 있으며 무엇을 만지거나 잡을 때 쓰는 몸의 부분.
hand
A body part connected at the end of the wrist that is used to touch or grab something.

다리, 다리, 다리, 발

다리 (noun) : 사람이나 동물의 몸통 아래에 붙어, 서고 걷고 뛰는 일을 하는 신체 부위.
leg
A body part attached to the bottom of the torso of a person or animal that is used to walk or run.

발 (noun) : 사람이나 동물의 다리 맨 끝부분.
foot
The bottom most part of a human's or animal's leg.

가슴, 허리, 엉덩이, 가슴, 허리, 엉덩이

가슴 (noun) : 인간이나 동물의 목과 배 사이에 있는 몸의 앞 부분.
chest
The front part of a human or animal's body, between the neck and the abdomen.

허리 (noun) : 사람이나 동물의 신체에서 갈비뼈 아래에서 엉덩이뼈까지의 부분.
waist
The part between the ribs and hip bones in the human or animal body.

엉덩이 (noun) : 허리와 허벅지 사이의 부분으로 앉았을 때 바닥에 닿는, 살이 많은 부위.
butt; buttocks
The fleshy part between the waist and thigh that touches the floor when one is sitting.

신나+게 흔들+어요.

신나다 (verb) : 흥이 나고 기분이 아주 좋아지다.
become happy; become delighted; become elated
To get excited and come to feel very good.

-게 : 앞의 말이 뒤에서 가리키는 일의 목적이나 결과, 방식, 정도 등이 됨을 나타내는 연결 어미.
-ge (no equivalent expression)
A connective ending used when the preceding statement is the purpose, result, method, amount, etc., of something mentioned in the following statement. **<method>**

흔들다 (verb) : 무엇을 좌우, 앞뒤로 자꾸 움직이게 하다.
wave; sway; flap; wag; shake
To make something move from side to side and back and forth, repeatedly.

-어요 : (두루높임으로) 어떤 사실을 서술하거나 질문, 명령, 권유함을 나타내는 종결 어미.
-eoyo (no equivalent expression)
(informal addressee-raising) A sentence-final ending used to describe a certain fact, ask a question, give an order, or advise. **<give an order>**

다 함께 춤+을 추+어요.
취요

다 (adverb) : 남거나 빠진 것이 없이 모두.
all; everything
With nothing left over or missing.

함께 (adverb) : 여럿이서 한꺼번에 같이.
together; along with
In the state of several people being all together.

춤 (noun) : 음악이나 규칙적인 박자에 맞춰 몸을 움직이는 것.
dance
An act of moving one's body to music or a regular beat.

을 : 서술어의 명사형 목적어임을 나타내는 조사.
no equivalent expression
A postpositional particle that indicates the noun object of the predicate.

추다 (verb) : 춤 동작을 하다.
dance
To perform the movements of a dance.

-어요 : (두루높임으로) 어떤 사실을 서술하거나 질문, 명령, 권유함을 나타내는 종결 어미.
-eoyo (no equivalent expression)
(informal addressee-raising) A sentence-final ending used to describe a certain fact, ask a question, give an order, or advise. **<give an order>**

즐겁+게 흔들+어요.

즐겁다 (adjective) : 마음에 들어 흐뭇하고 기쁘다.
joyful; pleasant
Pleased and satisfied with something.

-게 : 앞의 말이 뒤에서 가리키는 일의 목적이나 결과, 방식, 정도 등이 됨을 나타내는 연결 어미.
-ge (no equivalent expression)
A connective ending used when the preceding statement is the purpose, result, method, amount, etc., of something mentioned in the following statement. **<method>**

흔들다 (verb) : 무엇을 좌우, 앞뒤로 자꾸 움직이게 하다.
wave; sway; flap; wag; shake
To make something move from side to side and back and forth, repeatedly.

-어요 : (두루높임으로) 어떤 사실을 서술하거나 질문, 명령, 권유함을 나타내는 종결 어미.
-eoyo (no equivalent expression)
(informal addressee-raising) A sentence-final ending used to describe a certain fact, ask a question, give an order, or advise. **<give an order>**

우리 모두 춤+을 추+어요.
취요

우리 (pronoun) : 말하는 사람이 자기와 듣는 사람 또는 이를 포함한 여러 사람들을 가리키는 말.
we
A pronoun used when the speaker refers to himself/herself and the listener or listeners, or a group of people including the speaker and listener or listeners.

모두 (adverb) : 빠짐없이 다.
all of
Everyone or everything without exception.

춤 (noun) : 음악이나 규칙적인 박자에 맞춰 몸을 움직이는 것.
dance
An act of moving one's body to music or a regular beat.

을 : 서술어의 명사형 목적어임을 나타내는 조사.
no equivalent expression
A postpositional particle that indicates the noun object of the predicate.

추다 (verb) : 춤 동작을 하다.
dance
To perform the movements of a dance.

-어요 : (두루높임으로) 어떤 사실을 서술하거나 질문, 명령, 권유함을 나타내는 종결 어미.
-eoyo (no equivalent expression)
(informal addressee-raising) A sentence-final ending used to describe a certain fact, ask a question, give an order, or advise. **<give an order>**

< 3 절(verse) >

머리, 어깨, 무릎, 발, 무릎, 발, 머리, 어깨, 무릎, 발, 무릎, 발

머리 (noun) : 사람이나 동물의 몸에서 얼굴과 머리털이 있는 부분을 모두 포함한 목 위의 부분.
head
A part of the human or animal body above the neck that includes the face and hair.

어깨 (noun) : 목의 아래 끝에서 팔의 위 끝에 이르는 몸의 부분.
shoulder
The body part between the lower end of the neck and the upper end of the arm.

무릎 (noun) : 허벅지와 종아리 사이에 앞쪽으로 둥글게 튀어나온 부분.
knee
The round, protruded part between the thigh and the calf.

발 (noun) : 사람이나 동물의 다리 맨 끝부분.
foot
The bottom most part of a human's or animal's leg.

머리, 어깨, 무릎, 발, 머리, 어깨, 무릎, 발

머리 (noun) : 사람이나 동물의 몸에서 얼굴과 머리털이 있는 부분을 모두 포함한 목 위의 부분.
head
A part of the human or animal body above the neck that includes the face and hair.

어깨 (noun) : 목의 아래 끝에서 팔의 위 끝에 이르는 몸의 부분.
shoulder
The body part between the lower end of the neck and the upper end of the arm.

무릎 (noun) : 허벅지와 종아리 사이에 앞쪽으로 둥글게 튀어나온 부분.
knee
The round, protruded part between the thigh and the calf.

발 (noun) : 사람이나 동물의 다리 맨 끝부분.
foot
The bottom most part of a human's or animal's leg.

머리, 어깨, 무릎, 발, 머리, 어깨, 무릎, 발

머리 (noun) : 사람이나 동물의 몸에서 얼굴과 머리털이 있는 부분을 모두 포함한 목 위의 부분.
head
A part of the human or animal body above the neck that includes the face and hair.

어깨 (noun) : 목의 아래 끝에서 팔의 위 끝에 이르는 몸의 부분.
shoulder
The body part between the lower end of the neck and the upper end of the arm.

무릎 (noun) : 허벅지와 종아리 사이에 앞쪽으로 둥글게 튀어나온 부분.
knee
The round, protruded part between the thigh and the calf.

발 (noun) : 사람이나 동물의 다리 맨 끝부분.
foot
The bottom most part of a human's or animal's leg.

< 4 >

어때요?

나 어때요?
(How do I look?)

[발음(pronunciation)]

< 1 절(verse) >

청바지 입었는데 어때요?
청바지 이번는데 어때요?
cheongbaji ibeonneunde eottaeyo?

치마 입었는데 어때요?
치마 이번는데 어때요?
chima ibeonneunde eottaeyo?

반바지는?
반바지는?
banbajineun?

원피스는?
원피스는?
wonpiseuneun?

어때요? 어때요? 어때요? 어때요? 어때요?
어때요? 어때요? 어때요? 어때요? 어때요?
eottaeyo? eottaeyo? eottaeyo? eottaeyo? eottaeyo?

머리 묶었는데 어때요?
머리 무꺼는데 어때요?
meori mukkeonneunde eottaeyo?

머리 풀었는데 어때요?
머리 푸런는데 어때요?
meori pureonneunde eottaeyo?

긴 머리는?
긴 머리는?
gin meorineun?

짧은 머리는?
짤븐 머리는?
jjalbeun meorineun?

어때요? 어때요? 어때요? 어때요? 어때요?
어때요? 어때요? 어때요? 어때요? 어때요?
eottaeyo? eottaeyo? eottaeyo? eottaeyo? eottaeyo?

제 눈과 코와 입술이 얼마나 예뻐 보이나요?
제 눈과 코와 입쑤리 얼마나 예뻐 보이나요?
je nungwa kowa ipsuri eolmana yeppeo boinayo?

나 어때요?
나 어때요?
na eottaeyo?

나 예뻐요?
나 예뻐요?
na yeppeoyo?

어때요? 어때요? 어때요? 어때요? 어때요?
어때요? 어때요? 어때요? 어때요? 어때요?
eottaeyo? eottaeyo? eottaeyo? eottaeyo? eottaeyo?

< 2 절(verse) >

운동화 신었는데 어때요?
운동화 시넌는데 어때요?
undonghwa sineonneunde eottaeyo?

구두 신었는데 어때요?
구두 시넌는데 어때요?
gudu sineonneunde eottaeyo?

검은색은?
거믄새근?
geomeunsaegeun?

흰색은?
힌새근?
hinsaegeun?

어때요? 어때요? 어때요? 어때요? 어때요?
어때요? 어때요? 어때요? 어때요? 어때요?
eottaeyo? eottaeyo? eottaeyo? eottaeyo? eottaeyo?

목걸이 찼는데 어때요?
목꺼리 찬는데 어때요?
mokgeori channeunde eottaeyo?

반지 끼었는데 어때요?
반지 끼언는데 어때요?
banji kkieonneunde eottaeyo?

귀걸이는?
귀거리는?
gwigeorineun?

팔찌는?
팔찌는?
paljjineun?

어때요? 어때요? 어때요? 어때요? 어때요?
어때요? 어때요? 어때요? 어때요? 어때요?
eottaeyo? eottaeyo? eottaeyo? eottaeyo? eottaeyo?

제 눈과 코와 입술이 얼마나 예뻐 보이나요?
제 눈과 코와 입쑤리 얼마나 예뻐 보이나요?
je nungwa kowa ipsuri eolmana yeppeo boinayo?

나 어때요?
나 어때요?
na eottaeyo?

나 예뻐요?
나 예뻐요?
na yeppeoyo?

어때요? 어때요? 어때요? 어때요? 어때요?
어때요? 어때요? 어때요? 어때요? 어때요?
eottaeyo? eottaeyo? eottaeyo? eottaeyo? eottaeyo?

< 1 절(verse) >

청바지 입+었+는데 어떻+어요?
어때요

청바지 (noun) : 질긴 무명으로 만든 푸른색 바지.
jeans
A pair of blue pants made of strong cotton.

입다 (verb) : 옷을 몸에 걸치거나 두르다.
wear; be dressed; put on
To hang or drape clothes on or around one's body.

-었- : 어떤 사건이 과거에 완료되었거나 그 사건의 결과가 현재까지 지속되는 상황을 나타내는 어미.
-eot- (no equivalent expression)
An ending of a word used to indicate that an event was completed in the past or its result continues in the present.

-는데 : 뒤의 말을 하기 위하여 그 대상과 관련이 있는 상황을 미리 말함을 나타내는 연결 어미.
-neunde (no equivalent expression)
A connective ending used to talk in advance about a situation to follow.

어떻다 (adjective) : 생각, 느낌, 상태, 형편 등이 어찌 되어 있다.
such
Being such in one's thoughts, feelings, state, situation, etc.

-어요 : (두루높임으로) 어떤 사실을 서술하거나 질문, 명령, 권유함을 나타내는 종결 어미.
-eoyo (no equivalent expression)
(informal addressee-raising) A sentence-final ending used to describe a certain fact, **ask a question**, give an order, or advise.

치마 입+었+는데 어떻+어요?
어때요

치마 (noun) : 여자가 입는 아래 겉옷으로 다리가 들어가도록 된 부분이 없는 옷.
skirt
An outer lower garment that doesn't have pant legs, usually worn by women.

입다 (verb) : 옷을 몸에 걸치거나 두르다.
wear; be dressed; put on
To hang or drape clothes on or around one's body.

-었- : 어떤 사건이 과거에 완료되었거나 그 사건의 결과가 현재까지 지속되는 상황을 나타내는 어미.
-eot- (no equivalent expression)
An ending of a word used to indicate that an event was completed in the past or its result continues in the present.

-는데 : 뒤의 말을 하기 위하여 그 대상과 관련이 있는 상황을 미리 말함을 나타내는 연결 어미.
-neunde (no equivalent expression)
A connective ending used to talk in advance about a situation to follow.

어떻다 (adjective) : 생각, 느낌, 상태, 형편 등이 어찌 되어 있다.
such
Being such in one's thoughts, feelings, state, situation, etc.

-어요 : (두루높임으로) 어떤 사실을 서술하거나 질문, 명령, 권유함을 나타내는 종결 어미.
-eoyo (no equivalent expression)
(informal addressee-raising) A sentence-final ending used to describe a certain fact, **ask a question**, give an order, or advise.

반바지+는?

반바지 (noun) : 길이가 무릎 위나 무릎 정도까지 내려오는 짧은 바지.
short pants; shorts
Short trousers that end at the knee or above.

는 : 문장 속에서 어떤 대상이 화제임을 나타내는 조사.
neun (no equivalent expression)
A postpositional particle used to indicate that a certain subject is the topic of a sentence.

원피스+는?

원피스 (noun) : 윗옷과 치마가 하나로 붙어 있는 여자 겉옷.
one-piece dress
A woman's outer garment made of one piece.

는 : 문장 속에서 어떤 대상이 화제임을 나타내는 조사.
neun (no equivalent expression)
A postpositional particle used to indicate that a certain subject is the topic of a sentence.

어떻+어요?
어때요

어떻다 (adjective) : 생각, 느낌, 상태, 형편 등이 어찌 되어 있다.
such
Being such in one's thoughts, feelings, state, situation, etc.

-어요 : (두루높임으로) 어떤 사실을 서술하거나 질문, 명령, 권유함을 나타내는 종결 어미.
-eoyo (no equivalent expression)
(informal addressee-raising) A sentence-final ending used to describe a certain fact, **ask a question**, give an order, or advise.

머리 묶+었+는데 어떻+어요?
어때요

머리 (noun) : 머리에 난 털.
hair
The hair on the head.

묶다 (verb) : 끈 등으로 물건을 잡아매다.
tie up
To tie something with a cord, etc.

-었- : 어떤 사건이 과거에 완료되었거나 그 사건의 결과가 현재까지 지속되는 상황을 나타내는 어미.
-eot- (no equivalent expression)
An ending of a word used to indicate that an event was completed in the past or its result continues in the present.

-는데 : 뒤의 말을 하기 위하여 그 대상과 관련이 있는 상황을 미리 말함을 나타내는 연결 어미.
-neunde (no equivalent expression)
A connective ending used to talk in advance about a situation to follow.

어떻다 (adjective) : 생각, 느낌, 상태, 형편 등이 어찌 되어 있다.
such
Being such in one's thoughts, feelings, state, situation, etc.

-어요 : (두루높임으로) 어떤 사실을 서술하거나 질문, 명령, 권유함을 나타내는 종결 어미.
-eoyo (no equivalent expression)
(informal addressee-raising) A sentence-final ending used to describe a certain fact, **ask a question**, give an order, or advise.

머리 풀+었+는데 어떻+어요?
어때요

머리 (noun) : 머리에 난 털.
hair
The hair on the head.

풀다 (verb) : 매이거나 묶이거나 얽힌 것을 원래의 상태로 되게 하다.
untie
To return what has been tied, bound, or twisted back to its original state.

-었- : 어떤 사건이 과거에 완료되었거나 그 사건의 결과가 현재까지 지속되는 상황을 나타내는 어미.
-eot- (no equivalent expression)
An ending of a word used to indicate that an event was completed in the past or its result continues in the present.

-는데 : 뒤의 말을 하기 위하여 그 대상과 관련이 있는 상황을 미리 말함을 나타내는 연결 어미.
-neunde (no equivalent expression)
A connective ending used to talk in advance about a situation to follow.

어떻다 (adjective) : 생각, 느낌, 상태, 형편 등이 어찌 되어 있다.
such
Being such in one's thoughts, feelings, state, situation, etc.

-어요 : (두루높임으로) 어떤 사실을 서술하거나 질문, 명령, 권유함을 나타내는 종결 어미.
-eoyo (no equivalent expression)
(informal addressee-raising) A sentence-final ending used to describe a certain fact, **ask a question**, give an order, or advise.

길(기)+ㄴ 머리+는?
긴

길다 (adjective) : 물체의 한쪽 끝에서 다른 쪽 끝까지 두 끝이 멀리 떨어져 있다.
long; lengthy; extensive
Two ends of an object being far apart.

-ㄴ : 앞의 말이 관형어의 기능을 하게 만들고 현재의 상태를 나타내는 어미.
-n (no equivalent expression)
An ending of a word that makes the preceding statement function as an adnominal phrase and refers to the present state.

머리 (noun) : 머리에 난 털.
hair
The hair on the head.

는 : 문장 속에서 어떤 대상이 화제임을 나타내는 조사.
neun (no equivalent expression)
A postpositional particle used to indicate that a certain subject is the topic of a sentence.

짧+은 머리+는?

짧다 (adjective) : 공간이나 물체의 양 끝 사이가 가깝다.
short
The distance between the two ends of a space or object being close.

-은 : 앞의 말이 관형어의 기능을 하게 만들고 현재의 상태를 나타내는 어미.
-eun (no equivalent expression)
An ending of a word that makes the preceding word function as an adnominal phrase and refers to the present state.

머리 (noun) : 머리에 난 털.
hair
The hair on the head.

는 : 문장 속에서 어떤 대상이 화제임을 나타내는 조사.
neun (no equivalent expression)
A postpositional particle used to indicate that a certain subject is the topic of a sentence.

어떻+어요?
어때요

어떻다 (adjective) : 생각, 느낌, 상태, 형편 등이 어찌 되어 있다.
such
Being such in one's thoughts, feelings, state, situation, etc.

-어요 : (두루높임으로) 어떤 사실을 서술하거나 질문, 명령, 권유함을 나타내는 종결 어미.
-eoyo (no equivalent expression)
(informal addressee-raising) A sentence-final ending used to describe a certain fact, **ask a question**, give an order, or advise.

저+의 눈+과 코+와 입술+이 얼마나 예쁘(예ㅃ)+[어 보이]+나요?
제 예뻐 보이나요

저 (pronoun) : 말하는 사람이 듣는 사람에게 자신을 낮추어 가리키는 말.
I; me
The humble form used by the speaker to refer to himself/herself for the purpose of showing humility to the listener.

의 : 앞의 말이 뒤의 말에 대하여 소유, 소속, 소재, 관계, 기원, 주체의 관계를 가짐을 나타내는 조사.
ui (no equivalent expression)
A postpositional particle used to indicate that the referent of the following word is owned by, belongs to, is related to, originates from, or is the object of what the preceding word indicates.

눈 (noun) : 사람이나 동물의 얼굴에 있으며 빛의 자극을 받아 물체를 볼 수 있는 감각 기관.
eye
The sensory organ on the face of a person or animal that can see an object when stimulated by the light.

과 : 앞과 뒤의 명사를 같은 자격으로 이어 줄 때 쓰는 조사.
gwa (no equivalent expression)
A postpositional particle used to list the preceding and following nouns.

코 (noun) : 숨을 쉬고 냄새를 맡는 몸의 한 부분.
nose
The body part that is used for breathing and smelling.

와 : 앞과 뒤의 명사를 같은 자격으로 이어주는 조사.
wa (no equivalent expression)
A postpositional particle used to list the preceding and following nouns on an equal footing.

입술 (noun) : 사람의 입 주위를 둘러싸고 있는 붉고 부드러운 살.
lips
The red and soft flesh that surrounds the opening of the mouth.

이 : 어떤 상태나 상황의 대상이나 동작의 주체를 나타내는 조사.
i (no equivalent expression)
A postpositional particle referring to a subject under a certain state or situation, or the agent of an action.

얼마나 (adverb) : 어느 정도나.
how
How much.

예쁘다 (adjective) : 생긴 모양이 눈으로 보기에 좋을 만큼 아름답다.
pretty; beautiful; comely
The appearance of someone or something looking good and beautiful.

-어 보이다 : 겉으로 볼 때 앞의 말이 나타내는 것처럼 느껴지거나 추측됨을 나타내는 표현.
-eo boida (no equivalent expression)
An expression used to indicate that one feels or guesses something by appearance as mentioned in the preceding statement.

-나요 : (두루높임으로) 앞의 내용에 대해 상대방에게 물어볼 때 쓰는 표현.
-nayo (no equivalent expression)
(informal addressee-raising) An expression used to ask the listener about the preceding content.

나 어떻+어요?
어때요

나 (pronoun) : 말하는 사람이 친구나 아랫사람에게 자기를 가리키는 말.
I
A pronoun used to indicate oneself to a friend or a younger person.

어떻다 (adjective) : 생각, 느낌, 상태, 형편 등이 어찌 되어 있다.
such
Being such in one's thoughts, feelings, state, situation, etc.

-어요 : (두루높임으로) 어떤 사실을 서술하거나 질문, 명령, 권유함을 나타내는 종결 어미.
-eoyo (no equivalent expression)
(informal addressee-raising) A sentence-final ending used to describe a certain fact, **ask a question**, give an order, or advise.

나 예쁘(예ㅃ)+어요?
예뻐요

나 (pronoun) : 말하는 사람이 친구나 아랫사람에게 자기를 가리키는 말.
I
A pronoun used to indicate oneself to a friend or a younger person.

예쁘다 (adjective) : 생긴 모양이 눈으로 보기에 좋을 만큼 아름답다.
pretty; beautiful; comely
The appearance of someone or something looking good and beautiful.

-어요 : (두루높임으로) 어떤 사실을 서술하거나 질문, 명령, 권유함을 나타내는 종결 어미.
-eoyo (no equivalent expression)
(informal addressee-raising) A sentence-final ending used to describe a certain fact, **ask a question**, give an order, or advise.

어떻+어요?
어때요

어떻다 (adjective) : 생각, 느낌, 상태, 형편 등이 어찌 되어 있다.
such
Being such in one's thoughts, feelings, state, situation, etc.

-어요 : (두루높임으로) 어떤 사실을 서술하거나 질문, 명령, 권유함을 나타내는 종결 어미.
-eoyo (no equivalent expression)
(informal addressee-raising) A sentence-final ending used to describe a certain fact, **ask a question**, give an order, or advise.

< 2 절(verse) >

운동화 신+었+는데 어떻+어요?
어때요

운동화 (noun) : 운동을 할 때 신도록 만든 신발.
running shoes; sneakers
Shoes worn when doing an exercise.

신다 (verb) : 신발이나 양말 등의 속으로 발을 넣어 발의 전부나 일부를 덮다.
put on; wear
To put one's feet into a pair of shoes, socks, etc., and cover the whole or a part of the feet with them.

-었- : 어떤 사건이 과거에 완료되었거나 그 사건의 결과가 현재까지 지속되는 상황을 나타내는 어미.
-eot- (no equivalent expression)
An ending of a word used to indicate that an event was completed in the past or its result continues in the present.

-는데 : 뒤의 말을 하기 위하여 그 대상과 관련이 있는 상황을 미리 말함을 나타내는 연결 어미.
-neunde (no equivalent expression)
A connective ending used to talk in advance about a situation to follow.

어떻다 (adjective) : 생각, 느낌, 상태, 형편 등이 어찌 되어 있다.
such
Being such in one's thoughts, feelings, state, situation, etc.

-어요 : (두루높임으로) 어떤 사실을 서술하거나 질문, 명령, 권유함을 나타내는 종결 어미.
-eoyo (no equivalent expression)
(informal addressee-raising) A sentence-final ending used to describe a certain fact, **ask a question**, give an order, or advise.

구두 신+었+는데 어떻+어요?

어때요

구두 (noun) : 정장을 입었을 때 신는 가죽, 비닐 등으로 만든 신발.
shoes
Dress shoes made of leather or synthetic leather, worn with a suit.

신다 (verb) : 신발이나 양말 등의 속으로 발을 넣어 발의 전부나 일부를 덮다.
put on; wear
To put one's feet into a pair of shoes, socks, etc., and cover the whole or a part of the feet with them.

-었- : 어떤 사건이 과거에 완료되었거나 그 사건의 결과가 현재까지 지속되는 상황을 나타내는 어미.
-eot- (no equivalent expression)
An ending of a word used to indicate that an event was completed in the past or its result continues in the present.

-는데 : 뒤의 말을 하기 위하여 그 대상과 관련이 있는 상황을 미리 말함을 나타내는 연결 어미.
-neunde (no equivalent expression)
A connective ending used to talk in advance about a situation to follow.

어떻다 (adjective) : 생각, 느낌, 상태, 형편 등이 어찌 되어 있다.
such
Being such in one's thoughts, feelings, state, situation, etc.

-어요 : (두루높임으로) 어떤 사실을 서술하거나 질문, 명령, 권유함을 나타내는 종결 어미.
-eoyo (no equivalent expression)
(informal addressee-raising) A sentence-final ending used to describe a certain fact, **ask a question**, give an order, or advise.

검은색+은?

검은색 (noun) : 빛이 없을 때의 밤하늘과 같이 매우 어둡고 짙은 색.
black
A very dark color like a night sky with no light.

은 : 문장 속에서 어떤 대상이 화제임을 나타내는 조사.
eun (no equivalent expression)
A postpositional particle used to indicate that a certain subject is the topic of a sentence.

흰색+은?

흰색 (noun) : 눈이나 우유와 같은 밝은 색.
white
The bright color of snow or milk.

은 : 문장 속에서 어떤 대상이 화제임을 나타내는 조사.
eun (no equivalent expression)
A postpositional particle used to indicate that a certain subject is the topic of a sentence.

어떻+어요?
어때요

어떻다 (adjective) : 생각, 느낌, 상태, 형편 등이 어찌 되어 있다.
such
Being such in one's thoughts, feelings, state, situation, etc.

-어요 : (두루높임으로) 어떤 사실을 서술하거나 질문, 명령, 권유함을 나타내는 종결 어미.
-eoyo (no equivalent expression)
(informal addressee-raising) A sentence-final ending used to describe a certain fact, **ask a question**, give an order, or advise.

목걸이 차+았+는데 어떻+어요?
찼는데 어때요

목걸이 (noun) : 보석 등을 줄에 꿰어서 목에 거는 장식품.
necklace
A piece of jewelry with a string of jewels, etc., worn around the neck.

차다 (verb) : 물건을 허리나 팔목, 발목 등에 매어 달거나 걸거나 끼우다.
wear
To attach, hang, or put an object on one's waist, wrist, ankle, etc.

-았- : 어떤 사건이 과거에 완료되었거나 그 사건의 결과가 현재까지 지속되는 상황을 나타내는 어미.
-at- (no equivalent expression)
An ending of a word used to indicate that an event was completed in the past or its result continues in the present.

-는데 : 뒤의 말을 하기 위하여 그 대상과 관련이 있는 상황을 미리 말함을 나타내는 연결 어미.
-neunde (no equivalent expression)
A connective ending used to talk in advance about a situation to follow.

어떻다 (adjective) : 생각, 느낌, 상태, 형편 등이 어찌 되어 있다.
such
Being such in one's thoughts, feelings, state, situation, etc.

-어요 : (두루높임으로) 어떤 사실을 서술하거나 질문, 명령, 권유함을 나타내는 종결 어미.
-eoyo (no equivalent expression)
(informal addressee-raising) A sentence-final ending used to describe a certain fact, **ask a question**, give an order, or advise.

반지 끼+었+는데 어떻+어요?
어때요

반지 (noun) : 손가락에 끼는 동그란 장신구.
ring
A round accessory for wearing on one's finger.

끼다 (verb) : 무엇에 걸려 빠지지 않도록 꿰거나 꽂다.
stick in; lace
To thread or stick something in to prevent it from falling out.

-었- : 어떤 사건이 과거에 완료되었거나 그 사건의 결과가 현재까지 지속되는 상황을 나타내는 어미.
-eot- (no equivalent expression)
An ending of a word used to indicate that an event was completed in the past or its result continues in the present.

-는데 : 뒤의 말을 하기 위하여 그 대상과 관련이 있는 상황을 미리 말함을 나타내는 연결 어미.
-neunde (no equivalent expression)
A connective ending used to talk in advance about a situation to follow.

어떻다 (adjective) : 생각, 느낌, 상태, 형편 등이 어찌 되어 있다.
such
Being such in one's thoughts, feelings, state, situation, etc.

-어요 : (두루높임으로) 어떤 사실을 서술하거나 질문, 명령, 권유함을 나타내는 종결 어미.
-eoyo (no equivalent expression)
(informal addressee-raising) A sentence-final ending used to describe a certain fact, **ask a question**, give an order, or advise.

귀걸이+는?

귀걸이 (noun) : 귀에 다는 장식품.
earrings
Accessories for the ears.

는 : 문장 속에서 어떤 대상이 화제임을 나타내는 조사.
neun (no equivalent expression)
A postpositional particle used to indicate that a certain subject is the topic of a sentence.

팔찌+는?

팔찌 (noun) : 팔목에 끼는, 금, 은, 가죽 등으로 만든 장식품.
bracelet
A decoration item made of gold, silver, leather, etc., which is worn around one's wrist.

는 : 문장 속에서 어떤 대상이 화제임을 나타내는 조사.
neun (no equivalent expression)
A postpositional particle used to indicate that a certain subject is the topic of a sentence.

어떻+어요?

어때요

어떻다 (adjective) : 생각, 느낌, 상태, 형편 등이 어찌 되어 있다.
such
Being such in one's thoughts, feelings, state, situation, etc.

-어요 : (두루높임으로) 어떤 사실을 서술하거나 질문, 명령, 권유함을 나타내는 종결 어미.
-eoyo (no equivalent expression)
(informal addressee-raising) A sentence-final ending used to describe a certain fact, **ask a question**, give an order, or advise.

저+의 눈+과 코+와 입술+이 얼마나 예쁘(예ㅃ)+[어 보이]+나요?
제 예뻐 보이나요

저 (pronoun) : 말하는 사람이 듣는 사람에게 자신을 낮추어 가리키는 말.
I; me
The humble form used by the speaker to refer to himself/herself for the purpose of showing humility to the listener.

의 : 앞의 말이 뒤의 말에 대하여 소유, 소속, 소재, 관계, 기원, 주체의 관계를 가짐을 나타내는 조사.
ui (no equivalent expression)
A postpositional particle used to indicate that the referent of the following word is owned by, belongs to, is related to, originates from, or is the object of what the preceding word indicates.

눈 (noun) : 사람이나 동물의 얼굴에 있으며 빛의 자극을 받아 물체를 볼 수 있는 감각 기관.
eye
The sensory organ on the face of a person or animal that can see an object when stimulated by the light.

과 : 앞과 뒤의 명사를 같은 자격으로 이어 줄 때 쓰는 조사.
gwa (no equivalent expression)
A postpositional particle used to list the preceding and following nouns.

코 (noun) : 숨을 쉬고 냄새를 맡는 몸의 한 부분.
nose
The body part that is used for breathing and smelling.

와 : 앞과 뒤의 명사를 같은 자격으로 이어주는 조사.
wa (no equivalent expression)
A postpositional particle used to list the preceding and following nouns on an equal footing.

입술 (noun) : 사람의 입 주위를 둘러싸고 있는 붉고 부드러운 살.
lips
The red and soft flesh that surrounds the opening of the mouth.

이 : 어떤 상태나 상황의 대상이나 동작의 주체를 나타내는 조사.
i (no equivalent expression)
A postpositional particle referring to a subject under a certain state or situation, or the agent of an action.

얼마나 (adverb) : 어느 정도나.
how
How much.

예쁘다 (adjective) : 생긴 모양이 눈으로 보기에 좋을 만큼 아름답다.
pretty; beautiful; comely
The appearance of someone or something looking good and beautiful.

-어 보이다 : 겉으로 볼 때 앞의 말이 나타내는 것처럼 느껴지거나 추측됨을 나타내는 표현.
-eo boida (no equivalent expression)
An expression used to indicate that one feels or guesses something by appearance as mentioned in the preceding statement.

-나요 : (두루높임으로) 앞의 내용에 대해 상대방에게 물어볼 때 쓰는 표현.
-nayo (no equivalent expression)
(informal addressee-raising) An expression used to ask the listener about the preceding content.

나 어떻+어요?
어때요

나 (pronoun) : 말하는 사람이 친구나 아랫사람에게 자기를 가리키는 말.
I
A pronoun used to indicate oneself to a friend or a younger person.

어떻다 (adjective) : 생각, 느낌, 상태, 형편 등이 어찌 되어 있다.
such
Being such in one's thoughts, feelings, state, situation, etc.

-어요 : (두루높임으로) 어떤 사실을 서술하거나 질문, 명령, 권유함을 나타내는 종결 어미.
-eoyo (no equivalent expression)
(informal addressee-raising) A sentence-final ending used to describe a certain fact, **ask a question**, give an order, or advise.

나 예쁘(예ㅃ)+어요?
예뻐요

나 (pronoun) : 말하는 사람이 친구나 아랫사람에게 자기를 가리키는 말.
I
A pronoun used to indicate oneself to a friend or a younger person.

예쁘다 (adjective) : 생긴 모양이 눈으로 보기에 좋을 만큼 아름답다.
pretty; beautiful; comely
The appearance of someone or something looking good and beautiful.

-어요 : (두루높임으로) 어떤 사실을 서술하거나 질문, 명령, 권유함을 나타내는 종결 어미.
-eoyo (no equivalent expression)
(informal addressee-raising) A sentence-final ending used to describe a certain fact, **ask a question**, give an order, or advise.

어떻+어요?
어때요

어떻다 (adjective) : 생각, 느낌, 상태, 형편 등이 어찌 되어 있다.
such
Being such in one's thoughts, feelings, state, situation, etc.

-어요 : (두루높임으로) 어떤 사실을 서술하거나 질문, 명령, 권유함을 나타내는 종결 어미.
-eoyo (no equivalent expression)
(informal addressee-raising) A sentence-final ending used to describe a certain fact, **ask a question**, give an order, or advise.

< 5 >

하늘, 땅, 사람
(sky)
(ground; land)
(human; man)

[발음(pronunciation)]

< 1 절(verse) >

하늘에서 비가 내린다고 하는 걸 보니 하늘은 위인가요?
하느레서 비가 내린다고 하는 걸 보니 하느른 위인가요?
haneureseo biga naerindago haneun geol boni haneureun wiingayo?

그 비가 땅을 적신다고 하는 걸 보니 그럼 땅은 아래인가 보네요.
그 비가 땅을 적씬다고 하는 걸 보니 그럼 땅은 아래인가 보네요.
geu biga ttangeul jeoksindago haneun geol boni geureom ttangeun araeinga boneyo.

땅을 밟고 서서 하늘을 바라보는 사람은 하늘과 땅 사이에 있는 거겠군요.
땅을 밥꼬 서서 하느를 바라보는 사라믄 하늘과 땅 사이에 인는 거겓꾸뇨.
ttangeul bapgo seoseo haneureul baraboneun sarameun haneulgwa ttang saie inneun geogetgunyo.

그 사이에 갇혀 지지고 볶으며 오늘도 나는 살아가고 있네요.
그 사이에 가쳐 지지고 보끄며 오늘도 나는 사라가고 인네요.
geu saie gacheo jijigo bokkeumyeo oneuldo naneun saragago inneyo.

땅에 갇혀 사는 것은 이제 너무 지겨워요.
땅에 가쳐 사는 거슨 이제 너무 지겨워요.
ttange gacheo saneun geoseun ije neomu jigyeowoyo.

움츠린 가슴을 펴고 하늘 끝까지 날아올라 봐요.
움츠린 가스믈 펴고 하늘 끋까지 나라올라 봐요.
umcheurin gaseumeul pyeogo haneul kkeutkkaji naraolla bwayo.

우리 모두 거기서 행복하게 살아 봐요.
우리 모두 거기서 행보카게 사라 봐요.
uri modu geogiseo haengbokage sara bwayo.

< 후렴(refrain) >

이제부터는 지금부터는
이제부터는 지금부터는
ijebuteoneun jigeumbuteoneun

가슴이 시키는 대로 살아 봐요.
가스미 시키는 대로 사라 봐요.
gaseumi sikineun daero sara bwayo.

이제부터는 지금부터는
이제부터는 지금부터는
ijebuteoneun jigeumbuteoneun

가슴이 느끼는 대로 자유롭게
가스미 느끼는 대로 자유롭께
gaseumi neukkineun daero jayuropge

아무것도 신경 쓰지 마요.
아무걷또 신경 쓰지 마요.
amugeotdo singyeong sseuji mayo.

< 2 절(verse) >

아직까지 해가 뜨고 진 적은 한 번도 없었어요.
아직까지 해가 뜨고 진 저근 한 번도 업써써요.
ajikkkaji haega tteugo jin jeogeun han beondo eopseosseoyo.

이 땅에 사는 우리들만 어제도 오늘도 쉼 없이 돌고 돌고 또 돌아요.
이 땅에 사는 우리들만 어제도 오늘도 쉼 업씨 돌고 돌고 또 도라요.
i ttange saneun urideulman eojedo oneuldo swim eopsi dolgo dolgo tto dorayo.

배운 대로 남들이 시키는 대로 그렇게 사람들 사이에 숨어 살아가고 있죠.
배운 대로 남드리 시키는 대로 그러케 사람들 사이에 수머 사라가고 읻쬬.
baeun daero namdeuri sikineun daero geureoke saramdeul saie sumeo saragago itjyo.

그 사이에 갇혀 지지고 볶으며 오늘도 나는 살아가고 있네요.
그 사이에 가쳐 지지고 보끄며 오늘도 나는 사라가고 인네요.
geu saie gacheo jijigo bokkeumyeo oneuldo naneun saragago inneyo.

누가 시키는 대로 사는 것은 이제 너무 짜증이 나요.
누가 시키는 대로 사는 거슨 이제 너무 짜증이 나요.
nuga sikineun daero saneun geoseun ije neomu jjajeungi nayo.

바라고 원하는 생각들을 하늘 너머로 떠나보내요.
바라고 원하는 생각뜨를 하늘 너머로 떠나보내요.
barago wonhaneun saenggakdeureul haneul neomeoro tteonabonaeyo.

우리 모두 거기서 자유롭게 살아 봐요.
우리 모두 거기서 자유롭께 사라 봐요.
uri modu geogiseo jayuropge sara bwayo.

< 후렴(refrain) >

우- 워- 이제부터는 지금부터는
우- 워- 이제부터는 지금부터는
u- wo- ijebuteoneun jigeumbuteoneun

이제부터는 지금부터는
이제부터는 지금부터는
ijebuteoneun jigeumbuteoneun

가슴이 시키는 대로 살아 봐요.
가스미 시키는 대로 사라 봐요.
gaseumi sikineun daero sara bwayo.

이제부터는 지금부터는
이제부터는 지금부터는
ijebuteoneun jigeumbuteoneun

가슴이 느끼는 대로 자유롭게
가스미 느끼는 대로 자유롭께
gaseumi neukkineun daero jayuropge

이제부터는 지금부터는
이제부터는 지금부터는
ijebuteoneun jigeumbuteoneun

(우리 모두 거기서)
(우리 모두 거기서)
(uri modu geogiseo)

가슴이 시키는 대로 살아 봐요.
가스미 시키는 대로 사라 봐요.
gaseumi sikineun daero sara bwayo.

(자유롭게 살아요)
(자유롭께 사라요)
(jayuropge sarayo)

이제부터는 지금부터는
이제부터는 지금부터는
ijebuteoneun jigeumbuteoneun

(우리 모두 거기서)
(우리 모두 거기서)
(uri modu geogiseo)

가슴이 느끼는 대로 자유롭게
가스미 느끼는 대로 자유롭께
gaseumi neukkineun daero jayuropge

(자유롭게)
(자유롭께)
(jayuropge)

그런 사람이었어요.
그런 사라미어써요.
geureon saramieosseoyo.

그런 인생이었어요.
그런 인생이어써요.
geureon insaengieosseoyo.

그렇게 기억해 줘요.
그러케 기어캐 줘요.
geureoke gieokae jwoyo.

< 1 절(verse) >

하늘+에서 비+가 내리+ㄴ다고 하+[는 것(거)]+을 보+니
내린다고 하는 걸

하늘 (noun) : 땅 위로 펼쳐진 무한히 넓은 공간.
sky
The vast, limitless space that unfolds above the ground.

에서 : 앞말이 출발점의 뜻을 나타내는 조사.
eseo (no equivalent expression)
A postpositional particle used to indicate that the preceding word refers to the starting point of something.

비 (noun) : 높은 곳에서 구름을 이루고 있던 수증기가 식어서 뭉쳐 떨어지는 물방울.
rain
Water drops generated from cloud-forming vapors high in the sky that get cold, condense, and fall.

가 : 어떤 상태나 상황에 놓인 대상이나 동작의 주체를 나타내는 조사.
ga (no equivalent expression)
A postpositional particle referring to a subject under a certain state or situation, or the subject of an act.

내리다 (verb) : 눈이나 비 등이 오다.
fall; descend
To snow, rain, etc.

-ㄴ다고 : 다른 사람에게서 들은 내용을 간접적으로 전달하거나 주어의 생각, 의견 등을 나타내는 표현.
-ndago (no equivalent expression)
An expression used to pass along what the speaker heard from another person, or to present the subject's thoughts, opinions, etc.

하다 (verb) : 무엇에 대해 말하다.
say
To talk about something.

-는 것 : 명사가 아닌 것을 문장에서 명사처럼 쓰이게 하거나 '이다' 앞에 쓰일 수 있게 할 때 쓰는 표현.
-neun geot (no equivalent expression)
An expression used to enable a non-noun word to be used as a noun in a sentence or to be used in front of '이다' (be).

을 : 동작이 직접적으로 영향을 미치는 대상을 나타내는 조사.
eul (no equivalent expression)
A postpositional particle used to indicate the subject that an action has a direct influence on.

보다 (verb) : 무엇을 근거로 판단하다.
judge from
To judge based on evidence.

-니 : 뒤에 오는 말에 대하여 앞에 오는 말이 원인이나 근거, 전제가 됨을 나타내는 연결 어미.
-ni (no equivalent expression)
A connective ending used when the preceding statement is the cause, reason, or premise for the following statement.

하늘+은 위+이+ㄴ가요?
위인가요

하늘 (noun) : 땅 위로 펼쳐진 무한히 넓은 공간.
sky
The vast, limitless space that unfolds above the ground.

은 : 문장 속에서 어떤 대상이 화제임을 나타내는 조사.
eun (no equivalent expression)
A postpositional particle used to indicate that a certain subject is the topic of a sentence.

위 (noun) : 어떤 기준보다 더 높은 쪽. 또는 중간보다 더 높은 쪽.
top; higher part
A higher position than a certain standard; a higher position than the middle.

이다 : 주어가 지시하는 대상의 속성이나 부류를 지정하는 뜻을 나타내는 서술격 조사.
ida (no equivalent expression)
A predicate particle indicating the meaning of the attribute or category of the thing that the subject of the sentence refers to.

-ㄴ가요 : (두루높임으로) 현재의 사실에 대한 물음을 나타내는 종결 어미.
-ngayo (no equivalent expression)
(informal addressee-raising) A sentence-final ending referring to a question about a fact of the present.

그 비+가 땅+을 적시+ㄴ다고 하+[는 것(거)]+을 보+니
적신다고 하는 걸

그 (determiner) : 앞에서 이미 이야기한 대상을 가리킬 때 쓰는 말.
that; the
A term referring to something mentioned earlier.

비 (noun) : 높은 곳에서 구름을 이루고 있던 수증기가 식어서 뭉쳐 떨어지는 물방울.
rain
Water drops generated from cloud-forming vapors high in the sky that get cold, condense, and fall.

가 : 어떤 상태나 상황에 놓인 대상이나 동작의 주체를 나타내는 조사.
ga (no equivalent expression)
A postpositional particle referring to a subject under a certain state or situation, or the subject of an act.

땅 (noun) : 지구에서 물로 된 부분이 아닌 흙이나 돌로 된 부분.
ground; land
The part of the earth that consists of soil or stones instead of water.

을 : 동작이 직접적으로 영향을 미치는 대상을 나타내는 조사.
eul (no equivalent expression)
A postpositional particle used to indicate the subject that an action has a direct influence on.

적시다 (verb) : 물 등의 액체를 묻혀 젖게 하다.
wet
To cause something to come in contact with water and become wet.

-ㄴ다고 : 다른 사람에게서 들은 내용을 간접적으로 전달하거나 주어의 생각, 의견 등을 나타내는 표현.
-ndago (no equivalent expression)
An expression used to pass along what the speaker heard from another person, or to present the subject's thoughts, opinions, etc.

하다 (verb) : 무엇에 대해 말하다.
say
To talk about something.

-는 것 : 명사가 아닌 것을 문장에서 명사처럼 쓰이게 하거나 '이다' 앞에 쓰일 수 있게 할 때 쓰는 표현.
-neun geot (no equivalent expression)
An expression used to enable a non-noun word to be used as a noun in a sentence or to be used in front of '이다' (be).

을 : 동작이 직접적으로 영향을 미치는 대상을 나타내는 조사.
eul (no equivalent expression)
A postpositional particle used to indicate the subject that an action has a direct influence on.

보다 (verb) : 무엇을 근거로 판단하다.
judge from
To judge based on evidence.

-니 : 뒤에 오는 말에 대하여 앞에 오는 말이 원인이나 근거, 전제가 됨을 나타내는 연결 어미.
-ni (no equivalent expression)
A connective ending used when the preceding statement is the cause, reason, or premise for the following statement.

그럼 땅+은 아래+이+[ㄴ가 보]+네요.
아래인가 보네요

그럼 (adverb) : 앞의 내용이 뒤의 내용의 조건이 될 때 쓰는 말.
if so; in that case
A word used when the following statement is conditional upon the preceding one.

땅 (noun) : 지구에서 물로 된 부분이 아닌 흙이나 돌로 된 부분.
ground; land
The part of the earth that consists of soil or stones instead of water.

은 : 문장 속에서 어떤 대상이 화제임을 나타내는 조사.
eun (no equivalent expression)
A postpositional particle used to indicate that a certain subject is the topic of a sentence.

아래 (noun) : 일정한 기준보다 낮은 위치.
bottom; lower part
A lower position than a certain standard.

이다 : 주어가 지시하는 대상의 속성이나 부류를 지정하는 뜻을 나타내는 서술격 조사.
ida (no equivalent expression)
A predicate particle indicating the meaning of the attribute or category of the thing that the subject of the sentence refers to.

-ㄴ가 보다 : 앞의 말이 나타내는 사실을 추측함을 나타내는 표현.
-nga boda (no equivalent expression)
An expression used to guess about a fact mentioned in the preceding statement.

-네요 : (두루높임으로) 말하는 사람이 직접 경험하여 새롭게 알게 된 사실에 대해 감탄함을 나타낼 때 쓰는 표현.
-neyo (no equivalent expression)
(informal addressee-raising) An expression used to indicate that the speaker is impressed by a fact he/she learned anew from a past personal experience.

땅+을 밟+고 서+(어)서 하늘+을 바라보+는 사람+은
서서

땅 (noun) : 지구에서 물로 된 부분이 아닌 흙이나 돌로 된 부분.
ground; land
The part of the earth that consists of soil or stones instead of water.

을 : 동작이 직접적으로 영향을 미치는 대상을 나타내는 조사.
eul (no equivalent expression)
A postpositional particle used to indicate the subject that an action has a direct influence on.

밟다 (verb) : 어떤 대상에 발을 올려놓고 서거나 올려놓으면서 걷다.
pace; step; tread
To put feet on an object and stand on it or to tread on it.

-고 : 앞의 말이 나타내는 행동이나 그 결과가 뒤에 오는 행동이 일어나는 동안에 그대로 지속됨을 나타내는 연결 어미.
-go (no equivalent expression)
A connective ending used when an action or result of the preceding statement remains the same while the following action happens.

서다 (verb) : 사람이나 동물이 바닥에 발을 대고 몸을 곧게 하다.
stand
For a human or animal to place his/her feet on the ground and assume an upright position.

-어서 : 앞의 말과 뒤의 말이 순차적으로 일어남을 나타내는 연결 어미.
-eoseo (no equivalent expression)
A connective ending used to indicate that the preceding event and the following one happened sequentially.

하늘 (noun) : 땅 위로 펼쳐진 무한히 넓은 공간.
sky
The vast, limitless space that unfolds above the ground.

을 : 동작이 직접적으로 영향을 미치는 대상을 나타내는 조사.
eul (no equivalent expression)
A postpositional particle used to indicate the subject that an action has a direct influence on.

바라보다 (verb) : 바로 향해 보다.
look; stare; gaze
To look straight at something.

-는 : 앞의 말이 관형어의 기능을 하게 만들고 사건이나 동작이 현재 일어남을 나타내는 어미.

-neun (no equivalent expression)
An ending of a word that makes the preceding statement function as an adnominal phrase and implies that an event or action is happening in the present.

사람 (noun) : 생각할 수 있으며 언어와 도구를 만들어 사용하고 사회를 이루어 사는 존재.
human; man
A being that is capable of thinking, makes and uses languages and tools and lives by forming a society with others.

은 : 문장 속에서 어떤 대상이 화제임을 나타내는 조사.
eun (no equivalent expression)
A postpositional particle used to indicate that a certain subject is the topic of a sentence.

하늘+과 땅 사이+에 있+[는 것(거)]+(이)+겠+군요.
있는 거겠군요

하늘 (noun) : 땅 위로 펼쳐진 무한히 넓은 공간.
sky
The vast, limitless space that unfolds above the ground.

과 : 앞과 뒤의 명사를 같은 자격으로 이어 줄 때 쓰는 조사.
gwa (no equivalent expression)
A postpositional particle used to list the preceding and following nouns.

땅 (noun) : 지구에서 물로 된 부분이 아닌 흙이나 돌로 된 부분.
ground; land
The part of the earth that consists of soil or stones instead of water.

사이 (noun) : 한 물체에서 다른 물체까지 또는 한곳에서 다른 곳까지의 거리나 공간.
space; distance; gap
The distance or space between one object and another, or between one place and another.

에 : 앞말이 어떤 장소나 자리임을 나타내는 조사.
on; in; at
A postpositional particle to indicate that the preceding statement refers to a certain place or space.

있다 (adjective) : 사람이나 동물이 어느 곳에 머무르거나 사는 상태이다.
no equivalent expression
A person or animal staying or living in a certain place.

-는 것 : 명사가 아닌 것을 문장에서 명사처럼 쓰이게 하거나 '이다' 앞에 쓰일 수 있게 할 때 쓰는 표현.
-neun geot (no equivalent expression)
An expression used to enable a non-noun word to be used as a noun in a sentence or to be used in front of '이다' (be).

이다 : 주어가 지시하는 대상의 속성이나 부류를 지정하는 뜻을 나타내는 서술격 조사.
ida (no equivalent expression)
A predicate particle indicating the meaning of the attribute or category of the thing that the subject of the sentence refers to.

-겠- : 미래의 일이나 추측을 나타내는 어미.
-get- (no equivalent expression)
An ending of a word referring to a future event or assumption.

-군요 : (두루높임으로) 새롭게 알게 된 사실에 주목하거나 감탄함을 나타내는 표현.
-gunyo (no equivalent expression)
(informal addressee-raising) An expression used to indicate that the speaker notices or is impressed by a newly learned fact.

그 사이+에 갇히+어 [지지고 볶]+으며 오늘+도 나+는 살아가+[고 있]+네요.
갇혀

그 (determiner) : 앞에서 이미 이야기한 대상을 가리킬 때 쓰는 말.
that; the
A term referring to something mentioned earlier.

사이 (noun) : 한 물체에서 다른 물체까지 또는 한곳에서 다른 곳까지의 거리나 공간.
space; distance; gap
The distance or space between one object and another, or between one place and another.

에 : 앞말이 어떤 장소나 자리임을 나타내는 조사.
on; in; at
A postpositional particle to indicate that the preceding statement refers to a certain place or space.

갇히다 (verb) : 어떤 공간이나 상황에서 나가지 못하게 되다.
be locked up; be shut up; be imprisoned
To become stuck in a certain place or situation without an exit.

-어 : 앞의 말이 뒤의 말보다 먼저 일어났거나 뒤의 말에 대한 방법이나 수단이 됨을 나타내는 연결 어미.
-eo (no equivalent expression)
A connective ending used when the preceding statement happened before the following statement or was the ways or means to the following statement.

지지고 볶다 (idiom) : 온갖 것을 겪으며 함께 살아가다.
fry and roast
To live together going through all sorts of troubles.

-으며 : 두 가지 이상의 동작이나 상태가 함께 일어남을 나타내는 연결 어미.
-eumyeo (no equivalent expression)
A connective ending used when more than two actions or states happen at the same time.

오늘 (noun) : 지금 지나가고 있는 이날.
today
The day that is passing at the present time.

도 : 이미 있는 어떤 것에 다른 것을 더하거나 포함함을 나타내는 조사.
do (no equivalent expression)
A postpositional particle used to indicate an addition or inclusion of another thing to something that already exists.

나 (pronoun) : 말하는 사람이 친구나 아랫사람에게 자기를 가리키는 말.
I
A pronoun used to indicate oneself to a friend or a younger person.

는 : 문장 속에서 어떤 대상이 화제임을 나타내는 조사.
neun (no equivalent expression)
A postpositional particle used to indicate that a certain subject is the topic of a sentence.

살아가다 (verb) : 어떤 종류의 삶이나 시대 등을 견디며 생활해 나가다.
make a living
To continue to live by enduring a kind of life, period, etc.

-고 있다 : 앞의 말이 나타내는 행동이 계속 진행됨을 나타내는 표현.
-go itda (no equivalent expression)
An expression used to state that the act mentioned in the preceding statement is continued.

-네요 : (두루높임으로) 말하는 사람이 직접 경험하여 새롭게 알게 된 사실에 대해 감탄함을 나타낼 때 쓰는 표현.
-neyo (no equivalent expression)
(informal addressee-raising) An expression used to indicate that the speaker is impressed by a fact he/she learned anew from a past personal experience.

땅+에 갇히+어 살(사)+[는 것]+은 이제 너무 지겹(지겨우)+어요.

갇혀 사는 것은 지겨워요

땅 (noun) : 지구에서 물로 된 부분이 아닌 흙이나 돌로 된 부분.
ground; land
The part of the earth that consists of soil or stones instead of water.

에 : 앞말이 어떤 장소나 자리임을 나타내는 조사.
on; in; at
A postpositional particle to indicate that the preceding statement refers to a certain place or space.

갇히다 (verb) : 어떤 공간이나 상황에서 나가지 못하게 되다.
be locked up; be shut up; be imprisoned
To become stuck in a certain place or situation without an exit.

-어 : 앞의 말이 뒤의 말보다 먼저 일어났거나 뒤의 말에 대한 방법이나 수단이 됨을 나타내는 연결 어미.
-eo (no equivalent expression)
A connective ending used when the preceding statement happened before the following statement or was the ways or means to the following statement.

살다 (verb) : 사람이 생활을 하다.
live
For a person to lead a life.

-는 것 : 명사가 아닌 것을 문장에서 명사처럼 쓰이게 하거나 '이다' 앞에 쓰일 수 있게 할 때 쓰는 표현.
-neun geot (no equivalent expression)
An expression used to enable a non-noun word to be used as a noun in a sentence or to be used in front of '이다' (be).

은 : 문장 속에서 어떤 대상이 화제임을 나타내는 조사.
eun (no equivalent expression)
A postpositional particle used to indicate that a certain subject is the topic of a sentence.

이제 (adverb) : 지금의 시기가 되어.
now
Reaching this time.

너무 (adverb) : 일정한 정도나 한계를 훨씬 넘어선 상태로.
too
To an excessive degree.

지겹다 (adjective) : 같은 상태나 일이 반복되어 재미가 없고 지루하고 싫다.
boring; tedious
Dull and unpleasant due to the repetition of a state or work.

-어요 : (두루높임으로) 어떤 사실을 서술하거나 질문, 명령, 권유함을 나타내는 종결 어미.
-eoyo (no equivalent expression)
(informal addressee-raising) A sentence-final ending used to **describe** a certain fact, ask a question, give an order, or advise.

움츠리+ㄴ 가슴+을 펴+고 하늘 끝+까지 날아오르(날아올ㄹ)+[아 보]+아요.
움츠린 날아올라 봐요

움츠리다 (verb) : 몸이나 몸의 일부를 오그려 작아지게 하다.
shrink; withdraw; hunch
To make one's body or a part of the body retract and become smaller.

-ㄴ : 앞의 말이 관형어의 기능을 하게 만들고 사건이나 동작이 완료되어 그 상태가 유지되고 있음을 나타내는 어미.
-n (no equivalent expression)
An ending of a word that makes the preceding statement function as an adnominal phrase and indicates that an event or action has been completed and its state continues.

가슴 (noun) : 인간이나 동물의 목과 배 사이에 있는 몸의 앞 부분.
chest
The front part of a human or animal's body, between the neck and the abdomen.

을 : 동작이 직접적으로 영향을 미치는 대상을 나타내는 조사.
eul (no equivalent expression)
A postpositional particle used to indicate the subject that an action has a direct influence on.

펴다 (verb) : 굽은 것을 곧게 하다. 또는 움츠리거나 오므라든 것을 벌리다.
stretch; stand tall
To straighten what is bent; or to spread what is hunched or shrunk.

-고 : 앞의 말이 나타내는 행동이나 그 결과가 뒤에 오는 행동이 일어나는 동안에 그대로 지속됨을 나타내는 연결 어미.
-go (no equivalent expression)
A connective ending used when an action or result of the preceding statement remains the same while the following action happens.

하늘 (noun) : 땅 위로 펼쳐진 무한히 넓은 공간.
sky
The vast, limitless space that unfolds above the ground.

끝 (noun) : 공간에서의 마지막 장소.
end
The last place in a space.

까지 : 어떤 범위의 끝임을 나타내는 조사.
kkaji (no equivalent expression)
A postpositional particle referring to the end of a certain range.

날아오르다 (verb) : 날아서 위로 높이 올라가다.
fly up; soar
To fly up in the air.

-아 보다 : 앞의 말이 나타내는 행동을 시험 삼아 함을 나타내는 표현.
-a boda (no equivalent expression)
An expression used to indicate that one does the act mentioned in the preceding statement, as a test.

-아요 : (두루높임으로) 어떤 사실을 서술하거나 질문, 명령, 권유함을 나타내는 종결 어미.
-ayo (no equivalent expression)
(informal addressee-raising) A sentence-final ending used to describe a certain fact, ask a question, give an order, or **advise**.

우리 모두 거기+서 행복하+게 살+[아 보]+아요.

살아 봐요

우리 (pronoun) : 말하는 사람이 자기와 듣는 사람 또는 이를 포함한 여러 사람들을 가리키는 말.
we
A pronoun used when the speaker refers to himself/herself and the listener or listeners, or a group of people including the speaker and listener or listeners.

모두 (adverb) : 빠짐없이 다.
all of
Everyone or everything without exception.

거기 (pronoun) : 앞에서 이미 이야기한 곳을 가리키는 말.
there
A pronoun used to indicate the previously-mentioned place.

서 : 앞말이 행동이 이루어지고 있는 장소임을 나타내는 조사.
seo (no equivalent expression)
A postpositional particle used to indicate that the preceding word refers to a place where a certain act is being done.

행복하다 (adjective) : 삶에서 충분한 만족과 기쁨을 느껴 흐뭇하다.
happy; content; joyful
Being delighted as one feels enough satisfaction or enjoyment in life.

-게 : 앞의 말이 뒤에서 가리키는 일의 목적이나 결과, 방식, 정도 등이 됨을 나타내는 연결 어미.
-ge (no equivalent expression)
A connective ending used when the preceding statement is the purpose, result, **method**, amount, etc., of something mentioned in the following statement.

살다 (verb) : 사람이 생활을 하다.
live
For a person to lead a life.

-아 보다 : 앞의 말이 나타내는 행동을 시험 삼아 함을 나타내는 표현.
-a boda (no equivalent expression)
An expression used to indicate that one does the act mentioned in the preceding statement, as a test.

-아요 : (두루높임으로) 어떤 사실을 서술하거나 질문, 명령, 권유함을 나타내는 종결 어미.
-ayo (no equivalent expression)
(informal addressee-raising) A sentence-final ending used to describe a certain fact, ask a question, give an order, or **advise**.

< 후렴(refrain) >

이제+부터+는 지금+부터+는

이제 (noun) : 지금의 시기.
now
The present.

부터 : 어떤 일의 시작이나 처음을 나타내는 조사.
buteo (no equivalent expression)
A postpositional particle that indicates the start or beginning of something.

는 : 어떤 대상이 다른 것과 대조됨을 나타내는 조사.
neun (no equivalent expression)
A postpositional particle used to indicate that a certain subject contrasts with something else.

지금 (noun) : 말을 하고 있는 바로 이때.
now
The present moment as one speaks.

부터 : 어떤 일의 시작이나 처음을 나타내는 조사.
buteo (no equivalent expression)
A postpositional particle that indicates the start or beginning of something.

는 : 어떤 대상이 다른 것과 대조됨을 나타내는 조사.
neun (no equivalent expression)
A postpositional particle used to indicate that a certain subject contrasts with something else.

가슴+이 시키+[는 대로] 살+[아 보]+아요.
살아 봐요

가슴 (noun) : 마음이나 느낌.
heart; feeling
One's mind or emotion.

이 : 어떤 상태나 상황의 대상이나 동작의 주체를 나타내는 조사.
i (no equivalent expression)
A postpositional particle referring to a subject under a certain state or situation, or the agent of an action.

시키다 (verb) : 어떤 일이나 행동을 하게 하다.
order
To make a person do something.

-는 대로 : 앞에 오는 말이 뜻하는 현재의 행동이나 상황과 같음을 나타내는 표현.
-neun daero (no equivalent expression)
An expression used to indicate that something is the same as the present act or state mentioned in the preceding statement.

살다 (verb) : 사람이 생활을 하다.
live
For a person to lead a life.

-아 보다 : 앞의 말이 나타내는 행동을 시험 삼아 함을 나타내는 표현.
-a boda (no equivalent expression)
An expression used to indicate that one does the act mentioned in the preceding statement, as a test.

-아요 : (두루높임으로) 어떤 사실을 서술하거나 질문, 명령, 권유함을 나타내는 종결 어미.
-ayo (no equivalent expression)
(informal addressee-raising) A sentence-final ending used to describe a certain fact, ask a question, give an order, or advise.

이제+부터+는 지금+부터+는

이제 (noun) : 지금의 시기.
now
The present.

부터 : 어떤 일의 시작이나 처음을 나타내는 조사.
buteo (no equivalent expression)
A postpositional particle that indicates the start or beginning of something.

는 : 어떤 대상이 다른 것과 대조됨을 나타내는 조사.
neun (no equivalent expression)
A postpositional particle used to indicate that a certain subject contrasts with something else.

지금 (noun) : 말을 하고 있는 바로 이때.
now
The present moment as one speaks.

부터 : 어떤 일의 시작이나 처음을 나타내는 조사.
buteo (no equivalent expression)
A postpositional particle that indicates the start or beginning of something.

는 : 어떤 대상이 다른 것과 대조됨을 나타내는 조사.
neun (no equivalent expression)
A postpositional particle used to indicate that a certain subject contrasts with something else.

가슴+이 느끼+[는 대로] 자유롭+게

가슴 (noun) : 마음이나 느낌.
heart; feeling
One's mind or emotion.

이 : 어떤 상태나 상황의 대상이나 동작의 주체를 나타내는 조사.
i (no equivalent expression)
A postpositional particle referring to a subject under a certain state or situation, or the agent of an action.

느끼다 (verb) : 특정한 대상이나 상황을 어떻다고 생각하거나 인식하다.
think
To think about or perceive a certain subject or situation in a certain way.

-는 대로 : 앞에 오는 말이 뜻하는 현재의 행동이나 상황과 같음을 나타내는 표현.
-neun daero (no equivalent expression)
An expression used to indicate that something is the same as the present act or state mentioned in the preceding statement.

자유롭다 (adjective) : 무엇에 얽매이거나 구속되지 않고 자기 생각과 의지대로 할 수 있다.
free
Able to do as one thinks and at will without being bound or restricted by something.

-게 : 앞의 말이 뒤에서 가리키는 일의 목적이나 결과, 방식, 정도 등이 됨을 나타내는 연결 어미.
-ge (no equivalent expression)
A connective ending used when the preceding statement is the purpose, result, **method**, amount, etc., of something mentioned in the following statement.

아무것+도 [신경 쓰]+[지 말(마)]+(아)요.
신경 쓰지 마요

아무것 (noun) : 어떤 것의 조금이나 일부분.
anything
A little bit or part of something.

도 : 극단적인 경우를 들어 다른 경우는 말할 것도 없음을 나타내는 조사.
do (no equivalent expression)
A postpositional particle used when giving an extreme case in order to show that it is obvious in another case.

신경 쓰다 (idiom) : 사소한 일까지 세심하게 생각하다.
use one's nerve
To carefully think about every little trivial thing.

-지 말다 : 앞의 말이 나타내는 행동을 하지 못하게 함을 나타내는 표현.
-ji malda (no equivalent expression)
An expression used to prohibit the act mentioned in the preceding statement.

-아요 : (두루높임으로) 어떤 사실을 서술하거나 질문, 명령, 권유함을 나타내는 종결 어미.
-ayo (no equivalent expression)
(informal addressee-raising) A sentence-final ending used to describe a certain fact, ask a question, **give an order**, or advise.

< 2 절(verse) >

아직+까지 해+가 뜨+고 지+[ㄴ 적+은 한 번+도 없]+었+어요.

진 적은 한 번도 없었어요

아직 (adverb) : 어떤 일이나 상태 또는 어떻게 되기까지 시간이 더 지나야 함을 나타내거나, 어떤 일이나 상태가 끝나지 않고 계속 이어지고 있음을 나타내는 말.
yet; still
An adverb used to indicate that more time is needed to reach a certain state, or that something or a certain state has not ended, but is going on.

까지 : 어떤 범위의 끝임을 나타내는 조사.
kkaji (no equivalent expression)
A postpositional particle referring to the end of a certain range.

해 (noun) : 태양계의 중심에 있으며 온도가 매우 높고 스스로 빛을 내는 항성.
sun
The star at the center of a solar system which is extremely hot and emits light.

가 : 어떤 상태나 상황에 놓인 대상이나 동작의 주체를 나타내는 조사.
ga (no equivalent expression)
A postpositional particle referring to a subject under a certain state or situation, or the subject of an act.

뜨다 (verb) : 물 위나 공중에 있거나 위쪽으로 솟아오르다.
float; buoy
To stay on water or in the air, or to jump upward.

-고 : 두 가지 이상의 대등한 사실을 나열할 때 쓰는 연결 어미.
-go (no equivalent expression)
A connective ending used when listing more than two equal facts.

지다 (verb) : 해나 달이 서쪽으로 넘어가다.
set
For the sun or moon to go down westwards.

-ㄴ 적 없다 : 앞의 말이 나타내는 동작이 일어나거나 그 상태가 나타난 때가 없음을 나타내는 표현.
-n jeog eopda (no equivalent expression)
An expression used to indicate that the act or state mentioned in the preceding statement never existed.

은 : 문장 속에서 어떤 대상이 화제임을 나타내는 조사.
eun (no equivalent expression)
A postpositional particle used to indicate that a certain subject is the topic of a sentence.

한 (determiner) : 하나의.
one
One.

번 (noun) : 일의 횟수를 세는 단위.
beon (no equivalent expression)
A bound noun that serves as a unit for counting the frequency of a task.

도 : 극단적인 경우를 들어 다른 경우는 말할 것도 없음을 나타내는 조사.
do (no equivalent expression)
A postpositional particle used when giving an extreme case in order to show that it is obvious in another case.

-었- : 어떤 사건이 과거에 완료되었거나 그 사건의 결과가 현재까지 지속되는 상황을 나타내는 어미.
-eot- (no equivalent expression)
An ending of a word used to indicate that an event was completed in the past or its result continues in the present.

-어요 : (두루높임으로) 어떤 사실을 서술하거나 질문, 명령, 권유함을 나타내는 종결 어미.
-eoyo (no equivalent expression)
(informal addressee-raising) A sentence-final ending used to **describe** a certain fact, ask a question, give an order, or advise.

이 땅+에 살(사)+는 우리+들+만 어제+도 오늘+도
사는

이 (determiner) : 바로 앞에서 이야기한 대상을 가리킬 때 쓰는 말.
this
A pronoun referring to something mentioned in the immediately preceding sentence.

땅 (noun) : 지구에서 물로 된 부분이 아닌 흙이나 돌로 된 부분.
ground; land
The part of the earth that consists of soil or stones instead of water.

에 : 앞말이 어떤 장소나 자리임을 나타내는 조사.
on; in; at
A postpositional particle to indicate that the preceding statement refers to a certain place or space.

살다 (verb) : 사람이 생활을 하다.
live
For a person to lead a life.

-는 : 앞의 말이 관형어의 기능을 하게 만들고 사건이나 동작이 현재 일어남을 나타내는 어미.
-neun (no equivalent expression)
An ending of a word that makes the preceding statement function as an adnominal phrase and implies that an event or action is happening in the present.

우리 (pronoun) : 말하는 사람이 자기와 듣는 사람 또는 이를 포함한 여러 사람들을 가리키는 말.
we
A pronoun used when the speaker refers to himself/herself and the listener or listeners, or a group of people including the speaker and listener or listeners.

들 : '복수'의 뜻을 더하는 접미사.
-deul (no equivalent expression)
A suffix used to mean plural.

만 : 다른 것은 제외하고 어느 것을 한정함을 나타내는 조사.
man (no equivalent expression)
A postpositional particle used when limiting the field to one thing, excluding all the others.

어제 (noun) : 오늘의 하루 전날.
yesterday
The day before the present day.

도 : 둘 이상의 것을 나열함을 나타내는 조사.
do (no equivalent expression)
A postpositional particle used to list two or more things.

오늘 (noun) : 지금 지나가고 있는 이날.
today
The day that is passing at the present time.

도 : 둘 이상의 것을 나열함을 나타내는 조사.
do (no equivalent expression)
A postpositional particle used to list two or more things.

쉬+ㅁ 없이 돌+고 돌+고 또 돌+아요.
쉼

쉬다 (verb) : 하던 일이나 활동 등을 잠시 멈추다. 또는 그렇게 하다.
stop; close
To discontinue what one is doing for a moment; to make someone discontinue what he/she is doing for a moment.

-ㅁ : 앞의 말이 명사의 기능을 하게 하는 어미.
m (no equivalent expression)
An ending of a word that makes the preceding statement function as a noun.

없이 (adverb) : 어떤 일이나 증상 등이 나타나지 않게.
without
Without any matter, symptom, etc.

돌다 (verb) : 무엇을 중심으로 원을 그리면서 움직이다.
go round; rotate
To move around something in a circle.

-고 : 두 가지 이상의 대등한 사실을 나열할 때 쓰는 연결 어미.
-go (no equivalent expression)
A connective ending used when listing more than two equal facts.

돌다 (verb) : 무엇을 중심으로 원을 그리면서 움직이다.
go round; rotate
To move around something in a circle.

-고 : 두 가지 이상의 대등한 사실을 나열할 때 쓰는 연결 어미.
-go (no equivalent expression)
A connective ending used when listing more than two equal facts.

또 (adverb) : 어떤 일이나 행동이 다시.
once more
In the manner of happening or behaving again.

돌다 (verb) : 무엇을 중심으로 원을 그리면서 움직이다.
go round; rotate
To move around something in a circle.

-아요 : (두루높임으로) 어떤 사실을 서술하거나 질문, 명령, 권유함을 나타내는 종결 어미.
-ayo (no equivalent expression)
(informal addressee-raising) A sentence-final ending used to **describe** a certain fact, ask a question, give an order, or advise.

배우+[ㄴ 대로] 남+들+이 시키+[는 대로]

배운 대로

배우다 (verb) : 남의 행동이나 태도를 그대로 따르다.
follow; imitate; benchmark
To imitate someone's behavior or attitude.

-ㄴ 대로 : 앞에 오는 말이 뜻하는 과거의 행동이나 상황과 같음을 나타내는 표현.
-n daero (no equivalent expression)
An expression used to indicate that something is the same as a previous act or state mentioned in the preceding statement.

남 (noun) : 내가 아닌 다른 사람.
others; another person
A person other than me.

들 : '복수'의 뜻을 더하는 접미사.
-deul (no equivalent expression)
A suffix used to mean plural.

이 : 어떤 상태나 상황의 대상이나 동작의 주체를 나타내는 조사.
i (no equivalent expression)
A postpositional particle referring to a subject under a certain state or situation, or the agent of an action.

시키다 (verb) : 어떤 일이나 행동을 하게 하다.
order
To make a person do something.

-는 대로 : 앞에 오는 말이 뜻하는 현재의 행동이나 상황과 같음을 나타내는 표현.
-neun daero (no equivalent expression)
An expression used to indicate that something is the same as the present act or state mentioned in the preceding statement.

그렇+게 사람+들 사이+에 숨+어 살아가+[고 있]+죠.

그렇다 (adjective) : 상태, 모양, 성질 등이 그와 같다.
so; as such; like that
A state, appearance, characteristic, etc. being as such.

-게 : 앞의 말이 뒤에서 가리키는 일의 목적이나 결과, 방식, 정도 등이 됨을 나타내는 연결 어미.
-ge (no equivalent expression)
A connective ending used when the preceding statement is the purpose, result, **method**, amount, etc., of something mentioned in the following statement.

사람 (noun) : 특별히 정해지지 않은 자기 외의 남을 가리키는 말.
other; other person
The word that refers to an unspecified person other than oneself.

들 : '복수'의 뜻을 더하는 접미사.
-deul (no equivalent expression)
A suffix used to mean plural.

사이 (noun) : 한 물체에서 다른 물체까지 또는 한곳에서 다른 곳까지의 거리나 공간.
space; distance; gap
The distance or space between one object and another, or between one place and another.

에 : 앞말이 어떤 장소나 자리임을 나타내는 조사.
on; in; at
A postpositional particle to indicate that the preceding statement refers to a certain place or space.

숨다 (verb) : 남이 볼 수 없게 몸을 감추다.
hide
To hide one's body so that others cannot see it.

-어 : 앞의 말이 뒤의 말보다 먼저 일어났거나 뒤의 말에 대한 방법이나 수단이 됨을 나타내는 연결 어미.
-eo (no equivalent expression)
A connective ending used when the preceding statement happened before the following statement or was the ways or means to the following statement.

살아가다 (verb) : 어떤 종류의 삶이나 시대 등을 견디며 생활해 나가다.
make a living
To continue to live by enduring a kind of life, period, etc.

-고 있다 : 앞의 말이 나타내는 행동이 계속 진행됨을 나타내는 표현.
-go itda (no equivalent expression)
An expression used to state that the act mentioned in the preceding statement is continued.

-죠 : (두루높임으로) 말하는 사람이 자신에 대한 이야기나 자신의 생각을 친근하게 말할 때 쓰는 종결 어미.
-jyo (no equivalent expression)
(informal addressee-raising) A sentence-final ending used when the speaker talks about himself/herself or his/her thoughts in a friendly manner.

그 사이+에 갇히+어 [지지고 볶]+으며 오늘+도 나+는 살아가+[고 있]+네요.
갇혀

그 (determiner) : 앞에서 이미 이야기한 대상을 가리킬 때 쓰는 말.
that; the
A term referring to something mentioned earlier.

사이 (noun) : 한 물체에서 다른 물체까지 또는 한곳에서 다른 곳까지의 거리나 공간.
space; distance; gap
The distance or space between one object and another, or between one place and another.

에 : 앞말이 어떤 장소나 자리임을 나타내는 조사.
on; in; at
A postpositional particle to indicate that the preceding statement refers to a certain place or space.

갇히다 (verb) : 어떤 공간이나 상황에서 나가지 못하게 되다.
be locked up; be shut up; be imprisoned
To become stuck in a certain place or situation without an exit.

-어 : 앞의 말이 뒤의 말보다 먼저 일어났거나 뒤의 말에 대한 방법이나 수단이 됨을 나타내는 연결 어미.
-eo (no equivalent expression)
A connective ending used when the preceding statement happened before the following statement or was the ways or means to the following statement.

지지고 볶다 (idiom) : 온갖 것을 겪으며 함께 살아가다.
fry and roast
To live together going through all sorts of troubles.

-으며 : 두 가지 이상의 동작이나 상태가 함께 일어남을 나타내는 연결 어미.
-eumyeo (no equivalent expression)
A connective ending used when more than two actions or states happen at the same time.

오늘 (noun) : 지금 지나가고 있는 이날.
today
The day that is passing at the present time.

도 : 이미 있는 어떤 것에 다른 것을 더하거나 포함함을 나타내는 조사.
do (no equivalent expression)
A postpositional particle used to indicate an addition or inclusion of another thing to something that already exists.

나 (pronoun) : 말하는 사람이 친구나 아랫사람에게 자기를 가리키는 말.
I
A pronoun used to indicate oneself to a friend or a younger person.

는 : 문장 속에서 어떤 대상이 화제임을 나타내는 조사.
neun (no equivalent expression)
A postpositional particle used to indicate that a certain subject is the topic of a sentence.

살아가다 (verb) : 어떤 종류의 삶이나 시대 등을 견디며 생활해 나가다.
make a living
To continue to live by enduring a kind of life, period, etc.

-고 있다 : 앞의 말이 나타내는 행동이 계속 진행됨을 나타내는 표현.
-go itda (no equivalent expression)
An expression used to state that the act mentioned in the preceding statement is continued.

-네요 : (두루높임으로) 말하는 사람이 직접 경험하여 새롭게 알게 된 사실에 대해 감탄함을 나타낼 때 쓰는 표현.
-neyo (no equivalent expression)
(informal addressee-raising) An expression used to indicate that the speaker is impressed by a fact he/she learned anew from a past personal experience.

누(구)+가 시키+[는 대로] 살(사)+[는 것]+은 이제 너무 짜증+이 나+(아)요.
누가 사는 것은 나요

누구 (pronoun) : 굳이 이름을 밝힐 필요가 없는 사람을 가리키는 말.
no equivalent expression
A pronoun used to indicate a person whose name does not have to be necessarily disclosed.

가 : 어떤 상태나 상황에 놓인 대상이나 동작의 주체를 나타내는 조사.
ga (no equivalent expression)
A postpositional particle referring to a subject under a certain state or situation, or the subject of an act.

시키다 (verb) : 어떤 일이나 행동을 하게 하다.
order
To make a person do something.

-는 대로 : 앞에 오는 말이 뜻하는 현재의 행동이나 상황과 같음을 나타내는 표현.
-neun daero (no equivalent expression)
An expression used to indicate that something is the same as the present act or state mentioned in the preceding statement.

살다 (verb) : 사람이 생활을 하다.
live
For a person to lead a life.

-는 것 : 명사가 아닌 것을 문장에서 명사처럼 쓰이게 하거나 '이다' 앞에 쓰일 수 있게 할 때 쓰는 표현.
-neun geot (no equivalent expression)
An expression used to enable a non-noun word to be used as a noun in a sentence or to be used in front of '이다' (be).

은 : 문장 속에서 어떤 대상이 화제임을 나타내는 조사.
eun (no equivalent expression)
A postpositional particle used to indicate that a certain subject is the topic of a sentence.

이제 (adverb) : 지금의 시기가 되어.
now
Reaching this time.

너무 (adverb) : 일정한 정도나 한계를 훨씬 넘어선 상태로.
too
To an excessive degree.

짜증 (noun) : 마음에 들지 않아서 화를 내거나 싫은 느낌을 겉으로 드러내는 일. 또는 그런 성미.
irritation; annoyance
An act of expressing one's anger or dislike towards something because one is dissatisfied, or such a disposition.

이 : 어떤 상태나 상황의 대상이나 동작의 주체를 나타내는 조사.
i (no equivalent expression)
A postpositional particle referring to a subject under a certain state or situation, or the agent of an action.

나다 (verb) : 어떤 감정이나 느낌이 생기다.
feel
To feel a certain emotion or sensation.

-아요 : (두루높임으로) 어떤 사실을 서술하거나 질문, 명령, 권유함을 나타내는 종결 어미.
-ayo (no equivalent expression)
(informal addressee-raising) A sentence-final ending used to **describe** a certain fact, ask a question, give an order, or advise.

바라+고 원하+는 생각+들+을 하늘 너머+로 떠나보내+(어)요.

떠나보내요

바라다 (verb) : 생각이나 희망대로 어떤 일이 이루어지기를 기대하다.
want; hope; wish
To expect that something could be done as one's thought or hope.

-고 : 두 가지 이상의 대등한 사실을 나열할 때 쓰는 연결 어미.
-go (no equivalent expression)
A connective ending used when listing more than two equal facts.

원하다 (verb) : 무엇을 바라거나 하고자 하다.
want; wish; hope
To hope for something or desire to do something.

-는 : 앞의 말이 관형어의 기능을 하게 만들고 사건이나 동작이 현재 일어남을 나타내는 어미.
-neun (no equivalent expression)
An ending of a word that makes the preceding statement function as an adnominal phrase and implies that an event or action is happening in the present.

생각 (noun) : 사람이 머리를 써서 판단하거나 인식하는 것.
thought
The act of a human being using his/her brains to judge or perceive something.

들 : '복수'의 뜻을 더하는 접미사.
-deul (no equivalent expression)
A suffix used to mean plural.

을 : 동작이 직접적으로 영향을 미치는 대상을 나타내는 조사.
eul (no equivalent expression)
A postpositional particle used to indicate the subject that an action has a direct influence on.

하늘 (noun) : 땅 위로 펼쳐진 무한히 넓은 공간.
sky
The vast, limitless space that unfolds above the ground.

너머 (noun) : 경계나 가로막은 것을 넘어선 건너편.
beyond; over; the other side
The opposite side over a boundary or an obstacle.

로 : 움직임의 방향을 나타내는 조사.
ro (no equivalent expression)
A postpositional particle that indicates the direction of a movement.

떠나보내다 (verb) : 있던 곳을 떠나 다른 곳으로 가게 하다.
let go
To let someone leave a place where he/she has been and go to another place.

-어요 : (두루높임으로) 어떤 사실을 서술하거나 질문, 명령, 권유함을 나타내는 종결 어미.
-eoyo (no equivalent expression)
(informal addressee-raising) A sentence-final ending used to describe a certain fact, ask a question, give an order, or **advise**.

우리 모두 거기+서 자유롭+게 살+[아 보]+아요.
살아 봐요

우리 (pronoun) : 말하는 사람이 자기와 듣는 사람 또는 이를 포함한 여러 사람들을 가리키는 말.
we
A pronoun used when the speaker refers to himself/herself and the listener or listeners, or a group of people including the speaker and listener or listeners.

모두 (adverb) : 빠짐없이 다.
all of
Everyone or everything without exception.

거기 (pronoun) : 앞에서 이미 이야기한 곳을 가리키는 말.
there
A pronoun used to indicate the previously-mentioned place.

서 : 앞말이 행동이 이루어지고 있는 장소임을 나타내는 조사.
seo (no equivalent expression)
A postpositional particle used to indicate that the preceding word refers to a place where a certain act is being done.

자유롭다 (adjective) : 무엇에 얽매이거나 구속되지 않고 자기 생각과 의지대로 할 수 있다.
free
Able to do as one thinks and at will without being bound or restricted by something.

-게 : 앞의 말이 뒤에서 가리키는 일의 목적이나 결과, 방식, 정도 등이 됨을 나타내는 연결 어미.
-ge (no equivalent expression)
A connective ending used when the preceding statement is the purpose, result, **method**, amount, etc., of something mentioned in the following statement.

살다 (verb) : 사람이 생활을 하다.
live
For a person to lead a life.

-아 보다 : 앞의 말이 나타내는 행동을 시험 삼아 함을 나타내는 표현.
-a boda (no equivalent expression)
An expression used to indicate that one does the act mentioned in the preceding statement, as a test.

-아요 : (두루높임으로) 어떤 사실을 서술하거나 질문, 명령, 권유함을 나타내는 종결 어미.
-ayo (no equivalent expression)
(informal addressee-raising) A sentence-final ending used to describe a certain fact, ask a question, give an order, or **advise**.

< 후렴(refrain) >

이제+부터+는 지금+부터+는

이제 (noun) : 지금의 시기.
now
The present.

부터 : 어떤 일의 시작이나 처음을 나타내는 조사.
buteo (no equivalent expression)
A postpositional particle that indicates the start or beginning of something.

는 : 어떤 대상이 다른 것과 대조됨을 나타내는 조사.
neun (no equivalent expression)
A postpositional particle used to indicate that a certain subject contrasts with something else.

지금 (noun) : 말을 하고 있는 바로 이때.
now
The present moment as one speaks.

부터 : 어떤 일의 시작이나 처음을 나타내는 조사.
buteo (no equivalent expression)
A postpositional particle that indicates the start or beginning of something.

는 : 어떤 대상이 다른 것과 대조됨을 나타내는 조사.
neun (no equivalent expression)
A postpositional particle used to indicate that a certain subject contrasts with something else.

이제+부터+는 지금+부터+는

이제 (noun) : 지금의 시기.
now
The present.

부터 : 어떤 일의 시작이나 처음을 나타내는 조사.
buteo (no equivalent expression)
A postpositional particle that indicates the start or beginning of something.

는 : 어떤 대상이 다른 것과 대조됨을 나타내는 조사.
neun (no equivalent expression)
A postpositional particle used to indicate that a certain subject contrasts with something else.

지금 (noun) : 말을 하고 있는 바로 이때.
now
The present moment as one speaks.

부터 : 어떤 일의 시작이나 처음을 나타내는 조사.
buteo (no equivalent expression)
A postpositional particle that indicates the start or beginning of something.

는 : 어떤 대상이 다른 것과 대조됨을 나타내는 조사.
neun (no equivalent expression)
A postpositional particle used to indicate that a certain subject contrasts with something else.

가슴+이 시키+[는 대로] 살+[아 보]+아요.
살아 봐요

가슴 (noun) : 마음이나 느낌.
heart; feeling
One's mind or emotion.

이 : 어떤 상태나 상황의 대상이나 동작의 주체를 나타내는 조사.
i (no equivalent expression)
A postpositional particle referring to a subject under a certain state or situation, or the agent of an action.

시키다 (verb) : 어떤 일이나 행동을 하게 하다.
order
To make a person do something.

-는 대로 : 앞에 오는 말이 뜻하는 현재의 행동이나 상황과 같음을 나타내는 표현.
-neun daero (no equivalent expression)
An expression used to indicate that something is the same as the present act or state mentioned in the preceding statement.

살다 (verb) : 사람이 생활을 하다.
live
For a person to lead a life.

-아 보다 : 앞의 말이 나타내는 행동을 시험 삼아 함을 나타내는 표현.
-a boda (no equivalent expression)
An expression used to indicate that one does the act mentioned in the preceding statement, as a test.

-아요 : (두루높임으로) 어떤 사실을 서술하거나 질문, 명령, 권유함을 나타내는 종결 어미.
-ayo (no equivalent expression)
(informal addressee-raising) A sentence-final ending used to describe a certain fact, ask a question, give an order, or **advise**.

이제+부터+는 지금+부터+는

이제 (noun) : 지금의 시기.
now
The present.

부터 : 어떤 일의 시작이나 처음을 나타내는 조사.
buteo (no equivalent expression)
A postpositional particle that indicates the start or beginning of something.

는 : 어떤 대상이 다른 것과 대조됨을 나타내는 조사.
neun (no equivalent expression)
A postpositional particle used to indicate that a certain subject contrasts with something else.

지금 (noun) : 말을 하고 있는 바로 이때.
now
The present moment as one speaks.

부터 : 어떤 일의 시작이나 처음을 나타내는 조사.
buteo (no equivalent expression)
A postpositional particle that indicates the start or beginning of something.

는 : 어떤 대상이 다른 것과 대조됨을 나타내는 조사.
neun (no equivalent expression)
A postpositional particle used to indicate that a certain subject contrasts with something else.

가슴+이 느끼+[는 대로] 자유롭+게

가슴 (noun) : 마음이나 느낌.
heart; feeling
One's mind or emotion.

이 : 어떤 상태나 상황의 대상이나 동작의 주체를 나타내는 조사.
i (no equivalent expression)
A postpositional particle referring to a subject under a certain state or situation, or the agent of an action.

느끼다 (verb) : 특정한 대상이나 상황을 어떻다고 생각하거나 인식하다.
think
To think about or perceive a certain subject or situation in a certain way.

-는 대로 : 앞에 오는 말이 뜻하는 현재의 행동이나 상황과 같음을 나타내는 표현.
-neun daero (no equivalent expression)
An expression used to indicate that something is the same as the present act or state mentioned in the preceding statement.

자유롭다 (adjective) : 무엇에 얽매이거나 구속되지 않고 자기 생각과 의지대로 할 수 있다.
free
Able to do as one thinks and at will without being bound or restricted by something.

-게 : 앞의 말이 뒤에서 가리키는 일의 목적이나 결과, 방식, 정도 등이 됨을 나타내는 연결 어미.
-ge (no equivalent expression)
A connective ending used when the preceding statement is the purpose, result, **method**, amount, etc., of something mentioned in the following statement.

이제+부터+는 지금+부터+는

이제 (noun) : 지금의 시기.
now
The present.

부터 : 어떤 일의 시작이나 처음을 나타내는 조사.
buteo (no equivalent expression)
A postpositional particle that indicates the start or beginning of something.

는 : 어떤 대상이 다른 것과 대조됨을 나타내는 조사.
neun (no equivalent expression)
A postpositional particle used to indicate that a certain subject contrasts with something else.

지금 (noun) : 말을 하고 있는 바로 이때.
now
The present moment as one speaks.

부터 : 어떤 일의 시작이나 처음을 나타내는 조사.
buteo (no equivalent expression)
A postpositional particle that indicates the start or beginning of something.

는 : 어떤 대상이 다른 것과 대조됨을 나타내는 조사.
neun (no equivalent expression)
A postpositional particle used to indicate that a certain subject contrasts with something else.

(우리 모두 거기+서)

우리 (pronoun) : 말하는 사람이 자기와 듣는 사람 또는 이를 포함한 여러 사람들을 가리키는 말.
we
A pronoun used when the speaker refers to himself/herself and the listener or listeners, or a group of people including the speaker and listener or listeners.

모두 (adverb) : 빠짐없이 다.
all of
Everyone or everything without exception.

거기 (pronoun) : 앞에서 이미 이야기한 곳을 가리키는 말.
there
A pronoun used to indicate the previously-mentioned place.

서 : 앞말이 행동이 이루어지고 있는 장소임을 나타내는 조사.
seo (no equivalent expression)
A postpositional particle used to indicate that the preceding word refers to a place where a certain act is being done.

가슴+이 시키+[는 대로] 살+[아 보]+아요.
살아 봐요

가슴 (noun) : 마음이나 느낌.
heart; feeling
One's mind or emotion.

이 : 어떤 상태나 상황의 대상이나 동작의 주체를 나타내는 조사.
i (no equivalent expression)
A postpositional particle referring to a subject under a certain state or situation, or the agent of an action.

시키다 (verb) : 어떤 일이나 행동을 하게 하다.
order
To make a person do something.

-는 대로 : 앞에 오는 말이 뜻하는 현재의 행동이나 상황과 같음을 나타내는 표현.
-neun daero (no equivalent expression)
An expression used to indicate that something is the same as the present act or state mentioned in the preceding statement.

살다 (verb) : 사람이 생활을 하다.
live
For a person to lead a life.

-아 보다 : 앞의 말이 나타내는 행동을 시험 삼아 함을 나타내는 표현.
-a boda (no equivalent expression)
An expression used to indicate that one does the act mentioned in the preceding statement, as a test.

-아요 : (두루높임으로) 어떤 사실을 서술하거나 질문, 명령, 권유함을 나타내는 종결 어미.
-ayo (no equivalent expression)
(informal addressee-raising) A sentence-final ending used to describe a certain fact, ask a question, give an order, or **advise**.

(자유롭+게 살+아요)

자유롭다 (adjective) : 무엇에 얽매이거나 구속되지 않고 자기 생각과 의지대로 할 수 있다.
free
Able to do as one thinks and at will without being bound or restricted by something.

-게 : 앞의 말이 뒤에서 가리키는 일의 목적이나 결과, 방식, 정도 등이 됨을 나타내는 연결 어미.
-ge (no equivalent expression)
A connective ending used when the preceding statement is the purpose, result, **method**, amount, etc., of something mentioned in the following statement.

살다 (verb) : 사람이 생활을 하다.
live
For a person to lead a life.

-아요 : (두루높임으로) 어떤 사실을 서술하거나 질문, 명령, 권유함을 나타내는 종결 어미.
-ayo (no equivalent expression)
(informal addressee-raising) A sentence-final ending used to describe a certain fact, ask a question, give an order, or **advise**.

이제+부터+는 지금+부터+는

이제 (noun) : 지금의 시기.
now
The present.

부터 : 어떤 일의 시작이나 처음을 나타내는 조사.
buteo (no equivalent expression)
A postpositional particle that indicates the start or beginning of something.

는 : 어떤 대상이 다른 것과 대조됨을 나타내는 조사.
neun (no equivalent expression)
A postpositional particle used to indicate that a certain subject contrasts with something else.

지금 (noun) : 말을 하고 있는 바로 이때.
now
The present moment as one speaks.

부터 : 어떤 일의 시작이나 처음을 나타내는 조사.
buteo (no equivalent expression)
A postpositional particle that indicates the start or beginning of something.

는 : 어떤 대상이 다른 것과 대조됨을 나타내는 조사.
neun (no equivalent expression)
A postpositional particle used to indicate that a certain subject contrasts with something else.

(우리 모두 거기+서)

우리 (pronoun) : 말하는 사람이 자기와 듣는 사람 또는 이를 포함한 여러 사람들을 가리키는 말.
we
A pronoun used when the speaker refers to himself/herself and the listener or listeners, or a group of people including the speaker and listener or listeners.

모두 (adverb) : 빠짐없이 다.
all of
Everyone or everything without exception.

거기 (pronoun) : 앞에서 이미 이야기한 곳을 가리키는 말.
there
A pronoun used to indicate the previously-mentioned place.

서 : 앞말이 행동이 이루어지고 있는 장소임을 나타내는 조사.
seo (no equivalent expression)
A postpositional particle used to indicate that the preceding word refers to a place where a certain act is being done.

가슴+이 느끼+[는 대로] 자유롭+게

가슴 (noun) : 마음이나 느낌.
heart; feeling
One's mind or emotion.

이 : 어떤 상태나 상황의 대상이나 동작의 주체를 나타내는 조사.
i (no equivalent expression)
A postpositional particle referring to a subject under a certain state or situation, or the agent of an action.

느끼다 (verb) : 특정한 대상이나 상황을 어떻다고 생각하거나 인식하다.
think
To think about or perceive a certain subject or situation in a certain way.

-는 대로 : 앞에 오는 말이 뜻하는 현재의 행동이나 상황과 같음을 나타내는 표현.
-neun daero (no equivalent expression)
An expression used to indicate that something is the same as the present act or state mentioned in the preceding statement.

자유롭다 (adjective) : 무엇에 얽매이거나 구속되지 않고 자기 생각과 의지대로 할 수 있다.
free
Able to do as one thinks and at will without being bound or restricted by something.

-게 : 앞의 말이 뒤에서 가리키는 일의 목적이나 결과, 방식, 정도 등이 됨을 나타내는 연결 어미.
-ge (no equivalent expression)
A connective ending used when the preceding statement is the purpose, result, method, amount, etc., of something mentioned in the following statement.

(자유롭+게)

자유롭다 (adjective) : 무엇에 얽매이거나 구속되지 않고 자기 생각과 의지대로 할 수 있다.
free
Able to do as one thinks and at will without being bound or restricted by something.

-게 : 앞의 말이 뒤에서 가리키는 일의 목적이나 결과, 방식, 정도 등이 됨을 나타내는 연결 어미.
-ge (no equivalent expression)
A connective ending used when the preceding statement is the purpose, result, **method**, amount, etc., of something mentioned in the following statement.

그런 사람+이+었+어요.

그런 (determiner) : 상태, 모양, 성질 등이 그러한.
like that
A state, appearance, characteristic, etc. being as such.

사람 (noun) : 생각할 수 있으며 언어와 도구를 만들어 사용하고 사회를 이루어 사는 존재.
human; man
A being that is capable of thinking, makes and uses languages and tools and lives by forming a society with others.

이다 : 주어가 지시하는 대상의 속성이나 부류를 지정하는 뜻을 나타내는 서술격 조사.
ida (no equivalent expression)
A predicate particle indicating the meaning of the attribute or category of the thing that the subject of the sentence refers to.

-었- : 어떤 사건이 과거에 완료되었거나 그 사건의 결과가 현재까지 지속되는 상황을 나타내는 어미.
-eot- (no equivalent expression)
An ending of a word used to indicate that an event was completed in the past or its result continues in the present.

-어요 : (두루높임으로) 어떤 사실을 서술하거나 질문, 명령, 권유함을 나타내는 종결 어미.
-eoyo (no equivalent expression)
(informal addressee-raising) A sentence-final ending used to **describe** a certain fact, ask a question, give an order, or advise.

그런 인생+이+었+어요.

그런 (determiner) : 상태, 모양, 성질 등이 그러한.
like that
A state, appearance, characteristic, etc. being as such.

인생 (noun) : 사람이 세상을 살아가는 일.
life
The process of a person living in this world.

이다 : 주어가 지시하는 대상의 속성이나 부류를 지정하는 뜻을 나타내는 서술격 조사.
ida (no equivalent expression)
A predicate particle indicating the meaning of the attribute or category of the thing that the subject of the sentence refers to.

-었- : 어떤 사건이 과거에 완료되었거나 그 사건의 결과가 현재까지 지속되는 상황을 나타내는 어미.
-eot- (no equivalent expression)
An ending of a word used to indicate that an event was completed in the past or its result continues in the present.

-어요 : (두루높임으로) 어떤 사실을 서술하거나 질문, 명령, 권유함을 나타내는 종결 어미.
-eoyo (no equivalent expression)
(informal addressee-raising) A sentence-final ending used to **describe** a certain fact, ask a question, give an order, or advise.

그렇+게 기억하+[여 주]+어요.
기억해 줘요

그렇다 (adjective) : 상태, 모양, 성질 등이 그와 같다.
so; as such; like that
A state, appearance, characteristic, etc. being as such.

-게 : 앞의 말이 뒤에서 가리키는 일의 목적이나 결과, 방식, 정도 등이 됨을 나타내는 연결 어미.
-ge (no equivalent expression)
A connective ending used when the preceding statement is the purpose, result, **method**, amount, etc., of something mentioned in the following statement.

기억하다 (verb) : 이전의 모습, 사실, 지식, 경험 등을 잊지 않거나 다시 생각해 내다.
remember; recall
Not to forget or recall past figures, facts, knowledge or experiences.

-여 주다 : 남을 위해 앞의 말이 나타내는 행동을 함을 나타내는 표현.
-yeo juda (no equivalent expression)
An expression used to indicate that one does the act mentioned in the preceding statement for someone.

-어요 : (두루높임으로) 어떤 사실을 서술하거나 질문, 명령, 권유함을 나타내는 종결 어미.

-eoyo (no equivalent expression)

(informal addressee-raising) A sentence-final ending used to describe a certain fact, ask a question, **give an order**, or advise.

< 6 >

독주
(hard liquor)

[발음(pronunciation)]

< 1 절(verse) >

누구라도 한 잔 술을 따라 줘요
누구라도 한 잔 수를 따라 줘요
nugurado han jan sureul ttara jwoyo

비우고 싶은 것이 많아서
비우고 시픈 거시 마나서
biugo sipeun geosi manaseo

이 한 잔 마시고 나면 잊을 수 있을까요?
이 한 잔 마시고 나면 이즐 쑤 이쓸까요?
i han jan masigo namyeon ijeul su isseulkkayo?

버리고 싶은 것이 가득해서
버리고 시픈 거시 가드캐서
beorigo sipeun geosi gadeukaeseo

뜨거웠던 가슴, 마지막 온기가 사라지기 전에
뜨거월떤 가슴, 마지막 온기가 사라지기 저네
tteugeowotdeon gaseum, majimak ongiga sarajigi jeone

누구라도 독한 술 한 잔 따라 줘요.
누구라도 도칸 술 한 잔 따라 줘요.
nugurado dokan sul han jan ttara jwoyo.

< 후렴(refrain) >

이제부터 하얀 여백에 가득 찬
이제부터 하얀 여배게 가득 찬
ijebuteo hayan yeobaege gadeuk chan

내가 모르는 나를 지울 거예요
내가 모르는 나를 지울 꺼예요
naega moreuneun nareul jiul geoyeyo

오늘은 꼭 당신이 따라 준
오느른 꼭 당시니 따라 준
oneureun kkok dangsini ttara jun

한 잔의 가득한 독주를 비울 거예요.
한 자네 가드칸 독쭈를 비울 꺼예요.
han jane gadeukan dokjureul biul geoyeyo.

< 2 절(verse) >

누구라도 술 한 잔 따라 줘요
누구라도 술 한 잔 따라 줘요
nugurado sul han jan ttara jwoyo

추억에 취해 비틀거리기 전에
추어게 취해 비틀거리기 저네
chueoge chwihae biteulgeorigi jeone

이 한 잔 마시고 나면 지울 수 있을까요?
이 한 잔 마시고 나면 지울 쑤 이쓸까요?
i han jan masigo namyeon jiul su isseulkkayo?

그리움에 취해 잠들기 전에
그리우메 취해 잠들기 저네
geuriume chwihae jamdeulgi jeone

아직 어제를 살고 있는 이 꿈속에서 깨지 않도록
아직 어제를 살고 인는 이 꿈쏘게서 깨지 안토록
ajik eojereul salgo inneun i kkumsogeseo kkaeji antorok

누구라도 지독한 술 한 잔 따라 줘요.
누구라도 지도칸 술 한 잔 따라 줘요.
nugurado jidokan sul han jan ttara jwoyo.

< 후렴(refrain) >

이제부터 하얀 여백에 가득 찬
이제부터 하얀 여배게 가득 찬
ijebuteo hayan yeobaege gadeuk chan

내가 모르는 나를 지울 거예요
내가 모르는 나를 지울 꺼예요
naega moreuneun nareul jiul geoyeyo

오늘은 꼭 당신이 따라 준
오느른 꼭 당시니 따라 준
oneureun kkok dangsini ttara jun

한 잔의 가득한 독주를 비울 거예요.
한 자네 가드칸 독쭈를 비울 꺼예요.
han jane gadeukan dokjureul biul geoyeyo.

이제부터 하얀 여백에 가득 찬
이제부터 하얀 여배게 가득 찬
ijebuteo hayan yeobaege gadeuk chan

내가 모르는 나를 지울 거예요
내가 모르는 나를 지울 꺼예요
naega moreuneun nareul jiul geoyeyo

오늘은 꼭 당신이 따라 준
오느른 꼭 당시니 따라 준
oneureun kkok dangsini ttara jun

한 잔의 가득한 독주를 비울 거예요.
한 자네 가드칸 독쭈를 비울 꺼예요.
han jane gadeukan dokjureul biul geoyeyo.

< 1 절(verse) >

누구+라도 한 잔 술+을 따르(따ㄹ)+[아 주]+어요.

따라 줘요

누구 (pronoun) : 정해지지 않은 어떤 사람을 가리키는 말.
no equivalent expression
A pronoun used to indicate a random person.

라도 : 그것이 최선은 아니나 여럿 중에서는 그런대로 괜찮음을 나타내는 조사.
rado (no equivalent expression)
A postpositional word used to indicate that it is not the best option but the most acceptable among many options.

한 (determiner) : 하나의.
one
One.

잔 (noun) : 음료나 술 등을 담은 그릇을 기준으로 그 분량을 세는 단위.
cup; glass
A unit that measures the amount of alcoholic and non-alcoholic beverages by counting the number of containers holding the beverage.

술 (noun) : 맥주나 소주 등과 같이 알코올 성분이 들어 있어서 마시면 취하는 음료.
alcohol; liquor
A beverage that contains alcoholic ingredients so that one gets drunk if one drinks it, such as beer, soju, Korean distilled liquor, etc.

을 : 동작이 직접적으로 영향을 미치는 대상을 나타내는 조사.
eul (no equivalent expression)
A postpositional particle used to indicate the subject that an action has a direct influence on.

따르다 (verb) : 액체가 담긴 물건을 기울여 액체를 밖으로 조금씩 흐르게 하다.
pour; spill
To tilt an object that contains liquid and have the liquid flow out, little by little.

-아 주다 : 남을 위해 앞의 말이 나타내는 행동을 함을 나타내는 표현.
-a juda (no equivalent expression)
An expression used to indicate that one does the act mentioned in the preceding statement for someone.

-어요 : (두루높임으로) 어떤 사실을 서술하거나 질문, 명령, 권유함을 나타내는 종결 어미.
-eoyo (no equivalent expression)
(informal addressee-raising) A sentence-final ending used to describe a certain fact, ask a question, **give an order**, or advise.

비우+[고 싶]+[은 것]+이 많+아서

비우다 (verb) : 욕심이나 집착을 버리다.
empty (one's mind)
To rid oneself of greed or obsession.

-고 싶다 : 앞의 말이 나타내는 행동을 하기를 원함을 나타내는 표현.
-go sipda (no equivalent expression)
An expression used to state that the speaker wants to do the act mentioned in the preceding statement.

-은 것 : 명사가 아닌 것을 문장에서 명사처럼 쓰이게 하거나 '이다' 앞에 쓰일 수 있게 할 때 쓰는 표현.
-eun geot (no equivalent expression)
An expression used to enable a non-noun word to be used as a noun in the sentence or to be used in front of '이다' (be).

이 : 어떤 상태나 상황의 대상이나 동작의 주체를 나타내는 조사.
i (no equivalent expression)
A postpositional particle referring to a subject under a certain state or situation, or the agent of an action.

많다 (adjective) : 수나 양, 정도 등이 일정한 기준을 넘다.
plentiful; many; a lot of
A number, amount, etc., exceeding a certain standard.

-아서 : 이유나 근거를 나타내는 연결 어미.
-aseo (no equivalent expression)
A connective ending used for a reason or cause.

이 한 잔 마시+[고 나]+면 잊+[을 수 있]+을까요?

이 (determiner) : 바로 앞에서 이야기한 대상을 가리킬 때 쓰는 말.
this
A word that is used to refer to something which was just mentioned.

한 (determiner) : 하나의.
one
One.

잔 (noun) : 음료나 술 등을 담은 그릇을 기준으로 그 분량을 세는 단위.
cup; glass
A unit that measures the amount of alcoholic and non-alcoholic beverages by counting the number of containers holding the beverage.

마시다 (verb) : 물 등의 액체를 목구멍으로 넘어가게 하다.
drink
To make liquid such as water, etc., pass down one's throat.

-고 나다 : 앞에 오는 말이 나타내는 행동이 끝났음을 나타내는 표현.
-go nada (no equivalent expression)
An expression used to indicate that the act denoted in the preceding statement has finished.

-면 : 뒤에 오는 말에 대한 근거나 조건이 됨을 나타내는 연결 어미.
-myeon (no equivalent expression)
A connective ending used when the preceding statement becomes the reason or condition of the following statement.

잊다 (verb) : 어려움이나 고통, 또는 좋지 않은 지난 일을 마음속에 두지 않거나 신경 쓰지 않다.
forget; dismiss something from one's mind; think no more of
To put one's difficulties, pain, or bad things of the past out of one's mind, or not care about them.

-을 수 있다 : 어떤 행동이나 상태가 가능함을 나타내는 표현.
-eul su itda (no equivalent expression)
An expression used to indicate that an act or state is possible.

-을까요 : (두루높임으로) 아직 일어나지 않았거나 모르는 일에 대해서 말하는 사람이 추측하며 질문할 때 쓰는 표현.
-eulkkayo (no equivalent expression)
(informal addressee-raising) An expression used by the speaker to guess and ask about something not happening yet, or unknown.

버리+[고 싶]+[은 것]+이 가득하+여서
가득해서

버리다 (verb) : 마음속에 가졌던 생각을 스스로 잊다.
forget; let go
To forget the thoughts one had.

-고 싶다 : 앞의 말이 나타내는 행동을 하기를 원함을 나타내는 표현.
-go sipda (no equivalent expression)
An expression used to state that the speaker wants to do the act mentioned in the preceding statement.

-은 것 : 명사가 아닌 것을 문장에서 명사처럼 쓰이게 하거나 '이다' 앞에 쓰일 수 있게 할 때 쓰는 표현.
-eun geot (no equivalent expression)
An expression used to enable a non-noun word to be used as a noun in the sentence or to be used in front of '이다' (be).

이 : 어떤 상태나 상황의 대상이나 동작의 주체를 나타내는 조사.
i (no equivalent expression)
A postpositional particle referring to a subject under a certain state or situation, or the agent of an action.

가득하다 (adjective) : 어떤 감정이나 생각이 강하다.
felt strongly
An emotion or thought being strong.

-여서 : 이유나 근거를 나타내는 연결 어미.
-yeoseo (no equivalent expression)
A connective ending used to indicate a reason or cause.

뜨겁(뜨거우)+었던 가슴, 마지막 온기+가 사라지+[기 전에]
뜨거웠던

누구+라도 독하+ㄴ 술 한 잔 따르(따ㄹ)+[아 주]+어요.
독한 따라 줘요

뜨겁다 (adjective) : (비유적으로) 감정이나 열정 등이 격렬하고 강하다.
strong; warm; passionate
(figurative) Intense and strong in feeling, passion, etc.

-었던 : 과거의 사건이나 상태를 다시 떠올리거나 그 사건이나 상태가 완료되지 않고 중단되었다는 의미를 나타내는 표현.
-eotdeon (no equivalent expression)
An expression used to recall a past incident or state, and indicate that the incident or state is suspended, not completed.

가슴 (noun) : 마음이나 느낌.
heart; feeling
One's mind or emotion.

마지막 (noun) : 시간이나 순서의 맨 끝.
last
The very end of a time or order.

온기 (noun) : (비유적으로) 다정하거나 따뜻하게 베푸는 분위기나 마음.
warmth
(figurative) An atmosphere or attitude of sharing or giving something in a friendly or warm manner.

가 : 어떤 상태나 상황에 놓인 대상이나 동작의 주체를 나타내는 조사.
ga (no equivalent expression)
A postpositional particle referring to a subject under a certain state or situation, or the subject of an act.

사라지다 (verb) : 생각이나 감정 등이 없어지다.
disappear; evaporate
For a thought, feeling ,etc., to go away.

-기 전에 : 뒤에 오는 말이 나타내는 행동이 앞에 오는 말이 나타내는 행동보다 앞서는 것을 나타내는 표현.
-gi jeone (no equivalent expression)
An expression used to state that a certain act occurs earlier than the act in the preceding statement.

누구 (pronoun) : 정해지지 않은 어떤 사람을 가리키는 말.
no equivalent expression
A pronoun used to indicate a random person.

라도 : 그것이 최선은 아니나 여럿 중에서는 그런대로 괜찮음을 나타내는 조사.
rado (no equivalent expression)
A postpositional word used to indicate that it is not the best option but the most acceptable among many options.

독하다 (adjective) : 맛이나 냄새 등이 지나치게 자극적이다.
potent; strong
The taste, smell, etc., being too strong.

-ㄴ : 앞의 말이 관형어의 기능을 하게 만들고 현재의 상태를 나타내는 어미.
-n (no equivalent expression)
An ending of a word that makes the preceding statement function as an adnominal phrase and refers to the present state.

술 (noun) : 맥주나 소주 등과 같이 알코올 성분이 들어 있어서 마시면 취하는 음료.
alcohol; liquor
A beverage that contains alcoholic ingredients so that one gets drunk if one drinks it, such as beer, soju, Korean distilled liquor, etc.

한 (determiner) : 하나의.
one
One.

잔 (noun) : 음료나 술 등을 담은 그릇을 기준으로 그 분량을 세는 단위.
cup; glass
A unit that measures the amount of alcoholic and non-alcoholic beverages by counting the number of containers holding the beverage.

따르다 (verb) : 액체가 담긴 물건을 기울여 액체를 밖으로 조금씩 흐르게 하다.
pour; spill
To tilt an object that contains liquid and have the liquid flow out, little by little.

-아 주다 : 남을 위해 앞의 말이 나타내는 행동을 함을 나타내는 표현.
-a juda (no equivalent expression)
An expression used to indicate that one does the act mentioned in the preceding statement for someone.

-어요 : (두루높임으로) 어떤 사실을 서술하거나 질문, 명령, 권유함을 나타내는 종결 어미.
-eoyo (no equivalent expression)
(informal addressee-raising) A sentence-final ending used to describe a certain fact, ask a question, **give an order**, or advise.

< 후렴(refrain) >

이제+부터 하얗(하야)+ㄴ 여백+에 가득 차+ㄴ
하얀 찬

내+가 모르+는 나+를 지우+[ㄹ 것(거)]+이+에요.
지울 거예요

이제 (noun) : 말하고 있는 바로 이때.
now
This moment being spoken of.

부터 : 어떤 일의 시작이나 처음을 나타내는 조사.
buteo (no equivalent expression)
A postpositional particle that indicates the start or beginning of something.

하얗다 (adjective) : 눈이나 우유의 빛깔과 같이 밝고 선명하게 희다.
white
Clearly bright, white like the color of snow or milk.

-ㄴ : 앞의 말이 관형어의 기능을 하게 만들고 현재의 상태를 나타내는 어미.
-n (no equivalent expression)
An ending of a word that makes the preceding statement function as an adnominal phrase and refers to the present state.

여백 (noun) : 종이 등에 글씨를 쓰거나 그림을 그리고 남은 빈 자리.
blank; space; margin
A blank space left after writing or painting on a piece of paper, etc.

에 : 앞말이 어떤 장소나 자리임을 나타내는 조사.
on; in; at
A postpositional particle to indicate that the preceding statement refers to a certain place or space.

가득 (adverb) : 어떤 감정이나 생각이 강한 모양.
full
With a strong emotion or thought.

차다 (verb) : 감정이나 느낌 등이 가득하게 되다.
be full
To be full of feelings, emotions, etc.

-ㄴ : 앞의 말이 관형어의 기능을 하게 만들고 사건이나 동작이 완료되어 그 상태가 유지되고 있음을 나타내는 어미.
-n (no equivalent expression)
An ending of a word that makes the preceding statement function as an adnominal phrase and indicates that an event or action has been completed and its state continues.

내 (pronoun) : '나'에 조사 '가'가 붙을 때의 형태.
I
A form of '나' (I), when the postpositional particle '가' is attached to it.

가 : 어떤 상태나 상황에 놓인 대상이나 동작의 주체를 나타내는 조사.
ga (no equivalent expression)
A postpositional particle referring to a subject under a certain state or situation, or the subject of an act.

모르다 (verb) : 사람이나 사물, 사실 등을 알지 못하거나 이해하지 못하다.
not know
To have no knowledge or understanding of a person, object or fact.

-는 : 앞의 말이 관형어의 기능을 하게 만들고 사건이나 동작이 현재 일어남을 나타내는 어미.
-neun (no equivalent expression)
An ending of a word that makes the preceding statement function as an adnominal phrase and implies that an event or action is happening in the present.

나 (pronoun) : 말하는 사람이 친구나 아랫사람에게 자기를 가리키는 말.
I
A pronoun used to indicate oneself to a friend or a younger person.

를 : 동작이 직접적으로 영향을 미치는 대상을 나타내는 조사.
reul (no equivalent expression)
A postpositional particle used to indicate the subject that an act has a direct influence on.

지우다 (verb) : 생각이나 기억을 없애거나 잊다.
forget
To remove or get rid of one's thought or memory.

-ㄹ 것 : 명사가 아닌 것을 문장에서 명사처럼 쓰이게 하거나 '이다' 앞에 쓰일 수 있게 할 때 쓰는 표현.
-l geot (no equivalent expression)
An expression used to enable a non-noun word to be used as a noun in the sentence or to be used in front of '이다' (be).

이다 : 주어가 지시하는 대상의 속성이나 부류를 지정하는 뜻을 나타내는 서술격 조사.
ida (no equivalent expression)
A predicate particle indicating the meaning of the attribute or category of the thing that the subject of the sentence refers to.

-에요 : (두루높임으로) 어떤 사실을 서술하거나 질문함을 나타내는 종결 어미.
-eyo (no equivalent expression)
(informal addressee-raising) A sentence-final ending used when **describing** a certain fact or asking a question.

오늘+은 꼭 당신+이 따르(따르)+[아 주]+ㄴ
따라 준

오늘 (noun) : 지금 지나가고 있는 이날.
today
The day that is passing at the present time.

은 : 문장 속에서 어떤 대상이 화제임을 나타내는 조사.
eun (no equivalent expression)
A postpositional particle used to indicate that a certain subject is the topic of a sentence.

꼭 (adverb) : 어떤 일이 있어도 반드시.
without fail; at any cost; certainly
By all means under any circumstances.

당신 (pronoun) : (조금 높이는 말로) 듣는 사람을 가리키는 말.
you
(formal, slightly addressee-raising) A pronoun used to indicate the listener.

이 : 어떤 상태나 상황의 대상이나 동작의 주체를 나타내는 조사.
i (no equivalent expression)
A postpositional particle referring to a subject under a certain state or situation, or the agent of an action.

따르다 (verb) : 액체가 담긴 물건을 기울여 액체를 밖으로 조금씩 흐르게 하다.
pour; spill
To tilt an object that contains liquid and have the liquid flow out, little by little.

-아 주다 : 남을 위해 앞의 말이 나타내는 행동을 함을 나타내는 표현.
-a juda (no equivalent expression)
An expression used to indicate that one does the act mentioned in the preceding statement for someone.

-ㄴ : 앞의 말이 관형어의 기능을 하게 만들고 사건이나 동작이 완료되어 그 상태가 유지되고 있음을 나타내는 어미.
-n (no equivalent expression)
An ending of a word that makes the preceding statement function as an adnominal phrase and indicates that an event or action has been completed and its state continues.

한 잔+의 가득하+ㄴ 독주+를 비우+[ㄹ 것(거)]+이+에요.

가득한 비울 거예요

한 (determiner) : 하나의.
one
One.

잔 (noun) : 음료나 술 등을 담은 그릇을 기준으로 그 분량을 세는 단위.
cup; glass
A unit that measures the amount of alcoholic and non-alcoholic beverages by counting the number of containers holding the beverage.

의 : 앞의 말이 뒤의 말에 대하여 속성이나 수량을 한정하거나 같은 자격임을 나타내는 조사.
ui (no equivalent expression)
A postpositional particle used to indicate that the referent of the preceding word limits the properties or amount of the referent of the following word or that two words are on an equal footing.

가득하다 (adjective) : 양이나 수가 정해진 범위에 꽉 차 있다.
full; brimful
A quantity or number being full to the limit.

-ㄴ : 앞의 말이 관형어의 기능을 하게 만들고 현재의 상태를 나타내는 어미.
-n (no equivalent expression)
An ending of a word that makes the preceding statement function as an adnominal phrase and refers to the present state.

독주 (noun) : 매우 독한 술.
hard liquor
A liquor that is very strong.

를 : 동작이 직접적으로 영향을 미치는 대상을 나타내는 조사.
reul (no equivalent expression)
A postpositional particle used to indicate the subject that an act has a direct influence on.

비우다 (verb) : 안에 든 것을 없애 속을 비게 하다.
empty
To make something empty by eliminating its contents.

-ㄹ 것 : 명사가 아닌 것을 문장에서 명사처럼 쓰이게 하거나 '이다' 앞에 쓰일 수 있게 할 때 쓰는 표현.
-l geot (no equivalent expression)
An expression used to enable a non-noun word to be used as a noun in the sentence or to be used in front of '이다' (be).

이다 : 주어가 지시하는 대상의 속성이나 부류를 지정하는 뜻을 나타내는 서술격 조사.
ida (no equivalent expression)
A predicate particle indicating the meaning of the attribute or category of the thing that the subject of the sentence refers to.

-에요 : (두루높임으로) 어떤 사실을 서술하거나 질문함을 나타내는 종결 어미.
-eyo (no equivalent expression)
(informal addressee-raising) A sentence-final ending used when **describing** a certain fact or asking a question.

< 2 절(verse) >

누구+라도 술 한 잔 따르(따ㄹ)+[아 주]+어요.

따라 줘요

누구 (pronoun) : 정해지지 않은 어떤 사람을 가리키는 말.
no equivalent expression
A pronoun used to indicate a random person.

라도 : 그것이 최선은 아니나 여럿 중에서는 그런대로 괜찮음을 나타내는 조사.
rado (no equivalent expression)
A postpositional word used to indicate that it is not the best option but the most acceptable among many options.

술 (noun) : 맥주나 소주 등과 같이 알코올 성분이 들어 있어서 마시면 취하는 음료.
alcohol; liquor
A beverage that contains alcoholic ingredients so that one gets drunk if one drinks it, such as beer, soju, Korean distilled liquor, etc.

한 (determiner) : 하나의.
one
One.

잔 (noun) : 음료나 술 등을 담은 그릇을 기준으로 그 분량을 세는 단위.
cup; glass
A unit that measures the amount of alcoholic and non-alcoholic beverages by counting the number of containers holding the beverage.

따르다 (verb) : 액체가 담긴 물건을 기울여 액체를 밖으로 조금씩 흐르게 하다.
pour; spill
To tilt an object that contains liquid and have the liquid flow out, little by little.

-아 주다 : 남을 위해 앞의 말이 나타내는 행동을 함을 나타내는 표현.
-a juda (no equivalent expression)
An expression used to indicate that one does the act mentioned in the preceding statement for someone.

-어요 : (두루높임으로) 어떤 사실을 서술하거나 질문, 명령, 권유함을 나타내는 종결 어미.
-eoyo (no equivalent expression)
(informal addressee-raising) A sentence-final ending used to describe a certain fact, ask a question, **give an order**, or advise.

추억+에 취하+여 비틀거리+[기 전에]
취해

추억 (noun) : 지나간 일을 생각함. 또는 그런 생각이나 일.
memory
An act of looking back on a past incident, or such a thought or the incident itself.

에 : 앞말이 어떤 행위나 감정 등의 대상임을 나타내는 조사.
with; for; against
A postpositional particle to indicate that the preceding statement is the subject that is influenced by a certain action, emotion, etc.

취하다 (verb) : 무엇에 매우 깊이 빠져 마음을 빼앗기다.
be enchanted; be fascinated
To lose one's heart, as one fell for someone or something too much.

-여 : 앞에 오는 말이 뒤에 오는 말에 대한 원인이나 이유임을 나타내는 연결 어미.
-yeo (no equivalent expression)
A connective ending used when the preceding statement is the cause or reason for the following statement.

비틀거리다 (verb) : 몸을 가누지 못하고 계속 이리저리 쓰러질 듯이 걷다.
falter; totter
To walk without keeping one's balance, as if one is about to fall down.

-기 전에 : 뒤에 오는 말이 나타내는 행동이 앞에 오는 말이 나타내는 행동보다 앞서는 것을 나타내는 표현.
-gi jeone (no equivalent expression)
An expression used to state that a certain act occurs earlier than the act in the preceding statement.

이 한 잔 마시+[고 나]+면 지우+[ㄹ 수 있]+을까요?
지울 수 있을까요

이 (determiner) : 바로 앞에서 이야기한 대상을 가리킬 때 쓰는 말.
this
A word that is used to refer to something which was just mentioned.

한 (determiner) : 하나의.
one
One.

잔 (noun) : 음료나 술 등을 담은 그릇을 기준으로 그 분량을 세는 단위.
cup; glass
A unit that measures the amount of alcoholic and non-alcoholic beverages by counting the number of containers holding the beverage.

마시다 (verb) : 물 등의 액체를 목구멍으로 넘어가게 하다.
drink
To make liquid such as water, etc., pass down one's throat.

-고 나다 : 앞에 오는 말이 나타내는 행동이 끝났음을 나타내는 표현.
-go nada (no equivalent expression)
An expression used to indicate that the act denoted in the preceding statement has finished.

-면 : 뒤에 오는 말에 대한 근거나 조건이 됨을 나타내는 연결 어미.
-myeon (no equivalent expression)
A connective ending used when the preceding statement becomes the reason or condition of the following statement.

지우다 (verb) : 생각이나 기억을 없애거나 잊다.
forget
To remove or get rid of one's thought or memory.

-ㄹ 수 있다 : 어떤 행동이나 상태가 가능함을 나타내는 표현.
-l su itda (no equivalent expression)
An expression used to indicate that an act or state is possible.

-을까요 : (두루높임으로) 아직 일어나지 않았거나 모르는 일에 대해서 말하는 사람이 추측하며 질문할 때 쓰는 표현.
-eulkkayo (no equivalent expression)
(informal addressee-raising) An expression used by the speaker to guess and ask about something not happening yet, or unknown.

그리움+에 취하+여 잠들+[기 전에]
취해

그리움 (noun) : 어떤 대상을 몹시 보고 싶어 하는 안타까운 마음.
yearning; attachment; longing
A pitiable feeling that one misses someone very deeply.

에 : 앞말이 어떤 행위나 감정 등의 대상임을 나타내는 조사.
with; for; against
A postpositional particle to indicate that the preceding statement is the subject that is influenced by a certain action, emotion, etc.

취하다 (verb) : 무엇에 매우 깊이 빠져 마음을 빼앗기다.
be enchanted; be fascinated
To lose one's heart, as one fell for someone or something too much.

-여 : 앞에 오는 말이 뒤에 오는 말에 대한 원인이나 이유임을 나타내는 연결 어미.
-yeo (no equivalent expression)
A connective ending used when the preceding statement is the cause or reason for the following statement.

잠들다 (verb) : 잠을 자는 상태가 되다.
fall asleep; sink into a sleep
To come to be in the state of sleeping.

-기 전에 : 뒤에 오는 말이 나타내는 행동이 앞에 오는 말이 나타내는 행동보다 앞서는 것을 나타내는 표현.
-gi jeone (no equivalent expression)
An expression used to state that a certain act occurs earlier than the act in the preceding statement.

아직 어제+를 살+[고 있]+는 이 꿈속+에서 깨+[지 않]+도록

아직 (adverb) : 어떤 일이나 상태 또는 어떻게 되기까지 시간이 더 지나야 함을 나타내거나, 어떤 일이나 상태가 끝나지 않고 계속 이어지고 있음을 나타내는 말.
yet; still
An adverb used to indicate that more time is needed to reach a certain state, or that something or a certain state has not ended, but is going on.

어제 (noun) : 지나간 때.
yesterday
The time that has gone by.

를 : 동작이 직접적으로 영향을 미치는 대상을 나타내는 조사.
reul (no equivalent expression)
A postpositional particle used to indicate the subject that an act has a direct influence on.

살다 (verb) : 사람이 생활을 하다.
live
For a person to lead a life.

-고 있다 : 앞의 말이 나타내는 행동이 계속 진행됨을 나타내는 표현.
-go itda (no equivalent expression)
An expression used to state that the act mentioned in the preceding statement is continued.

-는 : 앞의 말이 관형어의 기능을 하게 만들고 사건이나 동작이 현재 일어남을 나타내는 어미.
-neun (no equivalent expression)
An ending of a word that makes the preceding statement function as an adnominal phrase and implies that an event or action is happening in the present.

이 (determiner) : 말하는 사람에게 가까이 있거나 말하는 사람이 생각하고 있는 대상을 가리킬 때 쓰는 말.
this
The word that is used to refer to a person who is close to the speaker or something that the speaker is thinking of.

꿈속 (noun) : 현실과 동떨어진 환상 속.
dream; fantasy
An illusion removed from reality.

에서 : 앞말이 행동이 이루어지고 있는 장소임을 나타내는 조사.
eseo (no equivalent expression)
A postpositional particle used to indicate that the preceding word refers to a place where a certain action is being done.

깨다 (verb) : 잠이 든 상태에서 벗어나 정신을 차리다. 또는 그렇게 하다.
wake up
To wake up from a sleeping state and come to one's senses; to do something in such a way.

-지 않다 : 앞의 말이 나타내는 행위나 상태를 부정하는 뜻을 나타내는 표현.
-ji anta (no equivalent expression)
An expression used to deny the act or state indicated in the preceding statement.

-도록 : 앞에 오는 말이 뒤에 오는 말에 대한 목적이나 결과, 방식, 정도임을 나타내는 연결 어미.
-dorok (no equivalent expression)
A connective ending used when the preceding statement is **the purpose**, result, method, amount, etc., of something mentioned in the following statement.

누구+라도 지독하+ㄴ 술 한 잔 따르(따르)+[아 주]+어요.
지독한 따라 줘요

누구 (pronoun) : 정해지지 않은 어떤 사람을 가리키는 말.
no equivalent expression
A pronoun used to indicate a random person.

라도 : 그것이 최선은 아니나 여럿 중에서는 그런대로 괜찮음을 나타내는 조사.
rado (no equivalent expression)
A postpositional word used to indicate that it is not the best option but the most acceptable among many options.

지독하다 (adjective) : 맛이나 냄새 등이 해롭거나 참기 어려울 정도로 심하다.
potent; overpowering
Having an intolerably harmful or strong taste, smell, etc.

-ㄴ : 앞의 말이 관형어의 기능을 하게 만들고 현재의 상태를 나타내는 어미.
-n (no equivalent expression)
An ending of a word that makes the preceding statement function as an adnominal phrase and refers to the present state.

술 (noun) : 맥주나 소주 등과 같이 알코올 성분이 들어 있어서 마시면 취하는 음료.
alcohol; liquor
A beverage that contains alcoholic ingredients so that one gets drunk if one drinks it, such as beer, soju, Korean distilled liquor, etc.

한 (determiner) : 하나의.
one
One.

잔 (noun) : 음료나 술 등을 담은 그릇을 기준으로 그 분량을 세는 단위.
cup; glass
A unit that measures the amount of alcoholic and non-alcoholic beverages by counting the number of containers holding the beverage.

따르다 (verb) : 액체가 담긴 물건을 기울여 액체를 밖으로 조금씩 흐르게 하다.
pour; spill
To tilt an object that contains liquid and have the liquid flow out, little by little.

-아 주다 : 남을 위해 앞의 말이 나타내는 행동을 함을 나타내는 표현.
-a juda (no equivalent expression)
An expression used to indicate that one does the act mentioned in the preceding statement for someone.

-어요 : (두루높임으로) 어떤 사실을 서술하거나 질문, 명령, 권유함을 나타내는 종결 어미.
-eoyo (no equivalent expression)
(informal addressee-raising) A sentence-final ending used to describe a certain fact, ask a question, **give an order**, or advise.

< 후렴(refrain) >

이제+부터 하얗(하야)+ㄴ 여백+에 가득 차+ㄴ
하얀 찬

이제 (noun) : 말하고 있는 바로 이때.
now
This moment being spoken of.

부터 : 어떤 일의 시작이나 처음을 나타내는 조사.
buteo (no equivalent expression)
A postpositional particle that indicates the start or beginning of something.

하얗다 (adjective) : 눈이나 우유의 빛깔과 같이 밝고 선명하게 희다.
white
Clearly bright, white like the color of snow or milk.

-ㄴ : 앞의 말이 관형어의 기능을 하게 만들고 현재의 상태를 나타내는 어미.
-n (no equivalent expression)
An ending of a word that makes the preceding statement function as an adnominal phrase and refers to the present state.

여백 (noun) : 종이 등에 글씨를 쓰거나 그림을 그리고 남은 빈 자리.
blank; space; margin
A blank space left after writing or painting on a piece of paper, etc.

에 : 앞말이 어떤 장소나 자리임을 나타내는 조사.
on; in; at
A postpositional particle to indicate that the preceding statement refers to a certain place or space.

가득 (adverb) : 어떤 감정이나 생각이 강한 모양.
full
With a strong emotion or thought.

차다 (verb) : 감정이나 느낌 등이 가득하게 되다.
be full
To be full of feelings, emotions, etc.

-ㄴ : 앞의 말이 관형어의 기능을 하게 만들고 사건이나 동작이 완료되어 그 상태가 유지되고 있음을 나타내는 어미.
-n (no equivalent expression)
An ending of a word that makes the preceding statement function as an adnominal phrase and indicates that an event or action has been completed and its state continues.

내+가 모르+는 나+를 지우+[ㄹ 것(거)]+이+에요.

지울 거예요

내 (pronoun) : '나'에 조사 '가'가 붙을 때의 형태.
I
A form of '나' (I), when the postpositional particle '가' is attached to it.

가 : 어떤 상태나 상황에 놓인 대상이나 동작의 주체를 나타내는 조사.
ga (no equivalent expression)
A postpositional particle referring to a subject under a certain state or situation, or the subject of an act.

모르다 (verb) : 사람이나 사물, 사실 등을 알지 못하거나 이해하지 못하다.
not know
To have no knowledge or understanding of a person, object or fact.

-는 : 앞의 말이 관형어의 기능을 하게 만들고 사건이나 동작이 현재 일어남을 나타내는 어미.
-neun (no equivalent expression)
An ending of a word that makes the preceding statement function as an adnominal phrase and implies that an event or action is happening in the present.

나 (pronoun) : 말하는 사람이 친구나 아랫사람에게 자기를 가리키는 말.
I
A pronoun used to indicate oneself to a friend or a younger person.

를 : 동작이 직접적으로 영향을 미치는 대상을 나타내는 조사.
reul (no equivalent expression)
A postpositional particle used to indicate the subject that an act has a direct influence on.

지우다 (verb) : 생각이나 기억을 없애거나 잊다.
forget
To remove or get rid of one's thought or memory.

-ㄹ 것 : 명사가 아닌 것을 문장에서 명사처럼 쓰이게 하거나 '이다' 앞에 쓰일 수 있게 할 때 쓰는 표현.
-l geot (no equivalent expression)
An expression used to enable a non-noun word to be used as a noun in the sentence or to be used in front of '이다' (be).

이다 : 주어가 지시하는 대상의 속성이나 부류를 지정하는 뜻을 나타내는 서술격 조사.
ida (no equivalent expression)
A predicate particle indicating the meaning of the attribute or category of the thing that the subject of the sentence refers to.

-에요 : (두루높임으로) 어떤 사실을 서술하거나 질문함을 나타내는 종결 어미.
-eyo (no equivalent expression)
(informal addressee-raising) A sentence-final ending used when **describing** a certain fact or asking a question.

오늘+은 꼭 당신+이 따르(따르)+[아 주]+ㄴ
따라 준

오늘 (noun) : 지금 지나가고 있는 이날.
today
The day that is passing at the present time.

은 : 문장 속에서 어떤 대상이 화제임을 나타내는 조사.
eun (no equivalent expression)
A postpositional particle used to indicate that a certain subject is the topic of a sentence.

꼭 (adverb) : 어떤 일이 있어도 반드시.
without fail; at any cost; certainly
By all means under any circumstances.

당신 (pronoun) : (조금 높이는 말로) 듣는 사람을 가리키는 말.
you
(formal, slightly addressee-raising) A pronoun used to indicate the listener.

이 : 어떤 상태나 상황의 대상이나 동작의 주체를 나타내는 조사.
i (no equivalent expression)
A postpositional particle referring to a subject under a certain state or situation, or the agent of an action.

따르다 (verb) : 액체가 담긴 물건을 기울여 액체를 밖으로 조금씩 흐르게 하다.
pour; spill
To tilt an object that contains liquid and have the liquid flow out, little by little.

-아 주다 : 남을 위해 앞의 말이 나타내는 행동을 함을 나타내는 표현.
-a juda (no equivalent expression)
An expression used to indicate that one does the act mentioned in the preceding statement for someone.

-ㄴ : 앞의 말이 관형어의 기능을 하게 만들고 사건이나 동작이 완료되어 그 상태가 유지되고 있음을 나타내는 어미.
-n (no equivalent expression)
An ending of a word that makes the preceding statement function as an adnominal phrase and indicates that an event or action has been completed and its state continues.

한 잔+의 가득하+ㄴ 독주+를 비우+[ㄹ 것(거)]+이+에요.
가득한 비울 거예요

한 (determiner) : 하나의.
one
One.

잔 (noun) : 음료나 술 등을 담은 그릇을 기준으로 그 분량을 세는 단위.
cup; glass
A unit that measures the amount of alcoholic and non-alcoholic beverages by counting the number of containers holding the beverage.

의 : 앞의 말이 뒤의 말에 대하여 속성이나 수량을 한정하거나 같은 자격임을 나타내는 조사.
ui (no equivalent expression)
A postpositional particle used to indicate that the referent of the preceding word limits the properties or amount of the referent of the following word or that two words are on an equal footing.

가득하다 (adjective) : 양이나 수가 정해진 범위에 꽉 차 있다.
full; brimful
A quantity or number being full to the limit.

-ㄴ : 앞의 말이 관형어의 기능을 하게 만들고 현재의 상태를 나타내는 어미.
-n (no equivalent expression)
An ending of a word that makes the preceding statement function as an adnominal phrase and refers to the present state.

독주 (noun) : 매우 독한 술.
hard liquor
A liquor that is very strong.

를 : 동작이 직접적으로 영향을 미치는 대상을 나타내는 조사.
reul (no equivalent expression)
A postpositional particle used to indicate the subject that an act has a direct influence on.

비우다 (verb) : 안에 든 것을 없애 속을 비게 하다.
empty
To make something empty by eliminating its contents.

-ㄹ 것 : 명사가 아닌 것을 문장에서 명사처럼 쓰이게 하거나 '이다' 앞에 쓰일 수 있게 할 때 쓰는 표현.
-l geot (no equivalent expression)
An expression used to enable a non-noun word to be used as a noun in the sentence or to be used in front of '이다' (be).

이다 : 주어가 지시하는 대상의 속성이나 부류를 지정하는 뜻을 나타내는 서술격 조사.
ida (no equivalent expression)
A predicate particle indicating the meaning of the attribute or category of the thing that the subject of the sentence refers to.

-에요 : (두루높임으로) 어떤 사실을 서술하거나 질문함을 나타내는 종결 어미.
-eyo (no equivalent expression)
(informal addressee-raising) A sentence-final ending used when **describing** a certain fact or asking a question.

이제+부터 하얗(하야)+ㄴ 여백+에 가득 차+ㄴ
하얀 찬

이제 (noun) : 말하고 있는 바로 이때.
now
This moment being spoken of.

부터 : 어떤 일의 시작이나 처음을 나타내는 조사.
buteo (no equivalent expression)
A postpositional particle that indicates the start or beginning of something.

하얗다 (adjective) : 눈이나 우유의 빛깔과 같이 밝고 선명하게 희다.
white
Clearly bright, white like the color of snow or milk.

-ㄴ : 앞의 말이 관형어의 기능을 하게 만들고 현재의 상태를 나타내는 어미.
-n (no equivalent expression)
An ending of a word that makes the preceding statement function as an adnominal phrase and refers to the present state.

여백 (noun) : 종이 등에 글씨를 쓰거나 그림을 그리고 남은 빈 자리.
blank; space; margin
A blank space left after writing or painting on a piece of paper, etc.

에 : 앞말이 어떤 장소나 자리임을 나타내는 조사.
on; in; at
A postpositional particle to indicate that the preceding statement refers to a certain place or space.

가득 (adverb) : 어떤 감정이나 생각이 강한 모양.
full
With a strong emotion or thought.

차다 (verb) : 감정이나 느낌 등이 가득하게 되다.
be full
To be full of feelings, emotions, etc.

-ㄴ : 앞의 말이 관형어의 기능을 하게 만들고 사건이나 동작이 완료되어 그 상태가 유지되고 있음을 나타내는 어미.
-n (no equivalent expression)
An ending of a word that makes the preceding statement function as an adnominal phrase and indicates that an event or action has been completed and its state continues.

내+가 모르+는 나+를 지우+[ㄹ 것(거)]+이+에요.
지울 거예요

내 (pronoun) : '나'에 조사 '가'가 붙을 때의 형태.
I
A form of '나' (I), when the postpositional particle '가' is attached to it.

가 : 어떤 상태나 상황에 놓인 대상이나 동작의 주체를 나타내는 조사.
ga (no equivalent expression)
A postpositional particle referring to a subject under a certain state or situation, or the subject of an act.

모르다 (verb) : 사람이나 사물, 사실 등을 알지 못하거나 이해하지 못하다.
not know
To have no knowledge or understanding of a person, object or fact.

-는 : 앞의 말이 관형어의 기능을 하게 만들고 사건이나 동작이 현재 일어남을 나타내는 어미.
-neun (no equivalent expression)
An ending of a word that makes the preceding statement function as an adnominal phrase and implies that an event or action is happening in the present.

나 (pronoun) : 말하는 사람이 친구나 아랫사람에게 자기를 가리키는 말.
I
A pronoun used to indicate oneself to a friend or a younger person.

를 : 동작이 직접적으로 영향을 미치는 대상을 나타내는 조사.
reul (no equivalent expression)
A postpositional particle used to indicate the subject that an act has a direct influence on.

지우다 (verb) : 생각이나 기억을 없애거나 잊다.
forget
To remove or get rid of one's thought or memory.

-ㄹ 것 : 명사가 아닌 것을 문장에서 명사처럼 쓰이게 하거나 '이다' 앞에 쓰일 수 있게 할 때 쓰는 표현.
-l geot (no equivalent expression)
An expression used to enable a non-noun word to be used as a noun in the sentence or to be used in front of '이다' (be).

이다 : 주어가 지시하는 대상의 속성이나 부류를 지정하는 뜻을 나타내는 서술격 조사.
ida (no equivalent expression)
A predicate particle indicating the meaning of the attribute or category of the thing that the subject of the sentence refers to.

-에요 : (두루높임으로) 어떤 사실을 서술하거나 질문함을 나타내는 종결 어미.
-eyo (no equivalent expression)
(informal addressee-raising) A sentence-final ending used when **describing** a certain fact or asking a question.

오늘+은 꼭 당신+이 따르(따ㄹ)+[아 주]+ㄴ
따라 준

오늘 (noun) : 지금 지나가고 있는 이날.
today
The day that is passing at the present time.

은 : 문장 속에서 어떤 대상이 화제임을 나타내는 조사.
eun (no equivalent expression)
A postpositional particle used to indicate that a certain subject is the topic of a sentence.

꼭 (adverb) : 어떤 일이 있어도 반드시.
without fail; at any cost; certainly
By all means under any circumstances.

당신 (pronoun) : (조금 높이는 말로) 듣는 사람을 가리키는 말.
you
(formal, slightly addressee-raising) A pronoun used to indicate the listener.

이 : 어떤 상태나 상황의 대상이나 동작의 주체를 나타내는 조사.
i (no equivalent expression)
A postpositional particle referring to a subject under a certain state or situation, or the agent of an action.

따르다 (verb) : 액체가 담긴 물건을 기울여 액체를 밖으로 조금씩 흐르게 하다.
pour; spill
To tilt an object that contains liquid and have the liquid flow out, little by little.

-아 주다 : 남을 위해 앞의 말이 나타내는 행동을 함을 나타내는 표현.
-a juda (no equivalent expression)
An expression used to indicate that one does the act mentioned in the preceding statement for someone.

-ㄴ : 앞의 말이 관형어의 기능을 하게 만들고 사건이나 동작이 완료되어 그 상태가 유지되고 있음을 나타내는 어미.
-n (no equivalent expression)
An ending of a word that makes the preceding statement function as an adnominal phrase and indicates that an event or action has been completed and its state continues.

한 잔+의 가득하+ㄴ 독주+를 비우+[ㄹ 것(거)]+이+에요.

가득한 비울 거예요

한 (determiner) : 하나의.
one
One.

잔 (noun) : 음료나 술 등을 담은 그릇을 기준으로 그 분량을 세는 단위.
cup; glass
A unit that measures the amount of alcoholic and non-alcoholic beverages by counting the number of containers holding the beverage.

의 : 앞의 말이 뒤의 말에 대하여 속성이나 수량을 한정하거나 같은 자격임을 나타내는 조사.
ui (no equivalent expression)
A postpositional particle used to indicate that the referent of the preceding word limits the properties or amount of the referent of the following word or that two words are on an equal footing.

가득하다 (adjective) : 양이나 수가 정해진 범위에 꽉 차 있다.
full; brimful
A quantity or number being full to the limit.

-ㄴ : 앞의 말이 관형어의 기능을 하게 만들고 현재의 상태를 나타내는 어미.
-n (no equivalent expression)
An ending of a word that makes the preceding statement function as an adnominal phrase and refers to the present state.

독주 (noun) : 매우 독한 술.
hard liquor
A liquor that is very strong.

를 : 동작이 직접적으로 영향을 미치는 대상을 나타내는 조사.
reul (no equivalent expression)
A postpositional particle used to indicate the subject that an act has a direct influence on.

비우다 (verb) : 안에 든 것을 없애 속을 비게 하다.
empty
To make something empty by eliminating its contents.

-ㄹ 것 : 명사가 아닌 것을 문장에서 명사처럼 쓰이게 하거나 '이다' 앞에 쓰일 수 있게 할 때 쓰는 표현.
-l geot (no equivalent expression)
An expression used to enable a non-noun word to be used as a noun in the sentence or to be used in front of '이다' (be).

이다 : 주어가 지시하는 대상의 속성이나 부류를 지정하는 뜻을 나타내는 서술격 조사.
ida (no equivalent expression)
A predicate particle indicating the meaning of the attribute or category of the thing that the subject of the sentence refers to.

-에요 : (두루높임으로) 어떤 사실을 서술하거나 질문함을 나타내는 종결 어미.
-eyo (no equivalent expression)
(informal addressee-raising) A sentence-final ending used when **describing** a certain fact or asking a question.

< 7 >

애창곡
(one's favorite song)

[발음(pronunciation)]

< 1 절(verse) >

내가 부르는 이 노래
내가 부르는 이 노래
naega bureuneun i norae

너에게 아직 다 못다 한 말
너에게 아직 다 몯따 한 말
neoege ajik da motda han mal

이 곡조엔 우리만 아는 속삭임
이 곡쪼엔 우리만 아는 속싸김
i gokjoen uriman aneun soksagim

내가 부르는 이 노래
내가 부르는 이 노래
naega bureuneun i norae

너에게 꼭 하고 싶은 말
너에게 꼭 하고 시픈 말
neoege kkok hago sipeun mal

이 선율엔 우리만 아는 귓속말
이 서뉴렌 우리만 아는 귇쏭말
i seonyuren uriman aneun gwitsongmal

아무리 화가 나도 삐져 있어도
아무리 화가 나도 삐저 이써도
amuri hwaga nado ppijeo isseodo

이 가락에 취해
이 가라게 취해
i garage chwihae

우린 서로 남몰래 눈을 맞춰요.
우린 서로 남몰래 누늘 맏춰요.
urin seoro nammollae nuneul matchwoyo.

내가 즐겨 부르는 이 노래
내가 즐겨 부르는 이 노래
naega jeulgyeo bureuneun i norae

이 음악이 흐르면
이 으마기 흐르면
i eumagi heureumyeon

너의 눈빛, 너의 표정
너에 눈삗, 너에 표정
neoe nunbit, neoe pyojeong

내 가슴이 살살 녹아요.
내 가스미 살살 노가요.
nae gaseumi salsal nogayo.

< 2 절(verse) >

내가 부르는 이 노래
내가 부르는 이 노래
naega bureuneun i norae

너에게만 들려줬던 말
너에게만 들려줟떤 말
neoegeman deullyeojwotdeon mal

이 곡조엔 둘이만 아는 짜릿함
이 곡쪼엔 두리만 아는 짜리탐
i gokjoen duriman aneun jjaritam

내가 부르는 이 노래
내가 부르는 이 노래
naega bureuneun i norae

너에게만 속삭였던 말
너에게만 속싸견떤 말
neoegeman soksagyeotdeon mal

이 선율엔 둘이만 아는 아찔함
이 서뉴렌 두리만 아는 아찔함
i seonyuren duriman aneun ajjilham

아무리 토라져도 삐져 있어도
아무리 토라저도 삐저 이써도
amuri torajeodo ppijeo isseodo

이 노랫말에 잠겨
이 노랜마레 잠겨
i noraenmare jamgyeo

우린 서로 남몰래 눈을 맞춰요.
우린 서로 남몰래 누늘 맏춰요.
urin seoro nammollae nuneul matchwoyo.

내가 즐겨 부르는 이 노래
내가 즐겨 부르는 이 노래
naega jeulgyeo bureuneun i norae

이 음악이 흐르면
이 으마기 흐르면
i eumagi heureumyeon

너의 눈빛, 너의 표정
너에 눈삗, 너에 표정
neoe nunbit, neoe pyojeong

내 가슴이 살살 녹아요.
내 가스미 살살 노가요.
nae gaseumi salsal nogayo.

< 3 절(verse) >

우리 둘이 부르는 이 노래
우리 두리 부르는 이 노래
uri duri bureuneun i norae

우리 둘만 아는 이 노래
우리 둘만 아는 이 노래
uri dulman aneun i norae

우리 둘이 영원히 함께 불러요
우리 두리 영원히 함께 불러요
uri duri yeongwonhi hamkke bulleoyo

이 음표에 우리 사랑 싣고
이 음표에 우리 사랑 싣꼬
i eumpyoe uri sarang sitgo

높고 낮게 길고 짧은 리듬
놉꼬 낟께 길고 짤븐 리듬
nopgo natge gilgo jjalbeun rideum

이 가락에 밤새도록 취해 봐요.
이 가라게 밤새도록 취해 봐요.
i garage bamsaedorok chwihae bwayo.

< 1 절(verse) >

내+가 부르+는 이 노래

내 (pronoun) : '나'에 조사 '가'가 붙을 때의 형태.
I
A form of '나' (I), when the postpositional particle '가' is attached to it.

가 : 어떤 상태나 상황에 놓인 대상이나 동작의 주체를 나타내는 조사.
ga (no equivalent expression)
A postpositional particle referring to a subject under a certain state or situation, or the subject of an act.

부르다 (verb) : 곡조에 따라 노래하다.
sing
To sing to a tune.

-는 : 앞의 말이 관형어의 기능을 하게 만들고 사건이나 동작이 현재 일어남을 나타내는 어미.
-neun (no equivalent expression)
An ending of a word that makes the preceding statement function as an adnominal phrase and implies that an event or action is happening in the present.

이 (determiner) : 말하는 사람에게 가까이 있거나 말하는 사람이 생각하고 있는 대상을 가리킬 때 쓰는 말.
this
The word that is used to refer to a person who is close to the speaker or something that the speaker is thinking of.

노래 (noun) : 운율에 맞게 지은 가사에 곡을 붙인 음악. 또는 그런 음악을 소리 내어 부름.
song; music; singing
A composition created by setting rhythmical lyrics to music; or the act of singing such a piece of music.

너+에게 아직 다 못다 하+ㄴ 말
한

너 (pronoun) : 듣는 사람이 친구나 아랫사람일 때, 그 사람을 가리키는 말.
no equivalent expression
A pronoun used to indicate the listener when he/she is the same age or younger.

에게 : 어떤 행동이 미치는 대상임을 나타내는 조사.
ege (no equivalent expression)
A postpositional particle referring to the subject that is influenced by a certain action.

아직 (adverb) : 어떤 일이나 상태 또는 어떻게 되기까지 시간이 더 지나야 함을 나타내거나, 어떤 일이나 상태가 끝나지 않고 계속 이어지고 있음을 나타내는 말.
yet; still
An adverb used to indicate that more time is needed to reach a certain state, or that something or a certain state has not ended, but is going on.

다 (adverb) : 남거나 빠진 것이 없이 모두.
all; everything
With nothing left over or missing.

못다 (adverb) : '어떤 행동을 완전히 다하지 못함'을 나타내는 말.
not yet
An adverb meaning that one has not finished a certain act.

하다 (verb) : 어떤 행동이나 동작, 활동 등을 행하다.
do; perform
To perform a certain move, action, activity, etc.

-ㄴ : 앞의 말이 관형어의 기능을 하게 만들고 사건이나 동작이 완료되어 그 상태가 유지되고 있음을 나타내는 어미.
-n (no equivalent expression)
An ending of a word that makes the preceding statement function as an adnominal phrase and indicates that an event or action has been completed and its state continues.

말 (noun) : 생각이나 느낌을 표현하고 전달하는 사람의 소리.
speech; words
Human voice through which thoughts or feelings are expressed and conveyed.

이 곡조+에+는 우리+만 알(아)+는 속삭임
곡조엔 아는

이 (determiner) : 말하는 사람에게 가까이 있거나 말하는 사람이 생각하고 있는 대상을 가리킬 때 쓰는 말.
this
The word that is used to refer to a person who is close to the speaker or something that the speaker is thinking of.

곡조 (noun) : 음악이나 노래의 흐름.
tune; melody
The flow of a piece of music or song.

에 : 앞말이 어떤 장소나 자리임을 나타내는 조사.
on; in; at
A postpositional particle to indicate that the preceding statement refers to a certain place or space.

는 : 문장 속에서 어떤 대상이 화제임을 나타내는 조사.
neun (no equivalent expression)
A postpositional particle used to indicate that a certain subject is the topic of a sentence.

우리 (pronoun) : 말하는 사람이 자기보다 높지 않은 사람에게 자기를 포함한 여러 사람들을 가리키는 말.
we
A pronoun used when the speaker refers to several people including himself/herself while speaking to a person senior to himself/herself.

만 : 다른 것은 제외하고 어느 것을 한정함을 나타내는 조사.
man (no equivalent expression)
A postpositional particle used when limiting the field to one thing, excluding all the others.

알다 (verb) : 교육이나 경험, 생각 등을 통해 사물이나 상황에 대한 정보 또는 지식을 갖추다.
know; understand
To have information or knowledge about an object or situation through education, experience, thoughts, etc.

-는 : 앞의 말이 관형어의 기능을 하게 만들고 사건이나 동작이 현재 일어남을 나타내는 어미.
-neun (no equivalent expression)
An ending of a word that makes the preceding statement function as an adnominal phrase and implies that an event or action is happening in the present.

속삭임 (noun) : 작고 낮은 목소리로 가만가만히 하는 이야기.
whisper
The act of talking quietly in a soft and low voice.

내+가 부르+는 이 노래

내 (pronoun) : '나'에 조사 '가'가 붙을 때의 형태.
I
A form of '나' (I), when the postpositional particle '가' is attached to it.

가 : 어떤 상태나 상황에 놓인 대상이나 동작의 주체를 나타내는 조사.
ga (no equivalent expression)
A postpositional particle referring to a subject under a certain state or situation, or the subject of an act.

부르다 (verb) : 곡조에 따라 노래하다.
sing
To sing to a tune.

-는 : 앞의 말이 관형어의 기능을 하게 만들고 사건이나 동작이 현재 일어남을 나타내는 어미.
-neun (no equivalent expression)
An ending of a word that makes the preceding statement function as an adnominal phrase and implies that an event or action is happening in the present.

이 (determiner) : 말하는 사람에게 가까이 있거나 말하는 사람이 생각하고 있는 대상을 가리킬 때 쓰는 말.
this
The word that is used to refer to a person who is close to the speaker or something that the speaker is thinking of.

노래 (noun) : 운율에 맞게 지은 가사에 곡을 붙인 음악. 또는 그런 음악을 소리 내어 부름.
song; music; singing
A composition created by setting rhythmical lyrics to music; or the act of singing such a piece of music.

너+에게 꼭 하+[고 싶]+은 말

너 (pronoun) : 듣는 사람이 친구나 아랫사람일 때, 그 사람을 가리키는 말.
no equivalent expression
A pronoun used to indicate the listener when he/she is the same age or younger.

에게 : 어떤 행동이 미치는 대상임을 나타내는 조사.
ege (no equivalent expression)
A postpositional particle referring to the subject that is influenced by a certain action.

꼭 (adverb) : 어떤 일이 있어도 반드시.
without fail; at any cost; certainly
By all means under any circumstances.

하다 (verb) : 어떤 행동이나 동작, 활동 등을 행하다.
do; perform
To perform a certain move, action, activity, etc.

-고 싶다 : 앞의 말이 나타내는 행동을 하기를 원함을 나타내는 표현.
-go sipda (no equivalent expression)
An expression used to state that the speaker wants to do the act mentioned in the preceding statement.

-은 : 앞의 말이 관형어의 기능을 하게 만들고 현재의 상태를 나타내는 어미.
-eun (no equivalent expression)
An ending of a word that makes the preceding word function as an adnominal phrase and refers to the present state.

말 (noun) : 생각이나 느낌을 표현하고 전달하는 사람의 소리.
speech; words
Human voice through which thoughts or feelings are expressed and conveyed.

이 선율+에+는 우리+만 알(아)+는 귓속말
선율엔 아는

이 (determiner) : 말하는 사람에게 가까이 있거나 말하는 사람이 생각하고 있는 대상을 가리킬 때 쓰는 말.
this
The word that is used to refer to a person who is close to the speaker or something that the speaker is thinking of.

선율 (noun) : 길고 짧거나 높고 낮은 소리가 어우러진 음의 흐름.
melody; tune
The flow of long and short or high and low notes.

에 : 앞말이 어떤 장소나 자리임을 나타내는 조사.
on; in; at
A postpositional particle to indicate that the preceding statement refers to a certain place or space.

는 : 문장 속에서 어떤 대상이 화제임을 나타내는 조사.
neun (no equivalent expression)
A postpositional particle used to indicate that a certain subject is the topic of a sentence.

우리 (pronoun) : 말하는 사람이 자기보다 높지 않은 사람에게 자기를 포함한 여러 사람들을 가리키는 말.
we
A pronoun used when the speaker refers to several people including himself/herself while speaking to a person senior to himself/herself.

만 : 다른 것은 제외하고 어느 것을 한정함을 나타내는 조사.
man (no equivalent expression)
A postpositional particle used when limiting the field to one thing, excluding all the others.

알다 (verb) : 교육이나 경험, 생각 등을 통해 사물이나 상황에 대한 정보 또는 지식을 갖추다.
know; understand
To have information or knowledge about an object or situation through education, experience, thoughts, etc.

-는 : 앞의 말이 관형어의 기능을 하게 만들고 사건이나 동작이 현재 일어남을 나타내는 어미.
-neun (no equivalent expression)
An ending of a word that makes the preceding statement function as an adnominal phrase and implies that an event or action is happening in the present.

귓속말 (noun) : 남의 귀에 입을 가까이 대고 작은 소리로 말함. 또는 그런 말.
whisper
The act of saying something quietly by putting one's mouth to another's ears, or such a whisper.

아무리 화+가 나+(아)도 삐지+[어 있]+어도
나도 삐져 있어도

아무리 (adverb) : 비록 그렇다 하더라도.
no matter how; however; whatever
Even so.

화 (noun) : 몹시 못마땅하거나 노여워하는 감정.
anger; fury
A feeling of strong frustration or anger.

가 : 어떤 상태나 상황에 놓인 대상이나 동작의 주체를 나타내는 조사.
ga (no equivalent expression)
A postpositional particle referring to a subject under a certain state or situation, or the subject of an act.

나다 (verb) : 어떤 감정이나 느낌이 생기다.
feel
To feel a certain emotion or sensation.

-아도 : 앞에 오는 말을 가정하거나 인정하지만 뒤에 오는 말에는 관계가 없거나 영향을 끼치지 않음을 나타내는 연결 어미.
-ado (no equivalent expression)
A connective ending used when assuming or recognizing the truth of the preceding statement, although it is not related to or does not influence the following statement.

삐지다 (verb) : 화가 나거나 서운해서 마음이 뒤틀리다.
become sullen; sulk
For one's mind to be twisted because one feels angry or hurt.

-어 있다 : 앞의 말이 나타내는 상태가 계속됨을 나타내는 표현.
-eo itda (no equivalent expression)
An expression used to indicate that the state mentioned in the preceding statement is continued.

-어도 : 앞에 오는 말을 가정하거나 인정하지만 뒤에 오는 말에는 관계가 없거나 영향을 끼치지 않음을 나타내는 연결 어미.
-eodo (no equivalent expression)
A connective ending used when assuming or recognizing the truth of the preceding statement, although it is not related to or does not influence the following statement.

이 가락+에 취하+여
취해

이 (determiner) : 말하는 사람에게 가까이 있거나 말하는 사람이 생각하고 있는 대상을 가리킬 때 쓰는 말.
this
The word that is used to refer to a person who is close to the speaker or something that the speaker is thinking of.

가락 (noun) : 음악에서 음의 높낮이의 흐름.
tune; melody
The flow of the highs and lows of a tune in music.

에 : 앞말이 어떤 행위나 감정 등의 대상임을 나타내는 조사.
with; for; against
A postpositional particle to indicate that the preceding statement is the subject that is influenced by a certain action, emotion, etc.

취하다 (verb) : 무엇에 매우 깊이 빠져 마음을 빼앗기다.
be enchanted; be fascinated
To lose one's heart, as one fell for someone or something too much.

-여 : 앞의 말이 뒤의 말보다 먼저 일어났거나 뒤의 말에 대한 방법이나 수단이 됨을 나타내는 연결 어미.
-yeo (no equivalent expression)
A connective ending used when the preceding statement happened before the following statement, or was the ways or means to the following statement.

우리+는 서로 남몰래 [눈을 맞추]+어요.
우린 눈을 맞춰요

우리 (pronoun) : 말하는 사람이 자기보다 높지 않은 사람에게 자기를 포함한 여러 사람들을 가리키는 말.
we
A pronoun used when the speaker refers to several people including himself/herself while speaking to a person senior to himself/herself.

는 : 문장 속에서 어떤 대상이 화제임을 나타내는 조사.
neun (no equivalent expression)
A postpositional particle used to indicate that a certain subject is the topic of a sentence.

서로 (adverb) : 관계를 맺고 있는 둘 이상의 대상이 함께. 또는 같이.
altogether
Together with or at the same time with one person who is one of two or more who are related.

남몰래 (adverb) : 다른 사람이 모르게.
secretly
So that others do not notice it.

눈을 맞추다 (idiom) : 서로 눈을 마주 보다.
contact each other's eyes
To look each other in the eyes.

-어요 : (두루높임으로) 어떤 사실을 서술하거나 질문, 명령, 권유함을 나타내는 종결 어미.
-eoyo (no equivalent expression)
(informal addressee-raising) A sentence-final ending used to describe a certain fact, ask a question, give an order, or advise.

내+가 즐기+어 부르+는 이 노래
즐겨

내 (pronoun) : '나'에 조사 '가'가 붙을 때의 형태.
I
A form of '나' (I), when the postpositional particle '가' is attached to it.

가 : 어떤 상태나 상황에 놓인 대상이나 동작의 주체를 나타내는 조사.
ga (no equivalent expression)
A postpositional particle referring to a subject under a certain state or situation, or the subject of an act.

즐기다 (verb) : 어떤 것을 좋아하여 자주 하다.
enjoy; appreciate; take pleasure in
To do something often out of one's fondness for it.

-어 : 앞의 말이 뒤의 말보다 먼저 일어났거나 뒤의 말에 대한 방법이나 수단이 됨을 나타내는 연결 어미.
-eo (no equivalent expression)
A connective ending used when the preceding statement happened before the following statement or was the ways or means to the following statement.

부르다 (verb) : 곡조에 따라 노래하다.
sing
To sing to a tune.

-는 : 앞의 말이 관형어의 기능을 하게 만들고 사건이나 동작이 현재 일어남을 나타내는 어미.
-neun (no equivalent expression)
An ending of a word that makes the preceding statement function as an adnominal phrase and implies that an event or action is happening in the present.

이 (determiner) : 말하는 사람에게 가까이 있거나 말하는 사람이 생각하고 있는 대상을 가리킬 때 쓰는 말.
this
The word that is used to refer to a person who is close to the speaker or something that the speaker is thinking of.

노래 (noun) : 운율에 맞게 지은 가사에 곡을 붙인 음악. 또는 그런 음악을 소리 내어 부름.
song; music; singing
A composition created by setting rhythmical lyrics to music; or the act of singing such a piece of music.

이 음악+이 흐르+면

이 (determiner) : 말하는 사람에게 가까이 있거나 말하는 사람이 생각하고 있는 대상을 가리킬 때 쓰는 말.

this

The word that is used to refer to a person who is close to the speaker or something that the speaker is thinking of.

음악 (noun) : 목소리나 악기로 박자와 가락이 있게 소리 내어 생각이나 감정을 표현하는 예술.

music

A field of art, in which one expresses one's thoughts or emotions by using one's voice or a musical instrument to make sounds with beats and melody.

이 : 어떤 상태나 상황의 대상이나 동작의 주체를 나타내는 조사.

i (no equivalent expression)

A postpositional particle referring to a subject under a certain state or situation, or the agent of an action.

흐르다 (verb) : 빛, 소리, 향기 등이 부드럽게 퍼지다.

flow

For light, sound, smell, etc., to spread gently.

-면 : 뒤에 오는 말에 대한 근거나 조건이 됨을 나타내는 연결 어미.

-myeon (no equivalent expression)

A connective ending used when the preceding statement becomes the reason or condition of the following statement.

너+의 눈빛, 너+의 표정

너 (pronoun) : 듣는 사람이 친구나 아랫사람일 때, 그 사람을 가리키는 말.

no equivalent expression

A pronoun used to indicate the listener when he/she is the same age or younger.

의 : 앞의 말이 뒤의 말에 대하여 소유, 소속, 소재, 관계, 기원, 주체의 관계를 가짐을 나타내는 조사.

ui (no equivalent expression)

A postpositional particle used to indicate that the referent of the following word is owned by, belongs to, is related to, originates from, or is the object of what the preceding word indicates.

눈빛 (noun) : 눈에 나타나는 감정.

look in one's eyes

Feelings that are revealed through the eyes.

너 (pronoun) : 듣는 사람이 친구나 아랫사람일 때, 그 사람을 가리키는 말.
no equivalent expression
A pronoun used to indicate the listener when he/she is the same age or younger.

의 : 앞의 말이 뒤의 말에 대하여 소유, 소속, 소재, 관계, 기원, 주체의 관계를 가짐을 나타내는 조사.
ui (no equivalent expression)
A postpositional particle used to indicate that the referent of the following word is owned by, belongs to, is related to, originates from, or is the object of what the preceding word indicates.

표정 (noun) : 마음속에 품은 감정이나 생각 등이 얼굴에 드러남. 또는 그런 모습.
facial expression
The state of one's face showing one's feeling, thought, etc., or such a face.

나+의 가슴+이 살살 녹+아요.
내

나 (pronoun) : 말하는 사람이 친구나 아랫사람에게 자기를 가리키는 말.
I
A pronoun used to indicate oneself to a friend or a younger person.

의 : 앞의 말이 뒤의 말에 대하여 소유, 소속, 소재, 관계, 기원, 주체의 관계를 가짐을 나타내는 조사.
ui (no equivalent expression)
A postpositional particle used to indicate that the referent of the following word is owned by, belongs to, is related to, originates from, or is the object of what the preceding word indicates.

가슴 (noun) : 마음이나 느낌.
heart; feeling
One's mind or emotion.

이 : 어떤 상태나 상황의 대상이나 동작의 주체를 나타내는 조사.
i (no equivalent expression)
A postpositional particle referring to a subject under a certain state or situation, or the agent of an action.

살살 (adverb) : 눈이나 설탕 등이 모르는 사이에 저절로 녹는 모양.
imperceptibly; softly
In the manner of snow, sugar, etc., melting away before one knows.

녹다 (verb) : 어떤 대상에게 몹시 반하거나 빠지다.
fall for
To fall for or be addicted to something.

-아요 : (두루높임으로) 어떤 사실을 서술하거나 질문, 명령, 권유함을 나타내는 종결 어미.
-ayo (no equivalent expression)
(informal addressee-raising) A sentence-final ending used to describe a certain fact, ask a question, give an order, or advise.

< 2 절(verse) >

내+가 부르+는 이 노래

내 (pronoun) : '나'에 조사 '가'가 붙을 때의 형태.
I
A form of '나' (I), when the postpositional particle '가' is attached to it.

가 : 어떤 상태나 상황에 놓인 대상이나 동작의 주체를 나타내는 조사.
ga (no equivalent expression)
A postpositional particle referring to a subject under a certain state or situation, or the subject of an act.

부르다 (verb) : 곡조에 따라 노래하다.
sing
To sing to a tune.

-는 : 앞의 말이 관형어의 기능을 하게 만들고 사건이나 동작이 현재 일어남을 나타내는 어미.
-neun (no equivalent expression)
An ending of a word that makes the preceding statement function as an adnominal phrase and implies that an event or action is happening in the present.

이 (determiner) : 말하는 사람에게 가까이 있거나 말하는 사람이 생각하고 있는 대상을 가리킬 때 쓰는 말.
this
The word that is used to refer to a person who is close to the speaker or something that the speaker is thinking of.

노래 (noun) : 운율에 맞게 지은 가사에 곡을 붙인 음악. 또는 그런 음악을 소리 내어 부름.
song; music; singing
A composition created by setting rhythmical lyrics to music; or the act of singing such a piece of music.

너+에게+만 들려주+었던 말
들려줬던

너 (pronoun) : 듣는 사람이 친구나 아랫사람일 때, 그 사람을 가리키는 말.
no equivalent expression
A pronoun used to indicate the listener when he/she is the same age or younger.

에게 : 어떤 행동이 미치는 대상임을 나타내는 조사.
ege (no equivalent expression)
A postpositional particle referring to the subject that is influenced by a certain action.

만 : 다른 것은 제외하고 어느 것을 한정함을 나타내는 조사.
man (no equivalent expression)
A postpositional particle used when limiting the field to one thing, excluding all the others.

들려주다 (verb) : 소리나 말을 듣게 해 주다.
sing; speak
To have someone listen to a sound or remark.

-었던 : 과거의 사건이나 상태를 다시 떠올리거나 그 사건이나 상태가 완료되지 않고 중단되었다는 의미를 나타내는 표현.
-eotdeon (no equivalent expression)
An expression used to recall a past incident or state, and indicate that the incident or state is suspended, not completed.

말 (noun) : 생각이나 느낌을 표현하고 전달하는 사람의 소리.
speech; words
Human voice through which thoughts or feelings are expressed and conveyed.

이 곡조+에+는 둘+이+만 알(아)+는 짜릿하+ㅁ
곡조엔 아는 짜릿함

이 (determiner) : 말하는 사람에게 가까이 있거나 말하는 사람이 생각하고 있는 대상을 가리킬 때 쓰는 말.
this
The word that is used to refer to a person who is close to the speaker or something that the speaker is thinking of.

곡조 (noun) : 음악이나 노래의 흐름.
tune; melody
The flow of a piece of music or song.

에 : 앞말이 어떤 장소나 자리임을 나타내는 조사.
on; in; at
A postpositional particle to indicate that the preceding statement refers to a certain place or space.

는 : 문장 속에서 어떤 대상이 화제임을 나타내는 조사.
neun (no equivalent expression)
A postpositional particle used to indicate that a certain subject is the topic of a sentence.

둘 (numeral) : 하나에 하나를 더한 수.
two
The cardinal number equal to the sum of 1 + 1.

이 : 어떤 상태나 상황의 대상이나 동작의 주체를 나타내는 조사.
i (no equivalent expression)
A postpositional particle referring to a subject under a certain state or situation, or the agent of an action.

만 : 다른 것은 제외하고 어느 것을 한정함을 나타내는 조사.
man (no equivalent expression)
A postpositional particle used when limiting the field to one thing, excluding all the others.

알다 (verb) : 교육이나 경험, 생각 등을 통해 사물이나 상황에 대한 정보 또는 지식을 갖추다.
know; understand
To have information or knowledge about an object or situation through education, experience, thoughts, etc.

-는 : 앞의 말이 관형어의 기능을 하게 만들고 사건이나 동작이 현재 일어남을 나타내는 어미.
-neun (no equivalent expression)
An ending of a word that makes the preceding statement function as an adnominal phrase and implies that an event or action is happening in the present.

짜릿하다 (adjective) : 심리적 자극을 받아 마음이 순간적으로 조금 흥분되고 떨리는 듯하다.
electrified; thrilled
Feeling slightly excited and tense temporarily out of a psychological stimulation.

-ㅁ : 앞의 말이 명사의 기능을 하게 하는 어미.
m (no equivalent expression)
An ending of a word that makes the preceding statement function as a noun.

내+가 부르+는 이 노래

내 (pronoun) : '나'에 조사 '가'가 붙을 때의 형태.
I
A form of '나' (I), when the postpositional particle '가' is attached to it.

가 : 어떤 상태나 상황에 놓인 대상이나 동작의 주체를 나타내는 조사.
ga (no equivalent expression)
A postpositional particle referring to a subject under a certain state or situation, or the subject of an act.

부르다 (verb) : 곡조에 따라 노래하다.
sing
To sing to a tune.

-는 : 앞의 말이 관형어의 기능을 하게 만들고 사건이나 동작이 현재 일어남을 나타내는 어미.
-neun (no equivalent expression)
An ending of a word that makes the preceding statement function as an adnominal phrase and implies that an event or action is happening in the present.

이 (determiner) : 말하는 사람에게 가까이 있거나 말하는 사람이 생각하고 있는 대상을 가리킬 때 쓰는 말.
this
The word that is used to refer to a person who is close to the speaker or something that the speaker is thinking of.

노래 (noun) : 운율에 맞게 지은 가사에 곡을 붙인 음악. 또는 그런 음악을 소리 내어 부름.
song; music; singing
A composition created by setting rhythmical lyrics to music; or the act of singing such a piece of music.

너+에게+만 속삭이+었던 말
속삭였던

너 (pronoun) : 듣는 사람이 친구나 아랫사람일 때, 그 사람을 가리키는 말.
no equivalent expression
A pronoun used to indicate the listener when he/she is the same age or younger.

에게 : 어떤 행동이 미치는 대상임을 나타내는 조사.
ege (no equivalent expression)
A postpositional particle referring to the subject that is influenced by a certain action.

만 : 다른 것은 제외하고 어느 것을 한정함을 나타내는 조사.
man (no equivalent expression)
A postpositional particle used when limiting the field to one thing, excluding all the others.

속삭이다 (verb) : 남이 알아듣지 못하게 작은 목소리로 가만가만 이야기하다.
whisper
To talk in a small voice repeatedly, so that others cannot hear.

-었던 : 과거의 사건이나 상태를 다시 떠올리거나 그 사건이나 상태가 완료되지 않고 중단되었다는 의미를 나타내는 표현.
-eotdeon (no equivalent expression)
An expression used to recall a past incident or state, and indicate that the incident or state is suspended, not completed.

말 (noun) : 생각이나 느낌을 표현하고 전달하는 사람의 소리.
speech; words
Human voice through which thoughts or feelings are expressed and conveyed.

이 선율+에+ㄴ 둘+이+만 알(아)+는 아찔하+ㅁ
선율엔 아는 아찔함

이 (determiner) : 말하는 사람에게 가까이 있거나 말하는 사람이 생각하고 있는 대상을 가리킬 때 쓰는 말.
this
The word that is used to refer to a person who is close to the speaker or something that the speaker is thinking of.

선율 (noun) : 길고 짧거나 높고 낮은 소리가 어우러진 음의 흐름.
melody; tune
The flow of long and short or high and low notes.

에 : 앞말이 어떤 장소나 자리임을 나타내는 조사.
on; in; at
A postpositional particle to indicate that the preceding statement refers to a certain place or space.

는 : 문장 속에서 어떤 대상이 화제임을 나타내는 조사.
neun (no equivalent expression)
A postpositional particle used to indicate that a certain subject is the topic of a sentence.

둘 (numeral) : 하나에 하나를 더한 수.
two
The cardinal number equal to the sum of 1 + 1.

이 : 어떤 상태나 상황의 대상이나 동작의 주체를 나타내는 조사.
i (no equivalent expression)
A postpositional particle referring to a subject under a certain state or situation, or the agent of an action.

만 : 다른 것은 제외하고 어느 것을 한정함을 나타내는 조사.
man (no equivalent expression)
A postpositional particle used when limiting the field to one thing, excluding all the others.

알다 (verb) : 교육이나 경험, 생각 등을 통해 사물이나 상황에 대한 정보 또는 지식을 갖추다.
know; understand
To have information or knowledge about an object or situation through education, experience, thoughts, etc.

-는 : 앞의 말이 관형어의 기능을 하게 만들고 사건이나 동작이 현재 일어남을 나타내는 어미.
-neun (no equivalent expression)
An ending of a word that makes the preceding statement function as an adnominal phrase and implies that an event or action is happening in the present.

아찔하다 (adjective) : 놀라거나 해서 갑자기 정신이 흐려지고 어지럽다.
dizzy; giddy
Feeling faint and light-headed suddenly in surprise.

-ㅁ : 앞의 말이 명사의 기능을 하게 하는 어미.
m (no equivalent expression)
An ending of a word that makes the preceding statement function as a noun.

아무리 토라지+어도 삐지+[어 있]+어도
토라져도 삐져 있어도

아무리 (adverb) : 비록 그렇다 하더라도.
no matter how; however; whatever
Even so.

토라지다 (verb) : 마음에 들지 않아 불만스러워 싹 돌아서다.
pout; sulk
To turn away, as one does not approve or is not satisfied with something.

-어도 : 앞에 오는 말을 가정하거나 인정하지만 뒤에 오는 말에는 관계가 없거나 영향을 끼치지 않음을 나타내는 연결 어미.
-eodo (no equivalent expression)
A connective ending used when assuming or recognizing the truth of the preceding statement, although it is not related to or does not influence the following statement.

삐지다 (verb) : 화가 나거나 서운해서 마음이 뒤틀리다.
become sullen; sulk
For one's mind to be twisted because one feels angry or hurt.

-어 있다 : 앞의 말이 나타내는 상태가 계속됨을 나타내는 표현.
-eo itda (no equivalent expression)
An expression used to indicate that the state mentioned in the preceding statement is continued.

-어도 : 앞에 오는 말을 가정하거나 인정하지만 뒤에 오는 말에는 관계가 없거나 영향을 끼치지 않음을 나타내는 연결 어미.
-eodo (no equivalent expression)
A connective ending used when assuming or recognizing the truth of the preceding statement, although it is not related to or does not influence the following statement.

이 노랫말+에 잠기+어
잠겨

이 (determiner) : 말하는 사람에게 가까이 있거나 말하는 사람이 생각하고 있는 대상을 가리킬 때 쓰는 말.
this
The word that is used to refer to a person who is close to the speaker or something that the speaker is thinking of.

노랫말 (noun) : 노래의 가락에 따라 부를 수 있게 만든 글이나 말.
lyrics
A writing or words written to be sung along to the melody of a song.

에 : 앞말이 어떤 행위나 감정 등의 대상임을 나타내는 조사.
with; for; against
A postpositional particle to indicate that the preceding statement is the subject that is influenced by a certain action, emotion, etc.

잠기다 (verb) : 생각이나 느낌 속에 빠지다.
be immersed; be sunk
To fall into a thought or feeling.

-어 : 앞의 말이 뒤의 말보다 먼저 일어났거나 뒤의 말에 대한 방법이나 수단이 됨을 나타내는 연결 어미.
-eo (no equivalent expression)
A connective ending used when the preceding statement happened before the following statement or was the ways or means to the following statement.

우리+는 서로 남몰래 [눈을 맞추]+어요.
우린 눈을 맞춰요

우리 (pronoun) : 말하는 사람이 자기보다 높지 않은 사람에게 자기를 포함한 여러 사람들을 가리키는 말.
we
A pronoun used when the speaker refers to several people including himself/herself while speaking to a person senior to himself/herself.

는 : 문장 속에서 어떤 대상이 화제임을 나타내는 조사.
neun (no equivalent expression)
A postpositional particle used to indicate that a certain subject is the topic of a sentence.

서로 (adverb) : 관계를 맺고 있는 둘 이상의 대상이 함께. 또는 같이.
altogether
Together with or at the same time with one person who is one of two or more who are related.

남몰래 (adverb) : 다른 사람이 모르게.
secretly
So that others do not notice it.

눈을 맞추다 (idiom) : 서로 눈을 마주 보다.
contact each other's eyes
To look each other in the eyes.

-어요 : (두루높임으로) 어떤 사실을 서술하거나 질문, 명령, 권유함을 나타내는 종결 어미.
-eoyo (no equivalent expression)
(informal addressee-raising) A sentence-final ending used to describe a certain fact, ask a question, give an order, or advise.

내+가 즐기+어 부르+는 이 노래
즐겨

내 (pronoun) : '나'에 조사 '가'가 붙을 때의 형태.
I
A form of '나' (I), when the postpositional particle '가' is attached to it.

가 : 어떤 상태나 상황에 놓인 대상이나 동작의 주체를 나타내는 조사.
ga (no equivalent expression)
A postpositional particle referring to a subject under a certain state or situation, or the subject of an act.

즐기다 (verb) : 어떤 것을 좋아하여 자주 하다.
enjoy; appreciate; take pleasure in
To do something often out of one's fondness for it.

-어 : 앞의 말이 뒤의 말보다 먼저 일어났거나 뒤의 말에 대한 방법이나 수단이 됨을 나타내는 연결 어미.
-eo (no equivalent expression)
A connective ending used when the preceding statement happened before the following statement or was the ways or means to the following statement.

부르다 (verb) : 곡조에 따라 노래하다.
sing
To sing to a tune.

-는 : 앞의 말이 관형어의 기능을 하게 만들고 사건이나 동작이 현재 일어남을 나타내는 어미.
-neun (no equivalent expression)
An ending of a word that makes the preceding statement function as an adnominal phrase and implies that an event or action is happening in the present.

이 (determiner) : 말하는 사람에게 가까이 있거나 말하는 사람이 생각하고 있는 대상을 가리킬 때 쓰는 말.
this
The word that is used to refer to a person who is close to the speaker or something that the speaker is thinking of.

노래 (noun) : 운율에 맞게 지은 가사에 곡을 붙인 음악. 또는 그런 음악을 소리 내어 부름.
song; music; singing
A composition created by setting rhythmical lyrics to music; or the act of singing such a piece of music.

이 음악+이 흐르+면

이 (determiner) : 말하는 사람에게 가까이 있거나 말하는 사람이 생각하고 있는 대상을 가리킬 때 쓰는 말.
this
The word that is used to refer to a person who is close to the speaker or something that the speaker is thinking of.

음악 (noun) : 목소리나 악기로 박자와 가락이 있게 소리 내어 생각이나 감정을 표현하는 예술.
music
A field of art, in which one expresses one's thoughts or emotions by using one's voice or a musical instrument to make sounds with beats and melody.

이 : 어떤 상태나 상황의 대상이나 동작의 주체를 나타내는 조사.
i (no equivalent expression)
A postpositional particle referring to a subject under a certain state or situation, or the agent of an action.

흐르다 (verb) : 빛, 소리, 향기 등이 부드럽게 퍼지다.
flow
For light, sound, smell, etc., to spread gently.

-면 : 뒤에 오는 말에 대한 근거나 조건이 됨을 나타내는 연결 어미.
-myeon (no equivalent expression)
A connective ending used when the preceding statement becomes the reason or condition of the following statement.

너+의 눈빛, 너+의 표정

너 (pronoun) : 듣는 사람이 친구나 아랫사람일 때, 그 사람을 가리키는 말.
no equivalent expression
A pronoun used to indicate the listener when he/she is the same age or younger.

의 : 앞의 말이 뒤의 말에 대하여 소유, 소속, 소재, 관계, 기원, 주체의 관계를 가짐을 나타내는 조사.
ui (no equivalent expression)
A postpositional particle used to indicate that the referent of the following word is owned by, belongs to, is related to, originates from, or is the object of what the preceding word indicates.

눈빛 (noun) : 눈에 나타나는 감정.
look in one's eyes
Feelings that are revealed through the eyes.

너 (pronoun) : 듣는 사람이 친구나 아랫사람일 때, 그 사람을 가리키는 말.
no equivalent expression
A pronoun used to indicate the listener when he/she is the same age or younger.

의 : 앞의 말이 뒤의 말에 대하여 소유, 소속, 소재, 관계, 기원, 주체의 관계를 가짐을 나타내는 조사.
ui (no equivalent expression)
A postpositional particle used to indicate that the referent of the following word is owned by, belongs to, is related to, originates from, or is the object of what the preceding word indicates.

표정 (noun) : 마음속에 품은 감정이나 생각 등이 얼굴에 드러남. 또는 그런 모습.
facial expression
The state of one's face showing one's feeling, thought, etc., or such a face.

나+의 가슴+이 살살 녹+아요.
내

나 (pronoun) : 말하는 사람이 친구나 아랫사람에게 자기를 가리키는 말.
I
A pronoun used to indicate oneself to a friend or a younger person.

의 : 앞의 말이 뒤의 말에 대하여 소유, 소속, 소재, 관계, 기원, 주체의 관계를 가짐을 나타내는 조사.
ui (no equivalent expression)
A postpositional particle used to indicate that the referent of the following word is owned by, belongs to, is related to, originates from, or is the object of what the preceding word indicates.

가슴 (noun) : 마음이나 느낌.
heart; feeling
One's mind or emotion.

이 : 어떤 상태나 상황의 대상이나 동작의 주체를 나타내는 조사.
i (no equivalent expression)
A postpositional particle referring to a subject under a certain state or situation, or the agent of an action.

살살 (adverb) : 눈이나 설탕 등이 모르는 사이에 저절로 녹는 모양.
imperceptibly; softly
In the manner of snow, sugar, etc., melting away before one knows.

녹다 (verb) : 어떤 대상에게 몹시 반하거나 빠지다.
fall for
To fall for or be addicted to something.

-아요 : (두루높임으로) 어떤 사실을 서술하거나 질문, 명령, 권유함을 나타내는 종결 어미.
-ayo (no equivalent expression)
(informal addressee-raising) A sentence-final ending used to describe a certain fact, ask a question, give an order, or advise.

< 3 절(verse) >

우리 둘+이 부르+는 이 노래

우리 (pronoun) : 말하는 사람이 자기보다 높지 않은 사람에게 자기를 포함한 여러 사람들을 가리키는 말.
we
A pronoun used when the speaker refers to several people including himself/herself while speaking to a person senior to himself/herself.

둘 (numeral) : 하나에 하나를 더한 수.
two
The cardinal number equal to the sum of 1 + 1.

이 : 어떤 상태나 상황의 대상이나 동작의 주체를 나타내는 조사.
i (no equivalent expression)
A postpositional particle referring to a subject under a certain state or situation, or the agent of an action.

부르다 (verb) : 곡조에 따라 노래하다.
sing
To sing to a tune.

-는 : 앞의 말이 관형어의 기능을 하게 만들고 사건이나 동작이 현재 일어남을 나타내는 어미.
-neun (no equivalent expression)
An ending of a word that makes the preceding statement function as an adnominal phrase and implies that an event or action is happening in the present.

이 (determiner) : 말하는 사람에게 가까이 있거나 말하는 사람이 생각하고 있는 대상을 가리킬 때 쓰는 말.
this
The word that is used to refer to a person who is close to the speaker or something that the speaker is thinking of.

노래 (noun) : 운율에 맞게 지은 가사에 곡을 붙인 음악. 또는 그런 음악을 소리 내어 부름.
song; music; singing
A composition created by setting rhythmical lyrics to music; or the act of singing such a piece of music.

우리 둘+만 알(아)+는 이 노래
아는

우리 (pronoun) : 말하는 사람이 자기보다 높지 않은 사람에게 자기를 포함한 여러 사람들을 가리키는 말.
we
A pronoun used when the speaker refers to several people including himself/herself while speaking to a person senior to himself/herself.

둘 (numeral) : 하나에 하나를 더한 수.
two
The cardinal number equal to the sum of 1 + 1.

만 : 다른 것은 제외하고 어느 것을 한정함을 나타내는 조사.
man (no equivalent expression)
A postpositional particle used when limiting the field to one thing, excluding all the others.

알다 (verb) : 교육이나 경험, 생각 등을 통해 사물이나 상황에 대한 정보 또는 지식을 갖추다.
know; understand
To have information or knowledge about an object or situation through education, experience, thoughts, etc.

-는 : 앞의 말이 관형어의 기능을 하게 만들고 사건이나 동작이 현재 일어남을 나타내는 어미.
-neun (no equivalent expression)
An ending of a word that makes the preceding statement function as an adnominal phrase and implies that an event or action is happening in the present.

이 (determiner) : 말하는 사람에게 가까이 있거나 말하는 사람이 생각하고 있는 대상을 가리킬 때 쓰는 말.
this
The word that is used to refer to a person who is close to the speaker or something that the speaker is thinking of.

노래 (noun) : 운율에 맞게 지은 가사에 곡을 붙인 음악. 또는 그런 음악을 소리 내어 부름.
song; music; singing
A composition created by setting rhythmical lyrics to music; or the act of singing such a piece of music.

우리 둘+이 영원히 함께 부르(불ㄹ)+어요.
불러요

우리 (pronoun) : 말하는 사람이 자기보다 높지 않은 사람에게 자기를 포함한 여러 사람들을 가리키는 말.
we
A pronoun used when the speaker refers to several people including himself/herself while speaking to a person senior to himself/herself.

둘 (numeral) : 하나에 하나를 더한 수.
two
The cardinal number equal to the sum of 1 + 1.

이 : 어떤 상태나 상황의 대상이나 동작의 주체를 나타내는 조사.
i (no equivalent expression)
A postpositional particle referring to a subject under a certain state or situation, or the agent of an action.

영원히 (adverb) : 끝없이 이어지는 상태로. 또는 언제까지나 변하지 않는 상태로.
eternally; everlastingly; forever
In a manner of a phenomenon or shape lasting endlessly; in a manner of forever not changing.

함께 (adverb) : 여럿이서 한꺼번에 같이.
together; along with
In the state of several people being all together.

부르다 (verb) : 곡조에 따라 노래하다.
sing
To sing to a tune.

-어요 : (두루높임으로) 어떤 사실을 서술하거나 질문, 명령, 권유함을 나타내는 종결 어미.
-eoyo (no equivalent expression)
(informal addressee-raising) A sentence-final ending used to describe a certain fact, ask a question, give an order, or advise.

이 음표+에 우리 사랑 실+고

이 (determiner) : 말하는 사람에게 가까이 있거나 말하는 사람이 생각하고 있는 대상을 가리킬 때 쓰는 말.

this

The word that is used to refer to a person who is close to the speaker or something that the speaker is thinking of.

음표 (noun) : 악보에서 음의 길이와 높낮이를 나타내는 기호.

musical note

The sign in a score, which indicates the length and height of pitches.

에 : 앞말이 어떤 행위나 작용이 미치는 대상임을 나타내는 조사.

on; in; to

A postpositional particle to indicate that the preceding statement is the subject to which a certain action or operation is applied.

우리 (pronoun) : 말하는 사람이 자기보다 높지 않은 사람에게 자기를 포함한 여러 사람들을 가리키는 말.

we

A pronoun used when the speaker refers to several people including himself/herself while speaking to a person senior to himself/herself.

사랑 (noun) : 상대에게 성적으로 매력을 느껴 열렬히 좋아하는 마음.

love

The state of being sexually attracted to and having strong affection for a person.

싣다 (verb) : 어떤 현상이나 뜻을 나타내거나 담다.

have; take

To show a certain phenomenon or contain a certain meaning.

-고 : 앞의 말이 나타내는 행동이나 그 결과가 뒤에 오는 행동이 일어나는 동안에 그대로 지속됨을 나타내는 연결 어미.

-go (no equivalent expression)

A connective ending used when an action or result of the preceding statement remains the same while the following action happens.

높+고 낮+게 길+고 짧+은 리듬

높다 (adjective) : 소리가 음의 차례에서 위쪽이거나 진동수가 크다.

high-pitched

A sound being at a high pitch or its number of vibrations being large.

-고 : 두 가지 이상의 대등한 사실을 나열할 때 쓰는 연결 어미.
-go (no equivalent expression)
A connective ending used when listing more than two equal facts.

낮다 (adjective) : 소리가 음의 차례에서 아래쪽이거나 진동수가 작다.
low
A sound being at a low pitch, or its number of vibrations being small.

-게 : 앞의 말이 뒤에서 가리키는 일의 목적이나 결과, 방식, 정도 등이 됨을 나타내는 연결 어미.
-ge (no equivalent expression)
A connective ending used when the preceding statement is the purpose, result, method, amount, etc., of something mentioned in the following statement.

길다 (adjective) : 한 때에서 다음의 한 때까지 이어지는 시간이 오래다.
long; prolonged; lengthy
The time from a certain moment to the next moment being long.

-고 : 두 가지 이상의 대등한 사실을 나열할 때 쓰는 연결 어미.
-go (no equivalent expression)
A connective ending used when listing more than two equal facts.

짧다 (adjective) : 한 때에서 다른 때까지의 동안이 오래지 않다.
short
The time period between two points in time being brief.

-은 : 앞의 말이 관형어의 기능을 하게 만들고 현재의 상태를 나타내는 어미.
-eun (no equivalent expression)
An ending of a word that makes the preceding word function as an adnominal phrase and refers to the present state.

리듬 (noun) : 소리의 높낮이, 길이, 세기 등이 일정하게 반복되는 것.
rhythm
A regularly repeated pattern of the length, stress, etc., of a sound.

이 가락+에 밤새+도록 취하+[여 보]+아요.

취해 봐요

이 (determiner) : 말하는 사람에게 가까이 있거나 말하는 사람이 생각하고 있는 대상을 가리킬 때 쓰는 말.
this
The word that is used to refer to a person who is close to the speaker or something that the speaker is thinking of.

가락 (noun) : 음악에서 음의 높낮이의 흐름.
tune; melody
The flow of the highs and lows of a tune in music.

에 : 앞말이 어떤 행위나 감정 등의 대상임을 나타내는 조사.
with; for; against
A postpositional particle to indicate that the preceding statement is the subject that is influenced by a certain action, emotion, etc.

밤새다 (verb) : 밤이 지나 아침이 오다.
stay up
For morning to come after a night.

-도록 : 앞에 오는 말이 뒤에 오는 말에 대한 목적이나 결과, 방식, 정도임을 나타내는 연결 어미.
-dorok (no equivalent expression)
A connective ending used when the preceding statement is the purpose, result, method, amount, etc., of something mentioned in the following statement.

취하다 (verb) : 무엇에 매우 깊이 빠져 마음을 빼앗기다.
be enchanted; be fascinated
To lose one's heart, as one fell for someone or something too much.

-여 보다 : 앞의 말이 나타내는 행동을 시험 삼아 함을 나타내는 표현.
-yeo boda (no equivalent expression)
An expression used to indicate that one does the act mentioned in the preceding statement, as a test.

-아요 : (두루높임으로) 어떤 사실을 서술하거나 질문, 명령, 권유함을 나타내는 종결 어미.
-ayo (no equivalent expression)
(informal addressee-raising) A sentence-final ending used to describe a certain fact, ask a question, give an order, or advise.

< 8 >

최고야

너는 최고야.

(you are the best.)

[발음(pronunciation)]

< 1 절(verse) >

엄마, 치킨 먹고 싶어.
엄마, 치킨 먹꼬 시퍼.
eomma, chikin meokgo sipeo.

아빠, 피자 먹고 싶어.
아빠, 피자 먹꼬 시퍼.
appa, pija meokgo sipeo.

치킨 먹고 싶어.
치킨 먹꼬 시퍼.
chikin meokgo sipeo.

피자 먹고 싶어.
피자 먹꼬 시퍼.
pija meokgo sipeo.

시켜 줘, 시켜 줘.
시켜 줘, 시켜 줘.
sikyeo jwo, sikyeo jwo.

전부 시켜 줘.
전부 시켜 줘.
jeonbu sikyeo jwo.

시켜, 뭐든지 시켜.
시켜, 뭐든지 시켜.
sikyeo, mwodeunji sikyeo.

시켜, 전부 다 시켜.
시켜, 전부 다 시켜.
sikyeo, jeonbu da sikyeo.

먹고 싶은 거, 맛보고 싶은 거 전부 다 시켜.
먹꼬 시픈 거, 맏뽀고 시픈 거 전부 다 시켜.
meokgo sipeun geo, matbogo sipeun geo jeonbu da sikyeo.

엄만 언제나 최고야.
엄만 언제나 최고야.
eomman eonjena choegoya.

최고, 최고, 최고
최고, 최고, 최고
choego, choego, choego

아빤 언제나 최고야.
아빤 언제나 최고야.
appan eonjena choegoya.

최고, 최고, 아빠 최고.
최고, 최고, 아빠 최고.
choego, choego, appa choego.

엄마 최고, 아빠 최고, 엄마 최고, 아빠 최고.
엄마 최고, 아빠 최고, 엄마 최고, 아빠 최고.
eomma choego, appa choego, eomma choego, appa choego.

< 2 절(verse) >

언니, 햄버거 먹고 싶어.
언니, 햄버거 먹꼬 시퍼.
eonni, haembeogeo meokgo sipeo.

오빠, 돈가스 먹고 싶어.
오빠, 돈가스 먹꼬 시퍼.
oppa, dongaseu meokgo sipeo.

햄버거 먹고 싶어.
햄버거 먹꼬 시퍼.
haembeogeo meokgo sipeo.

돈가스 먹고 싶어.
돈가스 먹꼬 시퍼.
dongaseu meokgo sipeo.

시켜 줘, 시켜 줘.
시켜 줘, 시켜 줘.
sikyeo jwo, sikyeo jwo.

전부 시켜 줘.
전부 시켜 줘.
jeonbu sikyeo jwo.

시켜, 뭐든지 시켜.
시켜, 뭐든지 시켜.
sikyeo, mwodeunji sikyeo.

시켜, 전부 다 시켜.
시켜, 전부 다 시켜.
sikyeo, jeonbu da sikyeo.

먹고 싶은 거, 맛보고 싶은 거 전부 다 시켜.
먹꼬 시픈 거, 맏뽀고 시픈 거 전부 다 시켜.
meokgo sipeun geo, matbogo sipeun geo jeonbu da sikyeo.

초밥도, 짜장면도, 짬뽕도, 탕수육도, 떡볶이도, 순대도, 김밥도, 냉면도.
초밥또, 짜장면도, 짬뽕도, 탕수육또, 떡뽀끼도, 순대도, 김밥또, 냉면도.
chobapdo, jjajangmyeondo, jjamppongdo, tangsuyukdo, tteokbokkido, sundaedo, gimbapdo, naengmyeondo.

시켜, 시켜, 뭐든지 시켜.
시켜, 시켜, 뭐든지 시켜.
sikyeo, sikyeo, mwodeunji sikyeo.

먹고 싶은 거 다 시켜.
먹꼬 시픈 거 다 시켜.
meokgo sipeun geo da sikyeo.

뭐든지 다 시켜 줄게.
뭐든지 다 시켜 줄께.
mwodeunji da sikyeo julge.

전부 다 시켜 줄게.
전부 다 시켜 줄께.
jeonbu da sikyeo julge.

언닌 언제나 최고야.
언닌 언제나 최고야.
eonnin eonjena choegoya.

최고, 최고, 최고.
최고, 최고, 최고.
choego, choego, choego.

오빤 언제나 최고야.
오빤 언제나 최고야.
oppan eonjena choegoya.

최고, 최고, 오빠 최고.
최고, 최고, 오빠 최고.
choego, choego, oppa choego.

엄마가 최고야, 엄마 최고.
엄마가 최고야, 엄마 최고.
eommaga choegoya, eomma choego.

아빠가 최고야, 아빠 최고.
아빠가 최고야, 아빠 최고.
appaga choegoya, appa choego.

최고, 최고, 언니 최고.
최고, 최고, 언니 최고.
choego, choego, eonni choego.

오빠가 최고야, 오빠 최고.
오빠가 최고야, 오빠 최고.
oppaga choegoya, oppa choego.

< 1 절(verse) >

엄마, 치킨 먹+[고 싶]+어.

엄마 (noun) : 격식을 갖추지 않아도 되는 상황에서 어머니를 이르거나 부르는 말.
mom
A word used to refer to or address one's mother in an informal situation.

치킨 (noun) : 토막을 낸 닭에 밀가루 등을 묻혀 기름에 튀기거나 구운 음식.
fried chicken
A dish made by coating chopped chicken with flour, and frying or baking it.

먹다 (verb) : 음식 등을 입을 통하여 배 속에 들여보내다.
eat; have; consume; take
To put food into one's mouth and take it in one's stomach.

-고 싶다 : 앞의 말이 나타내는 행동을 하기를 원함을 나타내는 표현.
no equivalent expression
An expression used to state that the speaker wants to do the act mentioned in the preceding statement.

-어 : (두루낮춤으로) 어떤 사실을 서술하거나 물음, 명령, 권유를 나타내는 종결 어미.
no equivalent expression
(informal addressee-lowering) A sentence-final ending used to describe a certain fact, ask a question, give an order, or advise. <description>

아빠, 피자 먹+[고 싶]+어.

아빠 (noun) : 격식을 갖추지 않아도 되는 상황에서 아버지를 이르거나 부르는 말.
dad; daddy
A word used to refer to or address a father in an informal situation.

피자 (noun) : 이탈리아에서 유래한 것으로 둥글고 납작한 밀가루 반죽 위에 토마토, 고기, 치즈 등을 얹어 구운 음식.
pizza
Food originating in Italy, made by baking a round, flat piece of dough topped with tomato, meat, cheese, etc.

먹다 (verb) : 음식 등을 입을 통하여 배 속에 들여보내다.
eat; have; consume; take
To put food into one's mouth and take it in one's stomach.

-고 싶다 : 앞의 말이 나타내는 행동을 하기를 원함을 나타내는 표현.
no equivalent expression
An expression used to state that the speaker wants to do the act mentioned in the preceding statement.

-어 : (두루낮춤으로) 어떤 사실을 서술하거나 물음, 명령, 권유를 나타내는 종결 어미.
no equivalent expression
(informal addressee-lowering) A sentence-final ending used to describe a certain fact, ask a question, give an order, or advise. <description>

치킨 먹+[고 싶]+어.

치킨 (noun) : 토막을 낸 닭에 밀가루 등을 묻혀 기름에 튀기거나 구운 음식.
fried chicken
A dish made by coating chopped chicken with flour, and frying or baking it.

먹다 (verb) : 음식 등을 입을 통하여 배 속에 들여보내다.
eat; have; consume; take
To put food into one's mouth and take it in one's stomach.

-고 싶다 : 앞의 말이 나타내는 행동을 하기를 원함을 나타내는 표현.
no equivalent expression
An expression used to state that the speaker wants to do the act mentioned in the preceding statement.

-어 : (두루낮춤으로) 어떤 사실을 서술하거나 물음, 명령, 권유를 나타내는 종결 어미.
no equivalent expression
(informal addressee-lowering) A sentence-final ending used to describe a certain fact, ask a question, give an order, or advise. <description>

피자 먹+[고 싶]+어.

피자 (noun) : 이탈리아에서 유래한 것으로 둥글고 납작한 밀가루 반죽 위에 토마토, 고기, 치즈 등을 얹어 구운 음식.
pizza
Food originating in Italy, made by baking a round, flat piece of dough topped with tomato, meat, cheese, etc.

먹다 (verb) : 음식 등을 입을 통하여 배 속에 들여보내다.
eat; have; consume; take
To put food into one's mouth and take it in one's stomach.

-고 싶다 : 앞의 말이 나타내는 행동을 하기를 원함을 나타내는 표현.
no equivalent expression
An expression used to state that the speaker wants to do the act mentioned in the preceding statement.

-어 : (두루낮춤으로) 어떤 사실을 서술하거나 물음, 명령, 권유를 나타내는 종결 어미.
no equivalent expression
(informal addressee-lowering) A sentence-final ending used to describe a certain fact, ask a question, give an order, or advise. <description>

시키+[어 주]+어, 시키+[어 주]+어.
시켜 줘 시켜 줘

시키다 (verb) : 음식이나 술, 음료 등을 주문하다.
order
To order food, alcohol, beverages, etc.

-어 주다 : 남을 위해 앞의 말이 나타내는 행동을 함을 나타내는 표현.
no equivalent expression
An expression used to indicate that one does the act mentioned in the preceding statement for someone.

-어 : (두루낮춤으로) 어떤 사실을 서술하거나 물음, 명령, 권유를 나타내는 종결 어미.
no equivalent expression
(informal addressee-lowering) A sentence-final ending used to describe a certain fact, ask a question, give an order, or advise. <order>

전부 시키+[어 주]+어.
시켜 줘

전부 (adverb) : 빠짐없이 다.
all
Wholly without anything omitted.

시키다 (verb) : 음식이나 술, 음료 등을 주문하다.
order
To order food, alcohol, beverages, etc.

-어 주다 : 남을 위해 앞의 말이 나타내는 행동을 함을 나타내는 표현.
no equivalent expression
An expression used to indicate that one does the act mentioned in the preceding statement for someone.

-어 : (두루낮춤으로) 어떤 사실을 서술하거나 물음, 명령, 권유를 나타내는 종결 어미.
no equivalent expression
(informal addressee-lowering) A sentence-final ending used to describe a certain fact, ask a question, give an order, or advise. <order>

시키+어, 뭐+든지 시키+어.
시켜 시켜

시키다 (verb) : 음식이나 술, 음료 등을 주문하다.
order
To order food, alcohol, beverages, etc.

-어 : (두루낮춤으로) 어떤 사실을 서술하거나 물음, 명령, 권유를 나타내는 종결 어미.
no equivalent expression
(informal addressee-lowering) A sentence-final ending used to describe a certain fact, ask a question, give an order, or advise. <order>

뭐 (pronoun) : 정해지지 않은 대상이나 굳이 이름을 밝힐 필요가 없는 대상을 가리키는 말.
what
A pronoun used to refer to a subject that does not need to be specified or named.

든지 : 어느 것이 선택되어도 차이가 없음을 나타내는 조사.
no equivalent expression
A postpositional particle used when it does not matter which one is chosen.

시키다 (verb) : 음식이나 술, 음료 등을 주문하다.
order
To order food, alcohol, beverages, etc.

-어 : (두루낮춤으로) 어떤 사실을 서술하거나 물음, 명령, 권유를 나타내는 종결 어미.
no equivalent expression
(informal addressee-lowering) A sentence-final ending used to describe a certain fact, ask a question, give an order, or advise. <order>

시키+어, 전부 다 시키+어.
시켜 시켜

시키다 (verb) : 음식이나 술, 음료 등을 주문하다.
order
To order food, alcohol, beverages, etc.

-어 : (두루낮춤으로) 어떤 사실을 서술하거나 물음, 명령, 권유를 나타내는 종결 어미.
no equivalent expression
(informal addressee-lowering) A sentence-final ending used to describe a certain fact, ask a question, give an order, or advise. <order>

전부 (adverb) : 빠짐없이 다.
all
Wholly without anything omitted.

다 (adverb) : 남거나 빠진 것이 없이 모두.
all; everything
With nothing left over or missing.

시키다 (verb) : 음식이나 술, 음료 등을 주문하다.
order
To order food, alcohol, beverages, etc.

-어 : (두루낮춤으로) 어떤 사실을 서술하거나 물음, 명령, 권유를 나타내는 종결 어미.
no equivalent expression
(informal addressee-lowering) A sentence-final ending used to describe a certain fact, ask a question, give an order, or advise. <order>

먹+[고 싶]+[은 거], 맛보+[고 싶]+[은 거] 전부 다 시키+어.
시켜

먹다 (verb) : 음식 등을 입을 통하여 배 속에 들여보내다.
eat; have; consume; take
To put food into one's mouth and take it in one's stomach.

-고 싶다 : 앞의 말이 나타내는 행동을 하기를 원함을 나타내는 표현.
no equivalent expression
An expression used to state that the speaker wants to do the act mentioned in the preceding statement.

-은 거 : 명사가 아닌 것을 문장에서 명사처럼 쓰이게 하거나 ‘이다’ 앞에 쓰일 수 있게 할 때 쓰는 표현.
no equivalent expression
An expression used to enable a non-noun word to be used as a noun in the sentence or to be used in front of '이다' (be).

맛보다 (verb) : 음식의 맛을 알기 위해 먹어 보다.
taste
To taste in order to figure out the taste of the food.

-고 싶다 : 앞의 말이 나타내는 행동을 하기를 원함을 나타내는 표현.
no equivalent expression
An expression used to state that the speaker wants to do the act mentioned in the preceding statement.

-은 거 : 명사가 아닌 것을 문장에서 명사처럼 쓰이게 하거나 ‘이다’ 앞에 쓰일 수 있게 할 때 쓰는 표현.
no equivalent expression
An expression used to enable a non-noun word to be used as a noun in the sentence or to be used in front of '이다' (be).

전부 (adverb) : 빠짐없이 다.
all
Wholly without anything omitted.

다 (adverb) : 남거나 빠진 것이 없이 모두.
all; everything
With nothing left over or missing.

시키다 (verb) : 음식이나 술, 음료 등을 주문하다.
order
To order food, alcohol, beverages, etc.

-어 : (두루낮춤으로) 어떤 사실을 서술하거나 물음, 명령, 권유를 나타내는 종결 어미.
no equivalent expression
(informal addressee-lowering) A sentence-final ending used to describe a certain fact, ask a question, give an order, or advise. <order>

엄마+는 언제나 최고+(이)+야.

엄만 최고야

엄마 (noun) : 격식을 갖추지 않아도 되는 상황에서 어머니를 이르거나 부르는 말.
mom
A word used to refer to or address one's mother in an informal situation.

는 : 문장 속에서 어떤 대상이 화제임을 나타내는 조사.
no equivalent expression
A postpositional particle used to indicate that a certain subject is the topic of a sentence.

언제나 (adverb) : 어느 때에나. 또는 때에 따라 달라지지 않고 변함없이.
always; all the time
Every time; invariably without changing with time.

최고 (noun) : 가장 좋거나 뛰어난 것.
the best
The state of being the best or the most advanced.

이다 : 주어가 지시하는 대상의 속성이나 부류를 지정하는 뜻을 나타내는 서술격 조사.
no equivalent expression
A predicate particle indicating the meaning of the attribute or category of the thing that the subject of the sentence refers to.

-야 : (두루낮춤으로) 어떤 사실에 대하여 서술하거나 물음을 나타내는 종결 어미.
no equivalent expression
(informal addressee-lowering) A sentence-final ending used to describe a certain fact or ask a question. <description>

최고, 최고, 최고.

최고 (noun) : 가장 좋거나 뛰어난 것.
the best
The state of being the best or the most advanced.

아빠+는 언제나 최고+(이)+야.
아빤 최고야

아빠 (noun) : 격식을 갖추지 않아도 되는 상황에서 아버지를 이르거나 부르는 말.
dad; daddy
A word used to refer to or address a father in an informal situation.

는 : 문장 속에서 어떤 대상이 화제임을 나타내는 조사.
no equivalent expression
A postpositional particle used to indicate that a certain subject is the topic of a sentence.

언제나 (adverb) : 어느 때에나. 또는 때에 따라 달라지지 않고 변함없이.
always; all the time
Every time; invariably without changing with time.

최고 (noun) : 가장 좋거나 뛰어난 것.
the best
The state of being the best or the most advanced.

이다 : 주어가 지시하는 대상의 속성이나 부류를 지정하는 뜻을 나타내는 서술격 조사.
no equivalent expression
A predicate particle indicating the meaning of the attribute or category of the thing that the subject of the sentence refers to.

-야 : (두루낮춤으로) 어떤 사실에 대하여 서술하거나 물음을 나타내는 종결 어미.
no equivalent expression
(informal addressee-lowering) A sentence-final ending used to describe a certain fact or ask a question. <description>

최고, 최고, 아빠 최고.

최고 (noun) : 가장 좋거나 뛰어난 것.
the best
The state of being the best or the most advanced.

아빠 (noun) : 격식을 갖추지 않아도 되는 상황에서 아버지를 이르거나 부르는 말.
dad; daddy
A word used to refer to or address a father in an informal situation.

최고 (noun) : 가장 좋거나 뛰어난 것.
the best
The state of being the best or the most advanced.

엄마 최고, 아빠 최고, 엄마 최고, 아빠 최고.

엄마 (noun) : 격식을 갖추지 않아도 되는 상황에서 어머니를 이르거나 부르는 말.
mom
A word used to refer to or address one's mother in an informal situation.

최고 (noun) : 가장 좋거나 뛰어난 것.
the best
The state of being the best or the most advanced.

아빠 (noun) : 격식을 갖추지 않아도 되는 상황에서 아버지를 이르거나 부르는 말.
dad; daddy
A word used to refer to or address a father in an informal situation.

최고 (noun) : 가장 좋거나 뛰어난 것.
the best
The state of being the best or the most advanced.

< 2 절(verse) >

언니, 햄버거 먹+[고 싶]+어.

언니 (noun) : 여자가 형제나 친척 형제들 중에서 자기보다 나이가 많은 여자를 이르거나 부르는 말.
older sister
A word used only by a female to refer to or address her female siblings or cousins older than herself.

햄버거 (noun) : 둥근 빵 사이에 고기와 채소와 치즈 등을 끼운 음식.
hamburger
Food made by putting meat, vegetables, cheese, etc., between two round buns.

먹다 (verb) : 음식 등을 입을 통하여 배 속에 들여보내다.
eat; have; consume; take
To put food into one's mouth and take it in one's stomach.

-고 싶다 : 앞의 말이 나타내는 행동을 하기를 원함을 나타내는 표현.
no equivalent expression
An expression used to state that the speaker wants to do the act mentioned in the preceding statement.

-어 : (두루낮춤으로) 어떤 사실을 서술하거나 물음, 명령, 권유를 나타내는 종결 어미.
no equivalent expression
(informal addressee-lowering) A sentence-final ending used to describe a certain fact, ask a question, give an order, or advise. <description>

오빠, 돈가스 먹+[고 싶]+어.

오빠 (noun) : 여자가 형제나 친척 형제들 중에서 자기보다 나이가 많은 남자를 이르거나 부르는 말.
elder brother
A word used only by a girl to refer to or address her male siblings or cousins older than herself.

돈가스 (noun) : 도톰하게 썬 돼지고기를 양념하여 빵가루를 묻히고 기름에 튀긴 음식.
pork cutlet
Thick slices of pork seasoned, coated with bread crumbs, and fried in oil.

먹다 (verb) : 음식 등을 입을 통하여 배 속에 들여보내다.
eat; have; consume; take
To put food into one's mouth and take it in one's stomach.

-고 싶다 : 앞의 말이 나타내는 행동을 하기를 원함을 나타내는 표현.
no equivalent expression
An expression used to state that the speaker wants to do the act mentioned in the preceding statement.

-어 : (두루낮춤으로) 어떤 사실을 서술하거나 물음, 명령, 권유를 나타내는 종결 어미.
no equivalent expression
(informal addressee-lowering) A sentence-final ending used to describe a certain fact, ask a question, give an order, or advise. <description>

햄버거 먹+[고 싶]+어.

햄버거 (noun) : 둥근 빵 사이에 고기와 채소와 치즈 등을 끼운 음식.
hamburger
Food made by putting meat, vegetables, cheese, etc., between two round buns.

먹다 (verb) : 음식 등을 입을 통하여 배 속에 들여보내다.
eat; have; consume; take
To put food into one's mouth and take it in one's stomach.

-고 싶다 : 앞의 말이 나타내는 행동을 하기를 원함을 나타내는 표현.
no equivalent expression
An expression used to state that the speaker wants to do the act mentioned in the preceding statement.

-어 : (두루낮춤으로) 어떤 사실을 서술하거나 물음, 명령, 권유를 나타내는 종결 어미.
no equivalent expression
(informal addressee-lowering) A sentence-final ending used to describe a certain fact, ask a question, give an order, or advise. <description>

돈가스 먹+[고 싶]+어.

돈가스 (noun) : 도톰하게 썬 돼지고기를 양념하여 빵가루를 묻히고 기름에 튀긴 음식.
pork cutlet
Thick slices of pork seasoned, coated with bread crumbs, and fried in oil.

먹다 (verb) : 음식 등을 입을 통하여 배 속에 들여보내다.
eat; have; consume; take
To put food into one's mouth and take it in one's stomach.

-고 싶다 : 앞의 말이 나타내는 행동을 하기를 원함을 나타내는 표현.
no equivalent expression
An expression used to state that the speaker wants to do the act mentioned in the preceding statement.

-어 : (두루낮춤으로) 어떤 사실을 서술하거나 물음, 명령, 권유를 나타내는 종결 어미.
no equivalent expression
(informal addressee-lowering) A sentence-final ending used to describe a certain fact, ask a question, give an order, or advise. <description>

시키+[어 주]+어, 시키+[어 주]+어.
시켜 줘　　　시켜 줘

시키다 (verb) : 음식이나 술, 음료 등을 주문하다.
order
To order food, alcohol, beverages, etc.

-어 주다 : 남을 위해 앞의 말이 나타내는 행동을 함을 나타내는 표현.
no equivalent expression
An expression used to indicate that one does the act mentioned in the preceding statement for someone.

-어 : (두루낮춤으로) 어떤 사실을 서술하거나 물음, 명령, 권유를 나타내는 종결 어미.
no equivalent expression
(informal addressee-lowering) A sentence-final ending used to describe a certain fact, ask a question, give an order, or advise. <order>

전부 시키+[어 주]+어.
시켜 줘

전부 (adverb) : 빠짐없이 다.
all
Wholly without anything omitted.

시키다 (verb) : 음식이나 술, 음료 등을 주문하다.
order
To order food, alcohol, beverages, etc.

-어 주다 : 남을 위해 앞의 말이 나타내는 행동을 함을 나타내는 표현.
no equivalent expression
An expression used to indicate that one does the act mentioned in the preceding statement for someone.

-어 : (두루낮춤으로) 어떤 사실을 서술하거나 물음, 명령, 권유를 나타내는 종결 어미.
no equivalent expression
(informal addressee-lowering) A sentence-final ending used to describe a certain fact, ask a question, give an order, or advise. <order>

시키+어, 뭐+든지 시키+어.
시켜 시켜

시키다 (verb) : 음식이나 술, 음료 등을 주문하다.
order
To order food, alcohol, beverages, etc.

-어 : (두루낮춤으로) 어떤 사실을 서술하거나 물음, 명령, 권유를 나타내는 종결 어미.
no equivalent expression
(informal addressee-lowering) A sentence-final ending used to describe a certain fact, ask a question, give an order, or advise. <order>

뭐 (pronoun) : 정해지지 않은 대상이나 굳이 이름을 밝힐 필요가 없는 대상을 가리키는 말.
what
A pronoun used to refer to a subject that does not need to be specified or named.

든지 : 어느 것이 선택되어도 차이가 없음을 나타내는 조사.
no equivalent expression
A postpositional particle used when it does not matter which one is chosen.

시키다 (verb) : 음식이나 술, 음료 등을 주문하다.
order
To order food, alcohol, beverages, etc.

-어 : (두루낮춤으로) 어떤 사실을 서술하거나 물음, 명령, 권유를 나타내는 종결 어미.
no equivalent expression
(informal addressee-lowering) A sentence-final ending used to describe a certain fact, ask a question, give an order, or advise. <order>

시키+어, 전부 다 시키+어.
시켜 시켜

시키다 (verb) : 음식이나 술, 음료 등을 주문하다.
order
To order food, alcohol, beverages, etc.

-어 : (두루낮춤으로) 어떤 사실을 서술하거나 물음, 명령, 권유를 나타내는 종결 어미.
no equivalent expression
(informal addressee-lowering) A sentence-final ending used to describe a certain fact, ask a question, give an order, or advise. <order>

전부 (adverb) : 빠짐없이 다.
all
Wholly without anything omitted.

다 (adverb) : 남거나 빠진 것이 없이 모두.
all; everything
With nothing left over or missing.

시키다 (verb) : 음식이나 술, 음료 등을 주문하다.
order
To order food, alcohol, beverages, etc.

-어 : (두루낮춤으로) 어떤 사실을 서술하거나 물음, 명령, 권유를 나타내는 종결 어미.
no equivalent expression
(informal addressee-lowering) A sentence-final ending used to describe a certain fact, ask a question, give an order, or advise. <order>

먹+[고 싶]+[은 거], 맛보+[고 싶]+[은 거] 전부 다 시키+어.
시켜

먹다 (verb) : 음식 등을 입을 통하여 배 속에 들여보내다.
eat; have; consume; take
To put food into one's mouth and take it in one's stomach.

-고 싶다 : 앞의 말이 나타내는 행동을 하기를 원함을 나타내는 표현.
no equivalent expression
An expression used to state that the speaker wants to do the act mentioned in the preceding statement.

-은 거 : 명사가 아닌 것을 문장에서 명사처럼 쓰이게 하거나 '이다' 앞에 쓰일 수 있게 할 때 쓰는 표현.
no equivalent expression
An expression used to enable a non-noun word to be used as a noun in the sentence or to be used in front of '이다' (be).

맛보다 (verb) : 음식의 맛을 알기 위해 먹어 보다.
taste
To taste in order to figure out the taste of the food.

-고 싶다 : 앞의 말이 나타내는 행동을 하기를 원함을 나타내는 표현.
no equivalent expression
An expression used to state that the speaker wants to do the act mentioned in the preceding statement.

-은 거 : 명사가 아닌 것을 문장에서 명사처럼 쓰이게 하거나 '이다' 앞에 쓰일 수 있게 할 때 쓰는 표현.
no equivalent expression
An expression used to enable a non-noun word to be used as a noun in the sentence or to be used in front of '이다' (be).

전부 (adverb) : 빠짐없이 다.
all
Wholly without anything omitted.

다 (adverb) : 남거나 빠진 것이 없이 모두.
all; everything
With nothing left over or missing.

시키다 (verb) : 음식이나 술, 음료 등을 주문하다.
order
To order food, alcohol, beverages, etc.

-어 : (두루낮춤으로) 어떤 사실을 서술하거나 물음, 명령, 권유를 나타내는 종결 어미.
no equivalent expression
(informal addressee-lowering) A sentence-final ending used to describe a certain fact, ask a question, give an order, or advise. <order>

초밥+도, 짜장면+도, 짬뽕+도, 탕수육+도.

초밥 (noun) : 식초와 소금으로 간을 하여 작게 뭉친 흰밥에 생선을 얹거나 김, 유부 등으로 싸서 만든 일본 음식.

sushi; roll

A Japanese dish made by placing fish on a small ball of rice seasoned with vinegar and salt, or by wrapping the rice ball with dried laver, fried tofu, etc.

도 : 둘 이상의 것을 나열함을 나타내는 조사.

no equivalent expression

A postpositional particle used to list two or more things.

짜장면 (noun) : 중국식 된장에 고기와 채소 등을 넣어 볶은 양념에 면을 비벼 먹는 음식.

jajangmyeon

A dish made by making sauce by stir-frying chopped meat, vegetables, etc., with Chinese soybean paste and then mixing noodles with the sauce.

도 : 둘 이상의 것을 나열함을 나타내는 조사.

no equivalent expression

A postpositional particle used to list two or more things.

짬뽕 (noun) : 여러 가지 해물과 야채를 볶고 매콤한 국물을 부어 만든 중국식 국수.

jjamppong

Chinese-style noodle dish made by pouring a spicy stock of stir-fried vegetables and seafood over noodles.

도 : 둘 이상의 것을 나열함을 나타내는 조사.

no equivalent expression

A postpositional particle used to list two or more things.

탕수육 (noun) : 튀김옷을 입혀 튀긴 고기에 식초, 간장, 설탕, 채소 등을 넣고 끓인 녹말 물을 부어 만든 중국요리.

sweet and sour pork

A Chinese dish made by frying flour-coated meat, and pouring a boiled mixture of vinegar, soybean sauce, sugar, vegetables, etc., over the meat.

도 : 둘 이상의 것을 나열함을 나타내는 조사.

no equivalent expression

A postpositional particle used to list two or more things.

떡볶이+도, 순대+도, 김밥+도, 냉면+도.

떡볶이 (noun) : 적당히 자른 가래떡에 간장이나 고추장 등의 양념과 여러 가지 채소를 넣고 볶은 음식.
tteokbokki
Boiled rice cake with seasoning, made by boiling garaetteok, rice cake stick, vegetables, seasonings such as soy sauce, gochujang, red chili paste, etc.

도 : 둘 이상의 것을 나열함을 나타내는 조사.
no equivalent expression
A postpositional particle used to list two or more things.

순대 (noun) : 당면, 두부, 찹쌀 등을 양념하여 돼지의 창자 속에 넣고 찐 음식.
sundae
A dish made by steaming seasoned sweet potato noodles, tofu, glutinous rice, etc. which are stuffed into a pig's intestine.

도 : 둘 이상의 것을 나열함을 나타내는 조사.
no equivalent expression
A postpositional particle used to list two or more things.

김밥 (noun) : 밥과 여러 가지 반찬을 김으로 말아 싸서 썰어 먹는 음식.
gimbap
A dish made by rolling rice and various other ingredients in dried laver seaweed and cutting them into bite-size slices.

도 : 둘 이상의 것을 나열함을 나타내는 조사.
no equivalent expression
A postpositional particle used to list two or more things.

냉면 (noun) : 국수를 냉국이나 김칫국 등에 말거나 고추장 양념에 비벼서 먹는 음식.
naengmyeon; cold buckwheat noodles
A dish made by putting noodles in naengguk, cold soup, kimchitguk, kimchi soup, or mixing gochujang, red chili paste, seasoning, etc.

도 : 둘 이상의 것을 나열함을 나타내는 조사.
no equivalent expression
A postpositional particle used to list two or more things.

시키+어, 시키+어, 뭐+든지 시키+어.
시켜 시켜 시켜

시키다 (verb) : 음식이나 술, 음료 등을 주문하다.
order
To order food, alcohol, beverages, etc.

-어 : (두루낮춤으로) 어떤 사실을 서술하거나 물음, 명령, 권유를 나타내는 종결 어미.
no equivalent expression
(informal addressee-lowering) A sentence-final ending used to describe a certain fact, ask a question, give an order, or advise. <order>

뭐 (pronoun) : 정해지지 않은 대상이나 굳이 이름을 밝힐 필요가 없는 대상을 가리키는 말.
what
A pronoun used to refer to a subject that does not need to be specified or named.

든지 : 어느 것이 선택되어도 차이가 없음을 나타내는 조사.
no equivalent expression
A postpositional particle used when it does not matter which one is chosen.

시키다 (verb) : 음식이나 술, 음료 등을 주문하다.
order
To order food, alcohol, beverages, etc.

-어 : (두루낮춤으로) 어떤 사실을 서술하거나 물음, 명령, 권유를 나타내는 종결 어미.
no equivalent expression
(informal addressee-lowering) A sentence-final ending used to describe a certain fact, ask a question, give an order, or advise. <order>

먹+[고 싶]+[은 거] 다 시키+어.
시켜

먹다 (verb) : 음식 등을 입을 통하여 배 속에 들여보내다.
eat; have; consume; take
To put food into one's mouth and take it in one's stomach.

-고 싶다 : 앞의 말이 나타내는 행동을 하기를 원함을 나타내는 표현.
no equivalent expression
An expression used to state that the speaker wants to do the act mentioned in the preceding statement.

-은 거 : 명사가 아닌 것을 문장에서 명사처럼 쓰이게 하거나 '이다' 앞에 쓰일 수 있게 할 때 쓰는 표현.
no equivalent expression
An expression used to enable a non-noun word to be used as a noun in the sentence or to be used in front of '이다' (be).

다 (adverb) : 남거나 빠진 것이 없이 모두.
all; everything
With nothing left over or missing.

시키다 (verb) : 음식이나 술, 음료 등을 주문하다.
order
To order food, alcohol, beverages, etc.

-어 : (두루낮춤으로) 어떤 사실을 서술하거나 물음, 명령, 권유를 나타내는 종결 어미.
no equivalent expression
(informal addressee-lowering) A sentence-final ending used to describe a certain fact, ask a question, give an order, or advise. <order>

뭐+든지 다 시키+[어 주]+ㄹ게.
시켜 줄게

뭐 (pronoun) : 정해지지 않은 대상이나 굳이 이름을 밝힐 필요가 없는 대상을 가리키는 말.
what
A pronoun used to refer to a subject that does not need to be specified or named.

든지 : 어느 것이 선택되어도 차이가 없음을 나타내는 조사.
no equivalent expression
A postpositional particle used when it does not matter which one is chosen.

다 (adverb) : 남거나 빠진 것이 없이 모두.
all; everything
With nothing left over or missing.

시키다 (verb) : 음식이나 술, 음료 등을 주문하다.
order
To order food, alcohol, beverages, etc.

-어 주다 : 남을 위해 앞의 말이 나타내는 행동을 함을 나타내는 표현.
no equivalent expression
An expression used to indicate that one does the act mentioned in the preceding statement for someone.

-ㄹ게 : (두루낮춤으로) 말하는 사람이 어떤 행동을 할 것을 듣는 사람에게 약속하거나 의지를 나타내는 종결 어미.
no equivalent expression
(informal addressee-lowering) A sentence-final ending used when the speaker promises or notifies the listener that he/she will do something.

전부 다 시키+[어 주]+ㄹ게.
시켜 줄게

전부 (adverb) : 빠짐없이 다.
all
Wholly without anything omitted.

다 (adverb) : 남거나 빠진 것이 없이 모두.
all; everything
With nothing left over or missing.

시키다 (verb) : 음식이나 술, 음료 등을 주문하다.
order
To order food, alcohol, beverages, etc.

-어 주다 : 남을 위해 앞의 말이 나타내는 행동을 함을 나타내는 표현.
no equivalent expression
An expression used to indicate that one does the act mentioned in the preceding statement for someone.

-ㄹ게 : (두루낮춤으로) 말하는 사람이 어떤 행동을 할 것을 듣는 사람에게 약속하거나 의지를 나타내는 종결 어미.
no equivalent expression
(informal addressee-lowering) A sentence-final ending used when the speaker promises or notifies the listener that he/she will do something.

언니+는 언제나 최고+(이)+야.

언닌 최고야

언니 (noun) : 여자가 형제나 친척 형제들 중에서 자기보다 나이가 많은 여자를 이르거나 부르는 말.
older sister
A word used only by a female to refer to or address her female siblings or cousins older than herself.

는 : 문장 속에서 어떤 대상이 화제임을 나타내는 조사.
no equivalent expression
A postpositional particle used to indicate that a certain subject is the topic of a sentence.

언제나 (adverb) : 어느 때에나. 또는 때에 따라 달라지지 않고 변함없이.
always; all the time
Every time; invariably without changing with time.

최고 (noun) : 가장 좋거나 뛰어난 것.
the best
The state of being the best or the most advanced.

이다 : 주어가 지시하는 대상의 속성이나 부류를 지정하는 뜻을 나타내는 서술격 조사.
no equivalent expression
A predicate particle indicating the meaning of the attribute or category of the thing that the subject of the sentence refers to.

-야 : (두루낮춤으로) 어떤 사실에 대하여 서술하거나 물음을 나타내는 종결 어미.
no equivalent expression
(informal addressee-lowering) A sentence-final ending used to describe a certain fact or ask a question. <description>

최고, 최고, 최고.

최고 (noun) : 가장 좋거나 뛰어난 것.
the best
The state of being the best or the most advanced.

오빠+는 언제나 최고+(이)+야.
오빤 최고야

오빠 (noun) : 여자가 형제나 친척 형제들 중에서 자기보다 나이가 많은 남자를 이르거나 부르는 말.
elder brother
A word used only by a girl to refer to or address her male siblings or cousins older than herself.

는 : 문장 속에서 어떤 대상이 화제임을 나타내는 조사.
no equivalent expression
A postpositional particle used to indicate that a certain subject is the topic of a sentence.

언제나 (adverb) : 어느 때에나. 또는 때에 따라 달라지지 않고 변함없이.
always; all the time
Every time; invariably without changing with time.

최고 (noun) : 가장 좋거나 뛰어난 것.
the best
The state of being the best or the most advanced.

이다 : 주어가 지시하는 대상의 속성이나 부류를 지정하는 뜻을 나타내는 서술격 조사.
no equivalent expression
A predicate particle indicating the meaning of the attribute or category of the thing that the subject of the sentence refers to.

-야 : (두루낮춤으로) 어떤 사실에 대하여 서술하거나 물음을 나타내는 종결 어미.
no equivalent expression
(informal addressee-lowering) A sentence-final ending used to describe a certain fact or ask a question. <description>

최고, 최고, 오빠 최고.

최고 (noun) : 가장 좋거나 뛰어난 것.
the best
The state of being the best or the most advanced.

오빠 (noun) : 여자가 형제나 친척 형제들 중에서 자기보다 나이가 많은 남자를 이르거나 부르는 말.
elder brother
A word used only by a girl to refer to or address her male siblings or cousins older than herself.

최고 (noun) : 가장 좋거나 뛰어난 것.
the best
The state of being the best or the most advanced.

엄마+가 최고+(이)+야, 엄마 최고.
최고야

엄마 (noun) : 격식을 갖추지 않아도 되는 상황에서 어머니를 이르거나 부르는 말.
mom
A word used to refer to or address one's mother in an informal situation.

가 : 어떤 상태나 상황에 놓인 대상이나 동작의 주체를 나타내는 조사.
no equivalent expression
A postpositional particle referring to a subject under a certain state or situation, or the subject of an act.

최고 (noun) : 가장 좋거나 뛰어난 것.
the best
The state of being the best or the most advanced.

이다 : 주어가 지시하는 대상의 속성이나 부류를 지정하는 뜻을 나타내는 서술격 조사.
no equivalent expression
A predicate particle indicating the meaning of the attribute or category of the thing that the subject of the sentence refers to.

-야 : (두루낮춤으로) 어떤 사실에 대하여 서술하거나 물음을 나타내는 종결 어미.
no equivalent expression
(informal addressee-lowering) A sentence-final ending used to describe a certain fact or ask a question. <description>

엄마 (noun) : 격식을 갖추지 않아도 되는 상황에서 어머니를 이르거나 부르는 말.
mom
A word used to refer to or address one's mother in an informal situation.

최고 (noun) : 가장 좋거나 뛰어난 것.
the best
The state of being the best or the most advanced.

아빠+가 최고+(이)+야, 아빠 최고.
최고야

아빠 (noun) : 격식을 갖추지 않아도 되는 상황에서 아버지를 이르거나 부르는 말.
dad; daddy
A word used to refer to or address a father in an informal situation.

가 : 어떤 상태나 상황에 놓인 대상이나 동작의 주체를 나타내는 조사.
no equivalent expression
A postpositional particle referring to a subject under a certain state or situation, or the subject of an act.

최고 (noun) : 가장 좋거나 뛰어난 것.
the best
The state of being the best or the most advanced.

이다 : 주어가 지시하는 대상의 속성이나 부류를 지정하는 뜻을 나타내는 서술격 조사.
no equivalent expression
A predicate particle indicating the meaning of the attribute or category of the thing that the subject of the sentence refers to.

-야 : (두루낮춤으로) 어떤 사실에 대하여 서술하거나 물음을 나타내는 종결 어미.
no equivalent expression
(informal addressee-lowering) A sentence-final ending used to describe a certain fact or ask a question. <description>

아빠 (noun) : 격식을 갖추지 않아도 되는 상황에서 아버지를 이르거나 부르는 말.
dad; daddy
A word used to refer to or address a father in an informal situation.

최고 **(noun)** : 가장 좋거나 뛰어난 것.
the best
The state of being the best or the most advanced.

최고, 최고, 언니 최고.

최고 **(noun)** : 가장 좋거나 뛰어난 것.
the best
The state of being the best or the most advanced.

언니 **(noun)** : 여자가 형제나 친척 형제들 중에서 자기보다 나이가 많은 여자를 이르거나 부르는 말.
older sister
A word used only by a female to refer to or address her female siblings or cousins older than herself.

최고 **(noun)** : 가장 좋거나 뛰어난 것.
the best
The state of being the best or the most advanced.

오빠+가 최고+(이)+야, 오빠 최고.
최고야

오빠 **(noun)** : 여자가 형제나 친척 형제들 중에서 자기보다 나이가 많은 남자를 이르거나 부르는 말.
elder brother
A word used only by a girl to refer to or address her male siblings or cousins older than herself.

가 : 어떤 상태나 상황에 놓인 대상이나 동작의 주체를 나타내는 조사.
no equivalent expression
A postpositional particle referring to a subject under a certain state or situation, or the subject of an act.

최고 **(noun)** : 가장 좋거나 뛰어난 것.
the best
The state of being the best or the most advanced.

이다 : 주어가 지시하는 대상의 속성이나 부류를 지정하는 뜻을 나타내는 서술격 조사.
no equivalent expression
A predicate particle indicating the meaning of the attribute or category of the thing that the subject of the sentence refers to.

-야 : (두루낮춤으로) 어떤 사실에 대하여 서술하거나 물음을 나타내는 종결 어미.
no equivalent expression
(informal addressee-lowering) A sentence-final ending used to describe a certain fact or ask a question. <description>

오빠 (noun) : 여자가 형제나 친척 형제들 중에서 자기보다 나이가 많은 남자를 이르거나 부르는 말.
elder brother
A word used only by a girl to refer to or address her male siblings or cousins older than herself.

최고 (noun) : 가장 좋거나 뛰어난 것.
the best
The state of being the best or the most advanced.

< 9 >

어쩌라고?

나한테 어떻게 하라고?
(What do you want me to do?)

[발음(pronunciation)]

< 1 절(verse) >

가라고, 가라고, 가라고.
가라고, 가라고, 가라고.
garago, garago, garago.

보기 싫으니까 가라고, 가라고.
보기 시르니까 가라고, 가라고.
bogi sireunikka garago, garago.

알았어.
아라써.
arasseo.

나 갈게.
나 갈게.
na galge.

가란다고 진짜 가.
가란다고 진짜 가.
garandago jinjja ga.

알았어.
아라써.
arasseo.

안 갈게.
안 갈께.
an galge.

가라는데 왜 안 가?
가라는데 왜 안 가?
garaneunde wae an ga?

알았어.
아라써.
arasseo.

가면 되지.
가면 되지.
gamyeon doeji.

가라고 하면 안 가야지.
가라고 하면 안 가야지.
garago hamyeon an gayaji.

짜증 나, 짜증 나, 짜증 나.
짜증 나, 짜증 나, 짜증 나.
jjajeung na, jjajeung na, jjajeung na.

어쩌라고? 어쩌라고? 어쩌라고? 어쩌라고?
어쩌라고? 어쩌라고? 어쩌라고? 어쩌라고?
eojjeorago? eojjeorago? eojjeorago? eojjeorago?

도대체 나보고 어쩌라고?
도대체 나보고 어쩌라고?
dodaeche nabogo eojjeorago?

도대체 나보고 어쩌라고?
도대체 나보고 어쩌라고?
dodaeche nabogo eojjeorago?

도대체 나보고 어쩌라고?
도대체 나보고 어쩌라고?
dodaeche nabogo eojjeorago?

어쩌라고?
어쩌라고?
eojjeorago?

< 2 절(verse) >

왜 안 가?
왜 안 가?
wae an ga?

왜 안 가?
왜 안 가?
wae an ga?

왜 안 가?
왜 안 가?
wae an ga?

가라는데 왜 안 가?
가라는데 왜 안 가?
garaneunde wae an ga?

왜 안 가?
왜 안 가?
wae an ga?

알았어.
아라써.
arasseo.

가면 되지.
가면 되지.
gamyeon doeji.

가란다고 진짜 가.
가란다고 진짜 가.
garandago jinjja ga.

가라는데 왜 안 가?
가라는데 왜 안 가?
garaneunde wae an ga?

가도 화내.
가도 화내.
gado hwanae.

안 가도 화내.
안 가도 화내.
an gado hwanae.

짜증 나, 짜증 나, 짜증 나.
짜증 나, 짜증 나, 짜증 나.
jjajeung na, jjajeung na, jjajeung na.

어쩌라고? 어쩌라고? 어쩌라고? 어쩌라고?
어쩌라고? 어쩌라고? 어쩌라고? 어쩌라고?
eojjeorago? eojjeorago? eojjeorago? eojjeorago?

도대체 나보고 어쩌라고?
도대체 나보고 어쩌라고?
dodaeche nabogo eojjeorago?

도대체 나보고 어쩌라고?
도대체 나보고 어쩌라고?
dodaeche nabogo eojjeorago?

도대체 나보고 어쩌라고?
도대체 나보고 어쩌라고?
dodaeche nabogo eojjeorago?

어쩌라고?
어쩌라고?
eojjeorago?

가라고, 가라고, 가라고.
가라고, 가라고, 가라고.
garago, garago, garago.

보기 싫으니까 가라고, 가라고.
보기 시르니까 가라고, 가라고.
bogi sireunikka garago, garago.

알았어.
아라써
arasseo.

나 갈게.
나 갈께
na galge.

어쩌라고?
어쩌라고?
eojjeorago?

< 1 절(verse) >

가+라고, 가+라고, 가+라고.

가다 (verb) : 한 곳에서 다른 곳으로 장소를 이동하다.
go; travel
To move from one place to another place.

-라고 : (두루낮춤으로) 말하는 사람의 생각이나 주장을 듣는 사람에게 강조하여 말함을 나타내는 종결 어미.
no equivalent expression
(informal addressee-lowering) A sentence-final ending used to emphatically state the speaker's thoughts or argument to the listener.

보+기 싫+으니까 가+라고, 가+라고.

보다 (verb) : 눈으로 대상의 존재나 겉모습을 알다.
see; look at; notice
To perceive with eyes the existence or appearance of an object.

-기 : 앞의 말이 명사의 기능을 하게 하는 어미.
no equivalent expression
An ending of a word used to make the preceding word function as a noun.

싫다 (adjective) : 어떤 일을 하고 싶지 않다.
unwilling; loath
Not wanting to do something.

-으니까 : 뒤에 오는 말에 대하여 앞에 오는 말이 원인이나 근거, 전제가 됨을 강조하여 나타내는 연결 어미.
no equivalent expression
A connective ending used to emphasize that the preceding statement is the cause, reason, or premise for the following statement.

가다 (verb) : 한 곳에서 다른 곳으로 장소를 이동하다.
go; travel
To move from one place to another place.

-라고 : (두루낮춤으로) 말하는 사람의 생각이나 주장을 듣는 사람에게 강조하여 말함을 나타내는 종결 어미.
no equivalent expression
(informal addressee-lowering) A sentence-final ending used to emphatically state the speaker's thoughts or argument to the listener.

알+았+어.

알다 (verb) : 상대방의 어떤 명령이나 요청에 대해 그대로 하겠다는 동의의 뜻을 나타내는 말.
will; say yes
To respond affirmatively to an order or request, agreeing to do as one has been told.

-았- : 어떤 사건이 과거에 완료되었거나 그 사건의 결과가 현재까지 지속되는 상황을 나타내는 어미.
no equivalent expression
An ending of a word used to indicate that an event was completed in the past or its result continues in the present.

-어 : (두루낮춤으로) 어떤 사실을 서술하거나 물음, 명령, 권유를 나타내는 종결 어미.
no equivalent expression
(informal addressee-lowering) A sentence-final ending used to describe a certain fact, ask a question, give an order, or advise. <description>

나 가+ㄹ게.
갈게

나 (pronoun) : 말하는 사람이 친구나 아랫사람에게 자기를 가리키는 말.
I
A pronoun used to indicate oneself to a friend or a younger person.

가다 (verb) : 한 곳에서 다른 곳으로 장소를 이동하다.
go; travel
To move from one place to another place.

-ㄹ게 : (두루낮춤으로) 말하는 사람이 어떤 행동을 할 것을 듣는 사람에게 약속하거나 의지를 나타내는 종결 어미.
no equivalent expression
(informal addressee-lowering) A sentence-final ending used when the speaker promises or notifies the listener that he/she will do something.

가+라고 하+ㄴ다고 진짜 가+(아).
가란다고 가

가다 (verb) : 한 곳에서 다른 곳으로 장소를 이동하다.
go; travel
To move from one place to another place.

-라고 : 다른 사람에게서 들은 내용을 간접적으로 전달하거나 주어의 생각, 의견 등을 나타내는 표현.
no equivalent expression
An expression used to pass along what the speaker heard from another person, or to present the subject's thoughts, opinions, etc.

하다 (verb) : 무엇에 대해 말하다.
say
To talk about something.

-ㄴ다고 : 어떤 행위의 목적, 의도를 나타내거나 어떤 상황의 이유, 원인을 나타내는 연결 어미.
no equivalent expression
A connective ending used when implying the purpose or intention of a certain action, or the reason or cause of a certain situation.

진짜 (adverb) : 꾸밈이나 거짓이 없이 참으로.
genuinely; really
Truly, without hypocrisy or dishonesty.

가다 (verb) : 한 곳에서 다른 곳으로 장소를 이동하다.
go; travel
To move from one place to another place.

-아 : (두루낮춤으로) 어떤 사실을 서술하거나 물음, 명령, 권유를 나타내는 종결 어미.
no equivalent expression
(informal addressee-lowering) A sentence-final ending used to describe a certain fact, ask a question, give an order, or advise. <description>

알+았+어.

알다 (verb) : 상대방의 어떤 명령이나 요청에 대해 그대로 하겠다는 동의의 뜻을 나타내는 말.
will; say yes
To respond affirmatively to an order or request, agreeing to do as one has been told.

-았- : 어떤 사건이 과거에 완료되었거나 그 사건의 결과가 현재까지 지속되는 상황을 나타내는 어미.
no equivalent expression
An ending of a word used to indicate that an event was completed in the past or its result continues in the present.

-어 : (두루낮춤으로) 어떤 사실을 서술하거나 물음, 명령, 권유를 나타내는 종결 어미.
no equivalent expression
(informal addressee-lowering) A sentence-final ending used to describe a certain fact, ask a question, give an order, or advise. <description>

안 가+ㄹ게.
갈게

안 (adverb) : 부정이나 반대의 뜻을 나타내는 말.
not
An adverb that has the meaning of negation or opposite.

가다 (verb) : 한 곳에서 다른 곳으로 장소를 이동하다.
go; travel
To move from one place to another place.

-ㄹ게 : (두루낮춤으로) 말하는 사람이 어떤 행동을 할 것을 듣는 사람에게 약속하거나 의지를 나타내는 종결 어미.
no equivalent expression
(informal addressee-lowering) A sentence-final ending used when the speaker promises or notifies the listener that he/she will do something.

가+라는데 왜 안 가+(아)?
가

가다 (verb) : 한 곳에서 다른 곳으로 장소를 이동하다.
go; travel
To move from one place to another place.

-라는데 : 명령이나 요청 등의 말을 전달하며 자신의 말을 이어 나타내는 표현.
no equivalent expression
An expression used to convey someone's remark, such as an order, request, etc., and to continue the sentence.

왜 (adverb) : 무슨 이유로. 또는 어째서.
why
For what reason; how come.

안 (adverb) : 부정이나 반대의 뜻을 나타내는 말.
not
An adverb that has the meaning of negation or opposite.

가다 (verb) : 한 곳에서 다른 곳으로 장소를 이동하다.
go; travel
To move from one place to another place.

-아 : (두루낮춤으로) 어떤 사실을 서술하거나 물음, 명령, 권유를 나타내는 종결 어미.
no equivalent expression
(informal addressee-lowering) A sentence-final ending used to describe a certain fact, ask a question, give an order, or advise. <question>

알+았+어.

알다 (verb) : 상대방의 어떤 명령이나 요청에 대해 그대로 하겠다는 동의의 뜻을 나타내는 말.
will; say yes
To respond affirmatively to an order or request, agreeing to do as one has been told.

-았- : 어떤 사건이 과거에 완료되었거나 그 사건의 결과가 현재까지 지속되는 상황을 나타내는 어미.
no equivalent expression
An ending of a word used to indicate that an event was completed in the past or its result continues in the present.

-어 : (두루낮춤으로) 어떤 사실을 서술하거나 물음, 명령, 권유를 나타내는 종결 어미.
no equivalent expression
(informal addressee-lowering) A sentence-final ending used to describe a certain fact, ask a question, give an order, or advise. <description>

가+[면 되]+지.

가다 (verb) : 한 곳에서 다른 곳으로 장소를 이동하다.
go; travel
To move from one place to another place.

-면 되다 : 조건이 되는 어떤 행동을 하거나 어떤 상태만 갖추어지면 문제가 없거나 충분함을 나타내는 표현.
no equivalent expression
An expression used to indicate that, as long as one does or reaches a certain act or state, there is no problem or it is enough.

-지 : (두루낮춤으로) 말하는 사람이 자신에 대한 이야기나 자신의 생각을 친근하게 말할 때 쓰는 종결 어미.
no equivalent expression
(informal addressee-lowering) A sentence-final ending used when the speaker talks about himself/herself or his/her thoughts in a friendly manner.

가+라고 하+면 안 가+(아)야지.
가야지

가다 (verb) : 한 곳에서 다른 곳으로 장소를 이동하다.
go; travel
To move from one place to another place.

-라고 : 다른 사람에게서 들은 내용을 간접적으로 전달하거나 주어의 생각, 의견 등을 나타내는 표현.
no equivalent expression
An expression used to pass along what the speaker heard from another person, or to present the subject's thoughts, opinions, etc.

하다 (verb) : 무엇에 대해 말하다.
say
To talk about something.

-면 : 뒤에 오는 말에 대한 근거나 조건이 됨을 나타내는 연결 어미.
no equivalent expression
A connective ending used when the preceding statement becomes the reason or condition of the following statement.

안 (adverb) : 부정이나 반대의 뜻을 나타내는 말.
not
An adverb that has the meaning of negation or opposite.

가다 (verb) : 한 곳에서 다른 곳으로 장소를 이동하다.
go; travel
To move from one place to another place.

-아야지 : (두루낮춤으로) 듣는 사람이나 다른 사람이 어떤 일을 해야 하거나 어떤 상태여야 함을 나타내는 종결 어미.
no equivalent expression
(informal addressee-lowering) A sentence-final ending used to indicate that the listener or another person is supposed to do a certain thing or be in a certain state.

짜증 나+(아), 짜증 나+(아), 짜증 나+(아).
나 나 나

짜증 (noun) : 마음에 들지 않아서 화를 내거나 싫은 느낌을 겉으로 드러내는 일. 또는 그런 성미.
irritation; annoyance
An act of expressing one's anger or dislike towards something because one is dissatisfied, or such a disposition.

나다 (verb) : 어떤 감정이나 느낌이 생기다.
feel
To feel a certain emotion or sensation.

-아 : (두루낮춤으로) 어떤 사실을 서술하거나 물음, 명령, 권유를 나타내는 종결 어미.
no equivalent expression
(informal addressee-lowering) A sentence-final ending used to describe a certain fact, ask a question, give an order, or advise. <description>

어쩌+라고? 어쩌+라고? 어쩌+라고? 어쩌+라고?

어쩌다 (verb) : 무엇을 어떻게 하다.
do
To do something in a certain way.

-라고 : (두루낮춤으로) 들은 사실을 되물으면서 확인함을 나타내는 종결 어미.
no equivalent expression
(informal addressee-lowering) A sentence-final ending used to ask again about a fact that one heard and confirm it.

도대체 나+보고 어쩌+라고?

도대체 (adverb) : 아주 궁금해서 묻는 말인데.
what on earth; how on earth; why on earth
Asking just out of curiosity.

나 (pronoun) : 말하는 사람이 친구나 아랫사람에게 자기를 가리키는 말.
I
A pronoun used to indicate oneself to a friend or a younger person.

보고 : 어떤 행동이 미치는 대상임을 나타내는 조사.
no equivalent expression
A postpositional particle used when something is the subject that an act has an influence on.

어쩌다 (verb) : 무엇을 어떻게 하다.
do
To do something in a certain way.

-라고 : (두루낮춤으로) 들은 사실을 되물으면서 확인함을 나타내는 종결 어미.
no equivalent expression
(informal addressee-lowering) A sentence-final ending used to ask again about a fact that one heard and confirm it.

어쩌+라고?

어쩌다 (verb) : 무엇을 어떻게 하다.
do
To do something in a certain way.

-라고 : (두루낮춤으로) 들은 사실을 되물으면서 확인함을 나타내는 종결 어미.
no equivalent expression
(informal addressee-lowering) A sentence-final ending used to ask again about a fact that one heard and confirm it.

< 2 절(verse) >

왜 안 가+(아)? 왜 안 가+(아)? 왜 안 가+(아)?
가 가 가

왜 (adverb) : 무슨 이유로. 또는 어째서.
why
For what reason; how come.

안 (adverb) : 부정이나 반대의 뜻을 나타내는 말.
not
An adverb that has the meaning of negation or opposite.

가다 (verb) : 한 곳에서 다른 곳으로 장소를 이동하다.
go; travel
To move from one place to another place.

-아 : (두루낮춤으로) 어떤 사실을 서술하거나 물음, 명령, 권유를 나타내는 종결 어미.
no equivalent expression
(informal addressee-lowering) A sentence-final ending used to describe a certain fact, ask a question, give an order, or advise. <question>

가+라는데 왜 안 가+(아)?
가

가다 (verb) : 한 곳에서 다른 곳으로 장소를 이동하다.
go; travel
To move from one place to another place.

-라는데 : 명령이나 요청 등의 말을 전달하며 자신의 말을 이어 나타내는 표현.
no equivalent expression
An expression used to convey someone's remark, such as an order, request, etc., and to continue the sentence.

왜 (adverb) : 무슨 이유로. 또는 어째서.
why
For what reason; how come.

안 (adverb) : 부정이나 반대의 뜻을 나타내는 말.
not
An adverb that has the meaning of negation or opposite.

가다 (verb) : 한 곳에서 다른 곳으로 장소를 이동하다.
go; travel
To move from one place to another place.

-아 : (두루낮춤으로) 어떤 사실을 서술하거나 물음, 명령, 권유를 나타내는 종결 어미.
no equivalent expression
(informal addressee-lowering) A sentence-final ending used to describe a certain fact, ask a question, give an order, or advise. <question>

왜 안 가+(아)?
가

왜 (adverb) : 무슨 이유로. 또는 어째서.
why
For what reason; how come.

안 (adverb) : 부정이나 반대의 뜻을 나타내는 말.
not
An adverb that has the meaning of negation or opposite.

가다 (verb) : 한 곳에서 다른 곳으로 장소를 이동하다.
go; travel
To move from one place to another place.

-아 : (두루낮춤으로) 어떤 사실을 서술하거나 물음, 명령, 권유를 나타내는 종결 어미.
no equivalent expression
(informal addressee-lowering) A sentence-final ending used to describe a certain fact, ask a question, give an order, or advise. <question>

알+았+어.

알다 (verb) : 상대방의 어떤 명령이나 요청에 대해 그대로 하겠다는 동의의 뜻을 나타내는 말.
will; say yes
To respond affirmatively to an order or request, agreeing to do as one has been told.

-았- : 어떤 사건이 과거에 완료되었거나 그 사건의 결과가 현재까지 지속되는 상황을 나타내는 어미.
no equivalent expression
An ending of a word used to indicate that an event was completed in the past or its result continues in the present.

-어 : (두루낮춤으로) 어떤 사실을 서술하거나 물음, 명령, 권유를 나타내는 종결 어미.
no equivalent expression
(informal addressee-lowering) A sentence-final ending used to describe a certain fact, ask a question, give an order, or advise. <description>

가+[면 되]+지.

가다 (verb) : 한 곳에서 다른 곳으로 장소를 이동하다.
go; travel
To move from one place to another place.

-면 되다 : 조건이 되는 어떤 행동을 하거나 어떤 상태만 갖추어지면 문제가 없거나 충분함을 나타내는 표현.
no equivalent expression
An expression used to indicate that, as long as one does or reaches a certain act or state, there is no problem or it is enough.

-지 : (두루낮춤으로) 말하는 사람이 자신에 대한 이야기나 자신의 생각을 친근하게 말할 때 쓰는 종결 어미.
no equivalent expression
(informal addressee-lowering) A sentence-final ending used when the speaker talks about himself/herself or his/her thoughts in a friendly manner.

가+라고 하+ㄴ다고 진짜 가+(아).
가란다고 가

가다 (verb) : 한 곳에서 다른 곳으로 장소를 이동하다.
go; travel
To move from one place to another place.

-라고 : 다른 사람에게서 들은 내용을 간접적으로 전달하거나 주어의 생각, 의견 등을 나타내는 표현.
no equivalent expression
An expression used to pass along what the speaker heard from another person, or to present the subject's thoughts, opinions, etc.

하다 (verb) : 무엇에 대해 말하다.
say
To talk about something.

-ㄴ다고 : 어떤 행위의 목적, 의도를 나타내거나 어떤 상황의 이유, 원인을 나타내는 연결 어미.
no equivalent expression
A connective ending used when implying the purpose or intention of a certain action, or the reason or cause of a certain situation.

진짜 (adverb) : 꾸밈이나 거짓이 없이 참으로.
genuinely; really
Truly, without hypocrisy or dishonesty.

가다 (verb) : 한 곳에서 다른 곳으로 장소를 이동하다.
go; travel
To move from one place to another place.

-아 : (두루낮춤으로) 어떤 사실을 서술하거나 물음, 명령, 권유를 나타내는 종결 어미.
no equivalent expression
(informal addressee-lowering) A sentence-final ending used to describe a certain fact, ask a question, give an order, or advise. <description>

가+라는데 왜 안 가+(아)?
가

가다 (verb) : 한 곳에서 다른 곳으로 장소를 이동하다.
go; travel
To move from one place to another place.

-라는데 : 명령이나 요청 등의 말을 전달하며 자신의 말을 이어 나타내는 표현.
no equivalent expression
An expression used to convey someone's remark, such as an order, request, etc., and to continue the sentence.

왜 (adverb) : 무슨 이유로. 또는 어째서.
why
For what reason; how come.

안 (adverb) : 부정이나 반대의 뜻을 나타내는 말.
not
An adverb that has the meaning of negation or opposite.

가다 (verb) : 한 곳에서 다른 곳으로 장소를 이동하다.
go; travel
To move from one place to another place.

-아 : (두루낮춤으로) 어떤 사실을 서술하거나 물음, 명령, 권유를 나타내는 종결 어미.
no equivalent expression
(informal addressee-lowering) A sentence-final ending used to describe a certain fact, ask a question, give an order, or advise. <question>

가+(아)도 화내+(어).
가도 화내

가다 (verb) : 한 곳에서 다른 곳으로 장소를 이동하다.
go; travel
To move from one place to another place.

-아도 : 앞에 오는 말을 가정하거나 인정하지만 뒤에 오는 말에는 관계가 없거나 영향을 끼치지 않음을 나타내는 연결 어미.
no equivalent expression
A connective ending used when assuming or recognizing the truth of the preceding statement, although it is not related to or does not influence the following statement.

화내다 (verb) : 몹시 기분이 상해 노여워하는 감정을 드러내다.
get angry with; be mad at
To show anger toward another, being upset with him/her.

-어 : (두루낮춤으로) 어떤 사실을 서술하거나 물음, 명령, 권유를 나타내는 종결 어미.
no equivalent expression
(informal addressee-lowering) A sentence-final ending used to describe a certain fact, ask a question, give an order, or advise. <description>

안 가+(아)도 화내+(어).
가도 화내

안 (adverb) : 부정이나 반대의 뜻을 나타내는 말.
not
An adverb that has the meaning of negation or opposite.

가다 (verb) : 한 곳에서 다른 곳으로 장소를 이동하다.
go; travel
To move from one place to another place.

-아도 : 앞에 오는 말을 가정하거나 인정하지만 뒤에 오는 말에는 관계가 없거나 영향을 끼치지 않음을 나타내는 연결 어미.
no equivalent expression
A connective ending used when assuming or recognizing the truth of the preceding statement, although it is not related to or does not influence the following statement.

화내다 (verb) : 몹시 기분이 상해 노여워하는 감정을 드러내다.
get angry with; be mad at
To show anger toward another, being upset with him/her.

-어 : (두루낮춤으로) 어떤 사실을 서술하거나 물음, 명령, 권유를 나타내는 종결 어미.
no equivalent expression
(informal addressee-lowering) A sentence-final ending used to describe a certain fact, ask a question, give an order, or advise. <description>

짜증 나+(아), 짜증 나+(아), 짜증 나+(아).
나 나 나

짜증 (noun) : 마음에 들지 않아서 화를 내거나 싫은 느낌을 겉으로 드러내는 일. 또는 그런 성미.
irritation; annoyance
An act of expressing one's anger or dislike towards something because one is dissatisfied, or such a disposition.

나다 (verb) : 어떤 감정이나 느낌이 생기다.
feel
To feel a certain emotion or sensation.

-아 : (두루낮춤으로) 어떤 사실을 서술하거나 물음, 명령, 권유를 나타내는 종결 어미.
no equivalent expression
(informal addressee-lowering) A sentence-final ending used to describe a certain fact, ask a question, give an order, or advise. <description>

어쩌+라고? 어쩌+라고? 어쩌+라고? 어쩌+라고?

어쩌다 (verb) : 무엇을 어떻게 하다.
do
To do something in a certain way.

-라고 : (두루낮춤으로) 들은 사실을 되물으면서 확인함을 나타내는 종결 어미.
no equivalent expression
(informal addressee-lowering) A sentence-final ending used to ask again about a fact that one heard and confirm it.

도대체 나+보고 어쩌+라고?

도대체 (adverb) : 아주 궁금해서 묻는 말인데.
what on earth; how on earth; why on earth
Asking just out of curiosity.

나 (pronoun) : 말하는 사람이 친구나 아랫사람에게 자기를 가리키는 말.
I
A pronoun used to indicate oneself to a friend or a younger person.

보고 : 어떤 행동이 미치는 대상임을 나타내는 조사.
no equivalent expression
A postpositional particle used when something is the subject that an act has an influence on.

어쩌다 (verb) : 무엇을 어떻게 하다.
do
To do something in a certain way.

-라고 : (두루낮춤으로) 들은 사실을 되물으면서 확인함을 나타내는 종결 어미.
no equivalent expression
(informal addressee-lowering) A sentence-final ending used to ask again about a fact that one heard and confirm it.

어쩌+라고?

어쩌다 (verb) : 무엇을 어떻게 하다.
do
To do something in a certain way.

-라고 : (두루낮춤으로) 들은 사실을 되물으면서 확인함을 나타내는 종결 어미.
no equivalent expression
(informal addressee-lowering) A sentence-final ending used to ask again about a fact that one heard and confirm it.

가+라고, 가+라고, 가+라고.

가다 (verb) : 한 곳에서 다른 곳으로 장소를 이동하다.
go; travel
To move from one place to another place.

-라고 : (두루낮춤으로) 말하는 사람의 생각이나 주장을 듣는 사람에게 강조하여 말함을 나타내는 종결 어미.
no equivalent expression
(informal addressee-lowering) A sentence-final ending used to emphatically state the speaker's thoughts or argument to the listener.

보+기 싫+으니까 가+라고, 가+라고.

보다 (verb) : 눈으로 대상의 존재나 겉모습을 알다.
see; look at; notice
To perceive with eyes the existence or appearance of an object.

-기 : 앞의 말이 명사의 기능을 하게 하는 어미.
no equivalent expression
An ending of a word used to make the preceding word function as a noun.

싫다 (adjective) : 어떤 일을 하고 싶지 않다.
unwilling; loath
Not wanting to do something.

-으니까 : 뒤에 오는 말에 대하여 앞에 오는 말이 원인이나 근거, 전제가 됨을 강조하여 나타내는 연결 어미.
no equivalent expression
A connective ending used to emphasize that the preceding statement is the cause, reason, or premise for the following statement.

가다 (verb) : 한 곳에서 다른 곳으로 장소를 이동하다.
go; travel
To move from one place to another place.

-라고 : (두루낮춤으로) 말하는 사람의 생각이나 주장을 듣는 사람에게 강조하여 말함을 나타내는 종결 어미.
no equivalent expression
(informal addressee-lowering) A sentence-final ending used to emphatically state the speaker's thoughts or argument to the listener.

알+았+어.

알다 (verb) : 상대방의 어떤 명령이나 요청에 대해 그대로 하겠다는 동의의 뜻을 나타내는 말.
will; say yes
To respond affirmatively to an order or request, agreeing to do as one has been told.

-았- : 어떤 사건이 과거에 완료되었거나 그 사건의 결과가 현재까지 지속되는 상황을 나타내는 어미.
no equivalent expression
An ending of a word used to indicate that an event was completed in the past or its result continues in the present.

-어 : (두루낮춤으로) 어떤 사실을 서술하거나 물음, 명령, 권유를 나타내는 종결 어미.
no equivalent expression
(informal addressee-lowering) A sentence-final ending used to describe a certain fact, ask a question, give an order, or advise. <description>

나 가+ㄹ게.
갈게

나 (pronoun) : 말하는 사람이 친구나 아랫사람에게 자기를 가리키는 말.
I
A pronoun used to indicate oneself to a friend or a younger person.

가다 (verb) : 한 곳에서 다른 곳으로 장소를 이동하다.
go; travel
To move from one place to another place.

-ㄹ게 : (두루낮춤으로) 말하는 사람이 어떤 행동을 할 것을 듣는 사람에게 약속하거나 의지를 나타내는 종결 어미.
no equivalent expression
(informal addressee-lowering) A sentence-final ending used when the speaker promises or notifies the listener that he/she will do something.

어쩌+라고?

어쩌다 (verb) : 무엇을 어떻게 하다.
do
To do something in a certain way.

-라고 : (두루낮춤으로) 들은 사실을 되물으면서 확인함을 나타내는 종결 어미.
no equivalent expression
(informal addressee-lowering) A sentence-final ending used to ask again about a fact that one heard and confirm it.

< 10 >

궁금해

나는 궁금해.
(I'm curious.)

[발음(pronunciation)]

< 1 절(verse) >

파도처럼 내 맘속으로 밀려 오다 바람처럼 흔적 없이 사라져.
파도처럼 내 맘소그로 밀려 오다 바람처럼 흔적 업씨 사라저.
padocheoreom nae mamsogeuro millyeooda baramcheoreom heunjeok eopsi sarajeo.

파도는 멈출 수가 없는 거니?
파도는 멈출 쑤가 엄는 거니?
padoneun meomchul suga eomneun geoni?

바람은 머물 수가 없는 거니?
바라믄 머물 쑤가 엄는 거니?
barameun meomul suga eomneun geoni?

피어나는 내 맘이 시들지 않게 그치지 않는 세찬 비를 뿌려줘.
피어나는 내 마미 시들지 안케 그치지 안는 세찬 비를 뿌려줘.
pieonaneun nae mami sideulji anke geuchiji anneun sechan bireul ppuryeojwo.

어떤 사람인지 궁금해.
어떤 사라민지 궁금해.
eotteon saraminji gunggeumhae.

너의 그 향기가 궁금해.
너에 그 향기가 궁금해.
neoe geu hyanggiga gunggeumhae.

어떤 사랑일지 너의 그 느낌이.
어떤 사랑일찌 너에 그 느끼미.
eotteon sarangilji neoe geu neukkimi.

궁금해, 궁금해, 궁금해, 궁금해, 궁금해.
궁금해, 궁금해, 궁금해, 궁금해, 궁금해.
gunggeumhae, gunggeumhae, gunggeumhae, gunggeumhae, gunggeumhae.

< 2 절(verse) >

감미로운 미소로 눈을 맞추면서 고개만 끄덕이다 말없이 사라져.
감미로운 미소로 누늘 맏추면서 고개만 끄더기다 마럽씨 사라저.
gammiroun misoro nuneul matchumyeonseo gogaeman kkeudeogida mareopsi sarajeo.

파도처럼 밀려드는 사랑이 보여.
파도처럼 밀려드는 사랑이 보여.
padocheoreom millyeodeuneun sarangi boyeo.

바람처럼 스치는 사랑이 느껴져.
바람처럼 스치는 사랑이 느껴저.
baramcheoreom seuchineun sarangi neukkyeojeo.

타오르는 열정이 꺼지지 않게 폭풍이 되어 내게 다가와 줘.
타오르는 열쩡이 꺼지지 안케 폭풍이 되어 내게 다가와 줘.
taoreuneun yeoljeongi kkeojiji anke pokpungi doeeo naege dagawa jwo.

어떤 사람인지 궁금해.
어떤 사라민지 궁금해.
eotteon saraminji gunggeumhae.

너의 그 향기가 궁금해.
너에 그 향기가 궁금해.
neoe geu hyanggiga gunggeumhae.

어떤 사랑일지 너의 그 느낌이.
어떤 사랑일찌 너에 그 느끼미.
eotteon sarangilji neoe geu neukkimi.

궁금해, 궁금해, 궁금해, 궁금해, 궁금해.
궁금해, 궁금해, 궁금해, 궁금해, 궁금해.
gunggeumhae, gunggeumhae, gunggeumhae, gunggeumhae, gunggeumhae.

< 3 절(verse) >

바람을 붙잡을 수 없더라도.
바라믈 붇짜블 쑤 업떠라도.
barameul butjabeul su eopdeorado.

파도가 비에 젖지 않더라도.
파도가 비에 젇찌 안터라도.
padoga bie jeotji anteorado.

내일은 가슴이 아프더라도.
내이른 가스미 아프더라도.
naeireun gaseumi apeudeorado.

미련과 후회만 남더라도.
미련과 후회만 남더라도.
miryeongwa huhoeman namdeorado.

어떤 사람인지 궁금해.
어떤 사라민지 궁금해.
eotteon saraminji gunggeumhae.

너의 그 향기가 궁금해.
너에 그 향기가 궁금해.
neoe geu hyanggiga gunggeumhae.

어떤 사랑일지 너의 그 느낌이.
어떤 사랑일찌 너에 그 느끼미.
eotteon sarangilji neoe geu neukkimi.

궁금해, 궁금해, 궁금해, 궁금해, 궁금해.
궁금해, 궁금해, 궁금해, 궁금해, 궁금해.
gunggeumhae, gunggeumhae, gunggeumhae, gunggeumhae, gunggeumhae.

< 1 절(verse) >

파도+처럼 나+의 맘속+으로 밀리+[어 오]+다
내 밀려 오다

파도 (noun) : 바다에 이는 물결.
wave
Waves forming in the sea.

처럼 : 모양이나 정도가 서로 비슷하거나 같음을 나타내는 조사.
no equivalent expression
A postpositional particle used when something is similar or identical to something else in shape or level.

나 (pronoun) : 말하는 사람이 친구나 아랫사람에게 자기를 가리키는 말.
I
A pronoun used to indicate oneself to a friend or a younger person.

의 : 앞의 말이 뒤의 말에 대하여 소유, 소속, 소재, 관계, 기원, 주체의 관계를 가짐을 나타내는 조사.
no equivalent expression
A postpositional particle used to indicate that the referent of the following word is owned by, belongs to, is related to, originates from, or is the object of what the preceding word indicates.

맘속 (noun) : 마음의 깊은 곳.
deep in one's heart
Deep down in one's heart.

으로 : 움직임의 방향을 나타내는 조사.
no equivalent expression
A postpositional particle that indicates the direction of movement.

밀리다 (verb) : 방향의 반대쪽에서 힘이 가해져서 움직여지다.
be pushed
To be moved as force is pressed from the opposite side.

-어 오다 : 앞의 말이 나타내는 행동이나 상태가 어떤 기준점으로 가까워지면서 계속 진행됨을 나타내는 표현.
no equivalent expression
An expression used to indicate that the act or state mentioned in the preceding statement is continued as a certain set point of time is approaching.

-다 : 어떤 행동이나 상태 등이 중단되고 다른 행동이나 상태로 바뀜을 나타내는 연결 어미.
no equivalent expression
A connective ending used when an action or state, etc., is stopped and changed to another action or state.

바람+처럼 흔적 없이 사라지+어.
사라져

바람 (noun) : 기압의 변화 또는 사람이나 기계에 의해 일어나는 공기의 움직임.
wind
The movement of air that is caused by changes in atmospheric pressure or by a human or machine.

처럼 : 모양이나 정도가 서로 비슷하거나 같음을 나타내는 조사.
no equivalent expression
A postpositional particle used when something is similar or identical to something else in shape or level.

흔적 (noun) : 사물이나 현상이 없어지거나 지나간 뒤에 남겨진 것.
trace; mark
A mark or trace left after an object or phenomenon disappears or passes by.

없이 (adverb) : 사람, 사물, 현상 등이 어떤 곳에 자리나 공간을 차지하고 존재하지 않게.
without
In a state in which a person, object, phenomenon, etc., does not exist or occupy a certain place or space.

사라지다 (verb) : 어떤 현상이나 물체의 자취 등이 없어지다.
disappear; vanish; go out of sight
For a certain phenomenon, the trace of something, etc., to be gone.

-어 : (두루낮춤으로) 어떤 사실을 서술하거나 물음, 명령, 권유를 나타내는 종결 어미.
no equivalent expression
(informal addressee-lowering) A sentence-final ending used to describe a certain fact, ask a question, give an order, or advise. <description>

파도+는 멈추+[ㄹ 수가 없]+[는 거]+(이)+니?
멈출 수가 없는 거니

파도 (noun) : 바다에 이는 물결.
wave
Waves forming in the sea.

는 : 문장 속에서 어떤 대상이 화제임을 나타내는 조사.
no equivalent expression
A postpositional particle used to indicate that a certain subject is the topic of a sentence.

멈추다 (verb) : 동작이나 상태가 계속되지 않다.
stop doing; quit
For a gesture or state not to continue.

-ㄹ 수가 없다 : 앞에 오는 말이 나타내는 일이 가능하지 않음을 나타내는 표현.
no equivalent expression
An expression used to express that the incident that occurred in the preceding statement is impossible.

-는 거 : 명사가 아닌 것을 문장에서 명사처럼 쓰이게 하거나 '이다' 앞에 쓰일 수 있게 할 때 쓰는 표현.
no equivalent expression
An expression used to enable a non-noun word to be used as a noun in a sentence or to be used in front of '이다' (be).

이다 : 주어가 지시하는 대상의 속성이나 부류를 지정하는 뜻을 나타내는 서술격 조사.
no equivalent expression
A predicate particle indicating the meaning of the attribute or category of the thing that the subject of the sentence refers to.

-니 : (아주낮춤으로) 물음을 나타내는 종결 어미.
no equivalent expression
(formal, highly addressee-lowering) A sentence-final ending referring to a question.

바람+은 머물+[(ㄹ) 수가 없]+[는 거]+(이)+니?
머물 수가 없는 거니

바람 (noun) : 기압의 변화 또는 사람이나 기계에 의해 일어나는 공기의 움직임.
wind
The movement of air that is caused by changes in atmospheric pressure or by a human or machine.

은 : 문장 속에서 어떤 대상이 화제임을 나타내는 조사.
no equivalent expression
A postpositional particle used to indicate that a certain subject is the topic of a sentence.

머물다 (verb) : 도중에 멈추거나 일시적으로 어떤 곳에 묵다.
stay temporarily; stop over; anchor
To stop in one's way or to stay at a place temporarily.

-ㄹ 수가 없다 : 앞에 오는 말이 나타내는 일이 가능하지 않음을 나타내는 표현.
no equivalent expression
An expression used to express that the incident that occurred in the preceding statement is impossible.

-는 거 : 명사가 아닌 것을 문장에서 명사처럼 쓰이게 하거나 '이다' 앞에 쓰일 수 있게 할 때 쓰는 표현.
no equivalent expression
An expression used to enable a non-noun word to be used as a noun in a sentence or to be used in front of '이다' (be).

이다 : 주어가 지시하는 대상의 속성이나 부류를 지정하는 뜻을 나타내는 서술격 조사.
no equivalent expression
A predicate particle indicating the meaning of the attribute or category of the thing that the subject of the sentence refers to.

-니 : (아주낮춤으로) 물음을 나타내는 종결 어미.
no equivalent expression
(formal, highly addressee-lowering) A sentence-final ending referring to a question.

피어나+는 나+의 맘+이 시들+[지 않]+게
내

피어나다 (verb) : 어떤 느낌이나 생각 등이 일어나다.
rise; come up; well up
For a certain feeling or thought, etc., to rise.

-는 : 앞의 말이 관형어의 기능을 하게 만들고 사건이나 동작이 현재 일어남을 나타내는 어미.
no equivalent expression
An ending of a word that makes the preceding statement function as an adnominal phrase and implies that an event or action is happening in the present.

나 (pronoun) : 말하는 사람이 친구나 아랫사람에게 자기를 가리키는 말.
I
A pronoun used to indicate oneself to a friend or a younger person.

의 : 앞의 말이 뒤의 말에 대하여 소유, 소속, 소재, 관계, 기원, 주체의 관계를 가짐을 나타내는 조사.
no equivalent expression
A postpositional particle used to indicate that the referent of the following word is owned by, belongs to, is related to, originates from, or is the object of what the preceding word indicates.

맘 (noun) : 좋아하는 마음이나 관심.
interest; taste
One's liking or interest for something.

이 : 어떤 상태나 상황의 대상이나 동작의 주체를 나타내는 조사.
no equivalent expression
A postpositional particle referring to a subject under a certain state or situation, or the agent of an action.

시들다 (verb) : 어떤 일에 대한 관심이나 기세가 이전보다 줄어들다.
wither away
For an interest in, or passion for a matter to decrease.

-지 않다 : 앞의 말이 나타내는 행위나 상태를 부정하는 뜻을 나타내는 표현.
no equivalent expression
An expression used to deny the act or state indicated in the preceding statement.

-게 : 앞의 말이 뒤에서 가리키는 일의 목적이나 결과, 방식, 정도 등이 됨을 나타내는 연결 어미.
no equivalent expression
A connective ending used when the preceding statement is the purpose, result, method, amount, etc., of something mentioned in the following statement.

그치+[지 않]+는 세차+ㄴ 비+를 뿌리+[어 주]+어.
세찬 뿌려 줘

그치다 (verb) : 계속되던 일, 움직임, 현상 등이 계속되지 않고 멈추다.
stop
For a continuing matter, movement, phenomenon, etc., to cease.

-지 않다 : 앞의 말이 나타내는 행위나 상태를 부정하는 뜻을 나타내는 표현.
no equivalent expression
An expression used to deny the act or state indicated in the preceding statement.

-는 : 앞의 말이 관형어의 기능을 하게 만들고 사건이나 동작이 현재 일어남을 나타내는 어미.
no equivalent expression
An ending of a word that makes the preceding statement function as an adnominal phrase and implies that an event or action is happening in the present.

세차다 (adjective) : 기운이나 일이 되어가는 형편 등이 힘 있고 거세다.
strong
Energy or the state of affairs being intense.

-ㄴ : 앞의 말이 관형어의 기능을 하게 만들고 현재의 상태를 나타내는 어미.
no equivalent expression
An ending of a word that makes the preceding statement function as an adnominal phrase and refers to the present state.

비 (noun) : 높은 곳에서 구름을 이루고 있던 수증기가 식어서 뭉쳐 떨어지는 물방울.
rain
Water drops generated from cloud-forming vapors high in the sky that get cold, condense, and fall.

를 : 동작이 직접적으로 영향을 미치는 대상을 나타내는 조사.
no equivalent expression
A postpositional particle used to indicate the subject that an act has a direct influence on.

뿌리다 (verb) : 눈이나 비 등이 날려 떨어지다. 또는 떨어지게 하다.
fall; blow and fall
For snow, rain, etc., to blow and fall, or cause them to fall.

-어 주다 : 남을 위해 앞의 말이 나타내는 행동을 함을 나타내는 표현.
no equivalent expression
An expression used to indicate that one does the act mentioned in the preceding statement for someone.

-어 : (두루낮춤으로) 어떤 사실을 서술하거나 물음, 명령, 권유를 나타내는 종결 어미.
no equivalent expression
(informal addressee-lowering) A sentence-final ending used to describe a certain fact, ask a question, give an order, or advise. <order>

어떤 사람+이+ㄴ지 궁금하+여.
사람인지 궁금해

어떤 (determiner) : 사람이나 사물의 특징, 내용, 성격, 성질, 모양 등이 무엇인지 물을 때 쓰는 말.
what
A word used when asking what characteristic, content, personality, quality, shape, etc., a person or object has.

사람 (noun) : 생각할 수 있으며 언어와 도구를 만들어 사용하고 사회를 이루어 사는 존재.
human; man
A being that is capable of thinking, makes and uses languages and tools and lives by forming a society with others.

이다 : 주어가 지시하는 대상의 속성이나 부류를 지정하는 뜻을 나타내는 서술격 조사.
no equivalent expression
A predicate particle indicating the meaning of the attribute or category of the thing that the subject of the sentence refers to.

-ㄴ지 : 뒤에 오는 말의 내용에 대한 막연한 이유나 판단을 나타내는 연결 어미.
no equivalent expression
A connective ending used to indicate an ambiguous reason or judgment about the following statement.

궁금하다 (adjective) : 무엇이 무척 알고 싶다.
curious
Having a strong desire to know about something.

-여 : (두루낮춤으로) 어떤 사실을 서술하거나 물음, 명령, 권유를 나타내는 종결 어미.
no equivalent expression
(informal addressee-lowering) A sentence-final ending used to describe a certain fact, ask a question, give an order, or advise.

너+의 그 향기+가 궁금하+여.
궁금해

너 (pronoun) : 듣는 사람이 친구나 아랫사람일 때, 그 사람을 가리키는 말.
no equivalent expression
A pronoun used to indicate the listener when he/she is the same age or younger.

의 : 앞의 말이 뒤의 말에 대하여 소유, 소속, 소재, 관계, 기원, 주체의 관계를 가짐을 나타내는 조사.
no equivalent expression
A postpositional particle used to indicate that the referent of the following word is owned by, belongs to, is related to, originates from, or is the object of what the preceding word indicates.

그 (determiner) : 듣는 사람에게 가까이 있거나 듣는 사람이 생각하고 있는 대상을 가리킬 때 쓰는 말.
that
A term referring to something near the listener or what the listener is thinking.

향기 (noun) : 좋은 냄새.
scent; fragrance
Good smell.

가 : 어떤 상태나 상황에 놓인 대상이나 동작의 주체를 나타내는 조사.
no equivalent expression
A postpositional particle referring to a subject under a certain state or situation, or the subject of an act.

궁금하다 (adjective) : 무엇이 무척 알고 싶다.
curious
Having a strong desire to know about something.

-여 : (두루낮춤으로) 어떤 사실을 서술하거나 물음, 명령, 권유를 나타내는 종결 어미.
no equivalent expression
(informal addressee-lowering) A sentence-final ending used to describe a certain fact, ask a question, give an order, or advise.

어떤 사랑+이+ㄹ지 너+의 그 느낌+이.
사랑일지

어떤 (determiner) : 사람이나 사물의 특징, 내용, 성격, 성질, 모양 등이 무엇인지 물을 때 쓰는 말.
what
A word used when asking what characteristic, content, personality, quality, shape, etc., a person or object has.

사랑 (noun) : 상대에게 성적으로 매력을 느껴 열렬히 좋아하는 마음.
love
The state of being sexually attracted to and having strong affection for a person.

이다 : 주어가 지시하는 대상의 속성이나 부류를 지정하는 뜻을 나타내는 서술격 조사.
no equivalent expression
A predicate particle indicating the meaning of the attribute or category of the thing that the subject of the sentence refers to.

-ㄹ지 : 어떠한 추측에 대한 막연한 의문을 갖고 그것을 뒤에 오는 말이 나타내는 사실이나 판단과 관련시킬 때 쓰는 연결 어미.
no equivalent expression
A connective ending used when having a doubt about a certain assumption and relating that to the fact or judgment of the following statement.

너 (pronoun) : 듣는 사람이 친구나 아랫사람일 때, 그 사람을 가리키는 말.
no equivalent expression
A pronoun used to indicate the listener when he/she is the same age or younger.

의 : 앞의 말이 뒤의 말에 대하여 소유, 소속, 소재, 관계, 기원, 주체의 관계를 가짐을 나타내는 조사.
no equivalent expression
A postpositional particle used to indicate that the referent of the following word is owned by, belongs to, is related to, originates from, or is the object of what the preceding word indicates.

그 (determiner) : 듣는 사람에게 가까이 있거나 듣는 사람이 생각하고 있는 대상을 가리킬 때 쓰는 말.
that
A term referring to something near the listener or what the listener is thinking.

느낌 (noun) : 몸이나 마음에서 일어나는 기분이나 감정.
feeling; sense; impression
A sense, mood, emotion, etc. felt in one's body and mind.

이 : 어떤 상태나 상황의 대상이나 동작의 주체를 나타내는 조사.
no equivalent expression
A postpositional particle referring to a subject under a certain state or situation, or the agent of an action.

궁금하+여, 궁금하+여, 궁금하+여, 궁금하+여, 궁금하+여.
궁금해 궁금해 궁금해 궁금해 궁금해

궁금하다 (adjective) : 무엇이 무척 알고 싶다.
curious
Having a strong desire to know about something.

-여 : (두루낮춤으로) 어떤 사실을 서술하거나 물음, 명령, 권유를 나타내는 종결 어미.
no equivalent expression
(informal addressee-lowering) A sentence-final ending used to describe a certain fact, ask a question, give an order, or advise.

< 2 절(verse) >

감미롭(감미로우)+ㄴ 미소+로 [눈을 맞추]+면서
감미로운

감미롭다 (adjective) : 달콤한 느낌이 있다.
mellow; sweet
A story, voice, song, etc., sounding sweet.

-ㄴ : 앞의 말이 관형어의 기능을 하게 만들고 현재의 상태를 나타내는 어미.
no equivalent expression
An ending of a word that makes the preceding statement function as an adnominal phrase and refers to the present state.

미소 (noun) : 소리 없이 빙긋이 웃는 웃음.
smile
A facial expression with the lips curved upwards and without sound.

로 : 어떤 일의 방법이나 방식을 나타내는 조사.
no equivalent expression
A postpositional particle that indicates a method or way to do something.

눈을 맞추다 (idiom) : 서로 눈을 마주 보다.
contact each other's eyes
To look each other in the eyes.

-면서 : 두 가지 이상의 동작이나 상태가 함께 일어남을 나타내는 연결 어미.
no equivalent expression
A connective ending used when more than two actions or states happen at the same time.

고개+만 끄덕이+다 말없이 사라지+어.
사라져

고개 (noun) : 목을 포함한 머리 부분.
head
A word referring to one's head, including the neck.

만 : 다른 것은 제외하고 어느 것을 한정함을 나타내는 조사.
no equivalent expression
A postpositional particle used when limiting the field to one thing, excluding all the others.

끄덕이다 (verb) : 머리를 가볍게 아래위로 움직이다.
nod; bow
To lightly move one's head up and down.

-다 : 어떤 행동이나 상태 등이 중단되고 다른 행동이나 상태로 바뀜을 나타내는 연결 어미.
no equivalent expression
A connective ending used when an action or state, etc., is stopped and changed to another action or state.

말없이 (adverb) : 아무 말도 하지 않고.
silently; in silence
Without saying anything.

사라지다 (verb) : 어떤 현상이나 물체의 자취 등이 없어지다.
disappear; vanish; go out of sight
For a certain phenomenon, the trace of something, etc., to be gone.

-어 : (두루낮춤으로) 어떤 사실을 서술하거나 물음, 명령, 권유를 나타내는 종결 어미.
no equivalent expression
(informal addressee-lowering) A sentence-final ending used to describe a certain fact, ask a question, give an order, or advise. <description>

파도+처럼 밀려들(밀려드)+는 사랑+이 보이+어.

밀려드는 **보여**

파도 (noun) : 바다에 이는 물결.
wave
Waves forming in the sea.

처럼 : 모양이나 정도가 서로 비슷하거나 같음을 나타내는 조사.
no equivalent expression
A postpositional particle used when something is similar or identical to something else in shape or level.

밀려들다 (verb) : 한꺼번에 많이 몰려 들어오다.
crowd; flood
For a crowd of people or things to come in at the same time.

-는 : 앞의 말이 관형어의 기능을 하게 만들고 사건이나 동작이 현재 일어남을 나타내는 어미.
no equivalent expression
An ending of a word that makes the preceding statement function as an adnominal phrase and implies that an event or action is happening in the present.

사랑 (noun) : 상대에게 성적으로 매력을 느껴 열렬히 좋아하는 마음.
love
The state of being sexually attracted to and having strong affection for a person.

이 : 어떤 상태나 상황의 대상이나 동작의 주체를 나타내는 조사.
no equivalent expression
A postpositional particle referring to a subject under a certain state or situation, or the agent of an action.

보이다 (verb) : 눈으로 대상의 존재나 겉모습을 알게 되다.
be viewed; be visible; be in sight
To come to know the presence or outward appearance of an object by looking at it.

-어 : (두루낮춤으로) 어떤 사실을 서술하거나 물음, 명령, 권유를 나타내는 종결 어미.
no equivalent expression
(informal addressee-lowering) A sentence-final ending used to describe a certain fact, ask a question, give an order, or advise. <description>

바람+처럼 스치+는 사랑+이 느끼+어지+어.

느껴져

바람 (noun) : 기압의 변화 또는 사람이나 기계에 의해 일어나는 공기의 움직임.
wind
The movement of air that is caused by changes in atmospheric pressure or by a human or machine.

처럼 : 모양이나 정도가 서로 비슷하거나 같음을 나타내는 조사.
no equivalent expression
A postpositional particle used when something is similar or identical to something else in shape or level.

스치다 (verb) : 냄새, 바람, 소리 등이 약하게 잠시 느껴지다.
pass gently; brush past
For a smell, wind, sound, etc., to be felt slightly for a moment.

-는 : 앞의 말이 관형어의 기능을 하게 만들고 사건이나 동작이 현재 일어남을 나타내는 어미.
no equivalent expression
An ending of a word that makes the preceding statement function as an adnominal phrase and implies that an event or action is happening in the present.

사랑 (noun) : 상대에게 성적으로 매력을 느껴 열렬히 좋아하는 마음.
love
The state of being sexually attracted to and having strong affection for a person.

이 : 어떤 상태나 상황의 대상이나 동작의 주체를 나타내는 조사.
no equivalent expression
A postpositional particle referring to a subject under a certain state or situation, or the agent of an action.

느끼다 (verb) : 마음속에서 어떤 감정을 경험하다.
feel
To experience a certain emotion in one's mind.

-어지다 : 앞에 오는 말이 나타내는 상태로 점점 되어 감을 나타내는 표현.
no equivalent expression
An expression used to indicate that someone or something gradually becomes the state mentioned in the preceding statement.

-어 : (두루낮춤으로) 어떤 사실을 서술하거나 물음, 명령, 권유를 나타내는 종결 어미.
no equivalent expression
(informal addressee-lowering) A sentence-final ending used to describe a certain fact, ask a question, give an order, or advise. <description>

타오르+는 열정+이 꺼지+[지 않]+게

타오르다 (verb) : 마음이 불같이 뜨거워지다.
get mad; become passionate
For one's mind to become hot like fire.

-는 : 앞의 말이 관형어의 기능을 하게 만들고 사건이나 동작이 현재 일어남을 나타내는 어미.
no equivalent expression
An ending of a word that makes the preceding statement function as an adnominal phrase and implies that an event or action is happening in the present.

열정 (noun) : 어떤 일에 뜨거운 애정을 가지고 열심히 하는 마음.
passion
The attitude of doing something hard with enthusiasm.

이 : 어떤 상태나 상황의 대상이나 동작의 주체를 나타내는 조사.
no equivalent expression
A postpositional particle referring to a subject under a certain state or situation, or the agent of an action.

꺼지다 (verb) : 어떤 감정이 풀어지거나 사라지다.
disappear
For an emotion to become soft or disappear.

-지 않다 : 앞의 말이 나타내는 행위나 상태를 부정하는 뜻을 나타내는 표현.
no equivalent expression
An expression used to deny the act or state indicated in the preceding statement.

-게 : 앞의 말이 뒤에서 가리키는 일의 목적이나 결과, 방식, 정도 등이 됨을 나타내는 연결 어미.
no equivalent expression
A connective ending used when the preceding statement is the purpose, result, method, amount, etc., of something mentioned in the following statement.

폭풍+이 되+어 나+에게 다가오+[아 주]+어.
내게 다가와 줘

폭풍 (noun) : 매우 세차게 부는 바람.
storm
A wind that blows extremely hard.

이 : 바뀌게 되는 대상이나 부정하는 대상임을 나타내는 조사.
no equivalent expression
A postpositional particle referring to the subject that is to be changed, or the subject that one denies.

되다 (verb) : 다른 것으로 바뀌거나 변하다.
become; turn
To change or transform into something or someone else.

-어 : 앞의 말이 뒤의 말보다 먼저 일어났거나 뒤의 말에 대한 방법이나 수단이 됨을 나타내는 연결 어미.
no equivalent expression
A connective ending used when the preceding statement happened before the following statement or was the ways or means to the following statement.

나 (pronoun) : 말하는 사람이 친구나 아랫사람에게 자기를 가리키는 말.
I
A pronoun used to indicate oneself to a friend or a younger person.

에게 : 어떤 행동이 미치는 대상임을 나타내는 조사.
no equivalent expression
A postpositional particle referring to the subject that is influenced by a certain action.

다가오다 (verb) : 어떤 대상이 있는 쪽으로 가까이 옮기어 오다.
approach; come near
To come closer to a subject.

-아 주다 : 남을 위해 앞의 말이 나타내는 행동을 함을 나타내는 표현.
no equivalent expression
An expression used to indicate that one does the act mentioned in the preceding statement for someone.

-어 : (두루낮춤으로) 어떤 사실을 서술하거나 물음, 명령, 권유를 나타내는 종결 어미.
no equivalent expression
(informal addressee-lowering) A sentence-final ending used to describe a certain fact, ask a question, give an order, or advise. <order>

어떤 사람+이+ㄴ지 궁금하+여.
사람인지 궁금해

어떤 (determiner) : 사람이나 사물의 특징, 내용, 성격, 성질, 모양 등이 무엇인지 물을 때 쓰는 말.
what
A word used when asking what characteristic, content, personality, quality, shape, etc., a person or object has.

사람 (noun) : 생각할 수 있으며 언어와 도구를 만들어 사용하고 사회를 이루어 사는 존재.
human; man
A being that is capable of thinking, makes and uses languages and tools and lives by forming a society with others.

이다 : 주어가 지시하는 대상의 속성이나 부류를 지정하는 뜻을 나타내는 서술격 조사.
no equivalent expression
A predicate particle indicating the meaning of the attribute or category of the thing that the subject of the sentence refers to.

-ㄴ지 : 뒤에 오는 말의 내용에 대한 막연한 이유나 판단을 나타내는 연결 어미.
no equivalent expression
A connective ending used to indicate an ambiguous reason or judgment about the following statement.

궁금하다 (adjective) : 무엇이 무척 알고 싶다.
curious
Having a strong desire to know about something.

-여 : (두루낮춤으로) 어떤 사실을 서술하거나 물음, 명령, 권유를 나타내는 종결 어미.
no equivalent expression
(informal addressee-lowering) A sentence-final ending used to describe a certain fact, ask a question, give an order, or advise.

너+의 그 향기+가 궁금하+여.
궁금해

너 (pronoun) : 듣는 사람이 친구나 아랫사람일 때, 그 사람을 가리키는 말.
no equivalent expression
A pronoun used to indicate the listener when he/she is the same age or younger.

의 : 앞의 말이 뒤의 말에 대하여 소유, 소속, 소재, 관계, 기원, 주체의 관계를 가짐을 나타내는 조사.
no equivalent expression
A postpositional particle used to indicate that the referent of the following word is owned by, belongs to, is related to, originates from, or is the object of what the preceding word indicates.

그 (determiner) : 듣는 사람에게 가까이 있거나 듣는 사람이 생각하고 있는 대상을 가리킬 때 쓰는 말.
that
A term referring to something near the listener or what the listener is thinking.

향기 (noun) : 좋은 냄새.
scent; fragrance
Good smell.

가 : 어떤 상태나 상황에 놓인 대상이나 동작의 주체를 나타내는 조사.
no equivalent expression
A postpositional particle referring to a subject under a certain state or situation, or the subject of an act.

궁금하다 (adjective) : 무엇이 무척 알고 싶다.
curious
Having a strong desire to know about something.

-여 : (두루낮춤으로) 어떤 사실을 서술하거나 물음, 명령, 권유를 나타내는 종결 어미.
no equivalent expression
(informal addressee-lowering) A sentence-final ending used to describe a certain fact, ask a question, give an order, or advise.

어떤 사랑+이+ㄹ지 너+의 그 느낌+이.
사랑일지

어떤 (determiner) : 사람이나 사물의 특징, 내용, 성격, 성질, 모양 등이 무엇인지 물을 때 쓰는 말.
what
A word used when asking what characteristic, content, personality, quality, shape, etc., a person or object has.

사랑 (noun) : 상대에게 성적으로 매력을 느껴 열렬히 좋아하는 마음.
love
The state of being sexually attracted to and having strong affection for a person.

이다 : 주어가 지시하는 대상의 속성이나 부류를 지정하는 뜻을 나타내는 서술격 조사.
no equivalent expression
A predicate particle indicating the meaning of the attribute or category of the thing that the subject of the sentence refers to.

-ㄹ지 : 어떠한 추측에 대한 막연한 의문을 갖고 그것을 뒤에 오는 말이 나타내는 사실이나 판단과 관련시킬 때 쓰는 연결 어미.
no equivalent expression
A connective ending used when having a doubt about a certain assumption and relating that to the fact or judgment of the following statement.

너 (pronoun) : 듣는 사람이 친구나 아랫사람일 때, 그 사람을 가리키는 말.
no equivalent expression
A pronoun used to indicate the listener when he/she is the same age or younger.

의 : 앞의 말이 뒤의 말에 대하여 소유, 소속, 소재, 관계, 기원, 주체의 관계를 가짐을 나타내는 조사.
no equivalent expression
A postpositional particle used to indicate that the referent of the following word is owned by, belongs to, is related to, originates from, or is the object of what the preceding word indicates.

그 (determiner) : 듣는 사람에게 가까이 있거나 듣는 사람이 생각하고 있는 대상을 가리킬 때 쓰는 말.
that
A term referring to something near the listener or what the listener is thinking.

느낌 (noun) : 몸이나 마음에서 일어나는 기분이나 감정.
feeling; sense; impression
A sense, mood, emotion, etc. felt in one's body and mind.

이 : 어떤 상태나 상황의 대상이나 동작의 주체를 나타내는 조사.
no equivalent expression
A postpositional particle referring to a subject under a certain state or situation, or the agent of an action.

궁금하+여, 궁금하+여, 궁금하+여, 궁금하+여, 궁금하+여.
궁금해 궁금해 궁금해 궁금해 궁금해

궁금하다 (adjective) : 무엇이 무척 알고 싶다.
curious
Having a strong desire to know about something.

-여 : (두루낮춤으로) 어떤 사실을 서술하거나 물음, 명령, 권유를 나타내는 종결 어미.
no equivalent expression
(informal addressee-lowering) A sentence-final ending used to describe a certain fact, ask a question, give an order, or advise.

< 3 절(verse) >

바람+을 붙잡+[을 수 없]+더라도.

바람 (noun) : 기압의 변화 또는 사람이나 기계에 의해 일어나는 공기의 움직임.
wind
The movement of air that is caused by changes in atmospheric pressure or by a human or machine.

을 : 동작이 직접적으로 영향을 미치는 대상을 나타내는 조사.
no equivalent expression
A postpositional particle used to indicate the subject that an action has a direct influence on.

붙잡다 (verb) : 무엇을 놓치지 않도록 단단히 잡다.
hold; grasp; grab
To hold something firmly so as not to lose it.

-을 수 없다 : 앞에 오는 말이 나타내는 일이 가능하지 않음을 나타내는 표현.
no equivalent expression
An expression used to indicate that the incident of the preceding statement is impossible.

-더라도 : 앞에 오는 말을 가정하거나 인정하지만 뒤에 오는 말에는 관계가 없거나 영향을 끼치지 않음을 나타내는 연결 어미.
no equivalent expression
A connective ending used when assuming or recognizing the truth of the preceding statement, but implying that it is not related to or does not influence the following statement.

파도+가 비+에 젖+[지 않]+더라도.

파도 (noun) : 바다에 이는 물결.
wave
Waves forming in the sea.

가 : 어떤 상태나 상황에 놓인 대상이나 동작의 주체를 나타내는 조사.
no equivalent expression
A postpositional particle referring to a subject under a certain state or situation, or the subject of an act.

비 (noun) : 높은 곳에서 구름을 이루고 있던 수증기가 식어서 뭉쳐 떨어지는 물방울.
rain
Water drops generated from cloud-forming vapors high in the sky that get cold, condense, and fall.

에 : 앞말이 어떤 일의 원인임을 나타내는 조사.
for; due to; because of
A postpositional particle to indicate that the preceding statement is the cause for something.

젖다 (verb) : 액체가 스며들어 축축해지다.
get wet
To become wet by absorbing liquid.

-지 않다 : 앞의 말이 나타내는 행위나 상태를 부정하는 뜻을 나타내는 표현.
no equivalent expression
An expression used to deny the act or state indicated in the preceding statement.

-더라도 : 앞에 오는 말을 가정하거나 인정하지만 뒤에 오는 말에는 관계가 없거나 영향을 끼치지 않음을 나타내는 연결 어미.
no equivalent expression
A connective ending used when assuming or recognizing the truth of the preceding statement, but implying that it is not related to or does not influence the following statement.

내일+은 가슴+이 아프+더라도.

내일 (noun) : 오늘의 다음 날.
days to come; future
The day after today.

은 : 문장 속에서 어떤 대상이 화제임을 나타내는 조사.
no equivalent expression
A postpositional particle used to indicate that a certain subject is the topic of a sentence.

가슴 (noun) : 마음이나 느낌.
heart; feeling
One's mind or emotion.

이 : 어떤 상태나 상황의 대상이나 동작의 주체를 나타내는 조사.
no equivalent expression
A postpositional particle referring to a subject under a certain state or situation, or the agent of an action.

아프다 (adjective) : 슬픔이나 연민으로 마음에 괴로운 느낌이 있다.
hurting; aching
Feeling pain in the heart due to sadness or a lingering attachment.

-더라도 : 앞에 오는 말을 가정하거나 인정하지만 뒤에 오는 말에는 관계가 없거나 영향을 끼치지 않음을 나타내는 연결 어미.
no equivalent expression
A connective ending used when assuming or recognizing the truth of the preceding statement, but implying that it is not related to or does not influence the following statement.

미련+과 후회+만 남+더라도.

미련 (noun) : 잊어버리거나 그만두어야 할 것을 깨끗이 잊거나 포기하지 못하고 여전히 끌리는 마음.
lingering attachment
A feeling of being still attached to something that should be forgotten or given up.

과 : 앞과 뒤의 명사를 같은 자격으로 이어 줄 때 쓰는 조사.
no equivalent expression
A postpositional particle used to list the preceding and following nouns.

후회 (noun) : 이전에 자신이 한 일이 잘못임을 깨닫고 스스로 자신의 잘못을 꾸짖음.
regret; remorse; repentance
An act of realizing that what one did was wrong and reprimanding oneself for having done it.

만 : 다른 것은 제외하고 어느 것을 한정함을 나타내는 조사.
no equivalent expression
A postpositional particle used when limiting the field to one thing, excluding all the others.

남다 (verb) : 잊히지 않다.
be left; be remembered
To not be forgotten.

-더라도 : 앞에 오는 말을 가정하거나 인정하지만 뒤에 오는 말에는 관계가 없거나 영향을 끼치지 않음을 나타내는 연결 어미.
no equivalent expression
A connective ending used when assuming or recognizing the truth of the preceding statement, but implying that it is not related to or does not influence the following statement.

어떤 사람+이+ㄴ지 궁금하+여.
사람인지 궁금해

어떤 (determiner) : 사람이나 사물의 특징, 내용, 성격, 성질, 모양 등이 무엇인지 물을 때 쓰는 말.
what
A word used when asking what characteristic, content, personality, quality, shape, etc., a person or object has.

사람 (noun) : 생각할 수 있으며 언어와 도구를 만들어 사용하고 사회를 이루어 사는 존재.
human; man
A being that is capable of thinking, makes and uses languages and tools and lives by forming a society with others.

이다 : 주어가 지시하는 대상의 속성이나 부류를 지정하는 뜻을 나타내는 서술격 조사.
no equivalent expression
A predicate particle indicating the meaning of the attribute or category of the thing that the subject of the sentence refers to.

-ㄴ지 : 뒤에 오는 말의 내용에 대한 막연한 이유나 판단을 나타내는 연결 어미.
no equivalent expression
A connective ending used to indicate an ambiguous reason or judgment about the following statement.

궁금하다 (adjective) : 무엇이 무척 알고 싶다.
curious
Having a strong desire to know about something.

-여 : (두루낮춤으로) 어떤 사실을 서술하거나 물음, 명령, 권유를 나타내는 종결 어미.
no equivalent expression
(informal addressee-lowering) A sentence-final ending used to describe a certain fact, ask a question, give an order, or advise.

너+의 그 향기+가 궁금하+여.
궁금해

너 (pronoun) : 듣는 사람이 친구나 아랫사람일 때, 그 사람을 가리키는 말.
no equivalent expression
A pronoun used to indicate the listener when he/she is the same age or younger.

의 : 앞의 말이 뒤의 말에 대하여 소유, 소속, 소재, 관계, 기원, 주체의 관계를 가짐을 나타내는 조사.
no equivalent expression
A postpositional particle used to indicate that the referent of the following word is owned by, belongs to, is related to, originates from, or is the object of what the preceding word indicates.

그 (determiner) : 듣는 사람에게 가까이 있거나 듣는 사람이 생각하고 있는 대상을 가리킬 때 쓰는 말.
that
A term referring to something near the listener or what the listener is thinking.

향기 (noun) : 좋은 냄새.
scent; fragrance
Good smell.

가 : 어떤 상태나 상황에 놓인 대상이나 동작의 주체를 나타내는 조사.
no equivalent expression
A postpositional particle referring to a subject under a certain state or situation, or the subject of an act.

궁금하다 (adjective) : 무엇이 무척 알고 싶다.
curious
Having a strong desire to know about something.

-여 : (두루낮춤으로) 어떤 사실을 서술하거나 물음, 명령, 권유를 나타내는 종결 어미.
no equivalent expression
(informal addressee-lowering) A sentence-final ending used to describe a certain fact, ask a question, give an order, or advise.

어떤 사랑+이+ㄹ지 너+의 그 느낌+이.
사랑일지

어떤 (determiner) : 사람이나 사물의 특징, 내용, 성격, 성질, 모양 등이 무엇인지 물을 때 쓰는 말.
what
A word used when asking what characteristic, content, personality, quality, shape, etc., a person or object has.

사랑 (noun) : 상대에게 성적으로 매력을 느껴 열렬히 좋아하는 마음.
love
The state of being sexually attracted to and having strong affection for a person.

이다 : 주어가 지시하는 대상의 속성이나 부류를 지정하는 뜻을 나타내는 서술격 조사.
no equivalent expression
A predicate particle indicating the meaning of the attribute or category of the thing that the subject of the sentence refers to.

-ㄹ지 : 어떠한 추측에 대한 막연한 의문을 갖고 그것을 뒤에 오는 말이 나타내는 사실이나 판단과 관련시킬 때 쓰는 연결 어미.
no equivalent expression
A connective ending used when having a doubt about a certain assumption and relating that to the fact or judgment of the following statement.

너 (pronoun) : 듣는 사람이 친구나 아랫사람일 때, 그 사람을 가리키는 말.
no equivalent expression
A pronoun used to indicate the listener when he/she is the same age or younger.

의 : 앞의 말이 뒤의 말에 대하여 소유, 소속, 소재, 관계, 기원, 주체의 관계를 가짐을 나타내는 조사.
no equivalent expression
A postpositional particle used to indicate that the referent of the following word is owned by, belongs to, is related to, originates from, or is the object of what the preceding word indicates.

그 (determiner) : 듣는 사람에게 가까이 있거나 듣는 사람이 생각하고 있는 대상을 가리킬 때 쓰는 말.
that
A term referring to something near the listener or what the listener is thinking.

느낌 (noun) : 몸이나 마음에서 일어나는 기분이나 감정.
feeling; sense; impression
A sense, mood, emotion, etc. felt in one's body and mind.

이 : 어떤 상태나 상황의 대상이나 동작의 주체를 나타내는 조사.
no equivalent expression
A postpositional particle referring to a subject under a certain state or situation, or the agent of an action.

궁금하+여, 궁금하+여, 궁금하+여, 궁금하+여, 궁금하+여.
궁금해 궁금해 궁금해 궁금해 궁금해

궁금하다 (adjective) : 무엇이 무척 알고 싶다.
curious
Having a strong desire to know about something.

-여 : (두루낮춤으로) 어떤 사실을 서술하거나 물음, 명령, 권유를 나타내는 종결 어미.
no equivalent expression
(informal addressee-lowering) A sentence-final ending used to describe a certain fact, ask a question, give an order, or advise.

< 참고 문헌 (reference) >

고려대학교 한국어대사전, 고려대학교 민족문화연구원, 2009
우리말샘, 국립국어원, 2016
표준국어대사전, 국립국어원, 1999
한국어교육 문법 자료편, 한글파크, 2016
한국어 교육학 사전, 하우, 2014
한국어기초사전, 국립국어원, 2016
한국어 문법 총론 Ⅰ, 집문당, 2015

노래로 배우는 한국어 1 English(translation)

발 행 | 2024년 6월 12일
저 자 | 주식회사 한글2119연구소
펴낸이 | 한건희
펴낸곳 | 주식회사 부크크
출판사등록 | 2014.07.15.(제2014-16호)
주 소 | 서울특별시 금천구 가산디지털1로 119 SK트윈타워 A동 305호
전 화 | 1670-8316
이메일 | info@bookk.co.kr

ISBN | 979-11-410-8926-9

www.bookk.co.kr